A HIS

VOLUME 3

THE RISE OF
THE COMMON PLAYER

A HISTORY OF ELIZABETHAN DRAMA
BY M. C. BRADBROOK

Volumes in the Series

These six books give a continuous history of Elizabethan drama; three are general books and three are on Shakespeare. The first two, *Themes and Conventions of Elizabethan Tragedy* and *The Growth and Structure of Elizabethan Comedy*, deal with the genres of tragedy and comedy, establishing the different kinds of drama as they developed between 1576 and 1642, with a close study of leading playwrights. The third, *The Rise of the Common Player*, deals with the social history of the playhouses and the actors, their relations with court and city. All three books were the first of their kind.

The study of Shakespeare in *Shakespeare and Elizabethan Poetry* is limited to the sixteenth century, and explores the connexion with the general poetic developments of that time. *Shakespeare the Craftsman* concentrates upon the crucial years at the turn of the century, when the drama established a lead over all other poetic genres, and when Shakespeare's own development was at its most intensive; the period culminates in *Hamlet*. *The Living Monument* deals with the Jacobean Shakespeare, his tragedies and final plays, against a background of the general development of theatrical art, including the court masque.

These books present a coherent account of the greatest period of English dramatic history, on a scale larger than any other history at present available: the emphasis throughout is on poetry seen in its social context. The series will be especially useful to students of English literature, drama or social history.

All these volumes are available in paperback from Cambridge University Press, either as a cased set or individually: some of them may also be purchased in hard covers – Volumes 1 and 6 from Cambridge University Press, and Volumes 2 and 3 from Chatto and Windus.

THE
RISE OF THE
COMMON PLAYER

*A Study of Actor and Society
in Shakespeare's England*

M. C. BRADBROOK

Professor Emerita of English in the University of Cambridge
and Fellow of Girton College

CAMBRIDGE UNIVERSITY PRESS

CAMBRIDGE

LONDON · NEW YORK · MELBOURNE

Published by the Syndics of the Cambridge University Press
The Pitt Building, Trumpington Street, Cambridge CB2 1RP
Bentley House, 200 Euston Road, London NW1 2DB
32 East 57th Street, New York, NY 10022, USA
296 Beaconsfield Parade, Middle Park, Melbourne 3206, Australia

First published by Chatto & Windus Ltd 1962
Reprinted 1964
First published by Cambridge University Press in paperback 1979

First printed in Great Britain by T & A Constable Ltd
Reprinted in Great Britain by W & J Mackay Limited, Chatham

ISBN 0 521 29527 0 paperback
ISBN 0 521 29531 9 set of six paperback volumes

CONTENTS

PLATES

PREFACE

THIS book has been written in the hope that it would interest both students of drama and students of social history. It is a continuation of the study I began in *Shakespeare and Elizabethan Poetry*; but instead of exploring the literary influences surrounding the plays, I have explored the social envelope within which they were made. This meant establishing the players' place in the social structure of the age, as it appears to one untrained as a historian, but stimulated by the revolutionary work on Tudor history which has appeared in recent years. Sir John Neale and his pupils have shown how the Elizabethan constitution may be interpreted in terms of social structure; Trevor Roper's and his opponents' 'quarrel of the gentry' throws strong emphasis on the economics of the courtier's life, and the importance of household display; the revolution in Tudor Government, as G. R. Elton pictures it, is reflected in miniature in the development of the Great Companies or players and of the Revels Office, substituting a bureaucratic organization for the old household rule. Players were a new, experimental social group; the opposition they met is a classic example of social prejudice and of the force of unexamined assumptions.

The material I have used had almost all been collected in the scholarly works of Chambers and Greg; the approach, I believe to be new. Laneham the Player, as it now appears, did not compose the letter which is the chief subject of Chapter VI; a notable piece of sleuthing has very recently ascribed it to another entertainer at Kenilworth (see p. 161); yet it illustrates their social status and the conflicts of the years when the first playhouse was being planned.[1]

The book is divided to correspond with the main social divisions of the drama in Elizabethan times. Apart from

---

[1] Quotations from this work are given in the original spelling, which is of significance for its origin; all other quotations are in modern spelling. In quoting from early books I have given the signature reference, not the page reference except when, as with Laneham, I have checked the pagination.

the first introductory chapter, which traces the actor's development from the time of Chaucer to the reign of Elizabeth, each part begins at the critical central point of Elizabeth's reign, in or about 1576. The four parts therefore run parallel to each other, covering the same period from different points of view, to reveal different aspects of the complex social structure.

Part I gives the social history of the public theatres, and of the troupes who played there, including a brief attempt to relate this social development to the corresponding development of literary forms.

In Part II, the same critical period is re-examined, but the focus is shifted to a study of typical individuals. Laneham is an example of the older type of player, a musician, writer and improviser as well as an actor; Tarlton is the first great star of the English stage; Wilson, a player poet, is first of the line that includes Shakespeare; Alleyn was not only the greatest tragic actor of his time, but the first actor to achieve dignity and fortune.

Part III is a study of the one attempt by fully incorporated household players to establish on a commercial basis the old noble Theatre of the Hall—the rise and fall of the choristers' troupes. As Common Players rose, household players declined; they go up and down together like two buckets in a well; in the end the choristers' theatre became assimilated to the common stages.

Lastly, Part IV shows something of the general dramatic sports of the age—royal and noble, popular and academic; for the Elizabethan theatre gained its strength from the common life; it was but one branch of a flowering tree, from whence it drew its sap and nurture; with the withering of these lesser forms, the greater theatre too declined.

The growth of drama had been slow; but suddenly within the last quarter of the sixteenth century, the language burst into flower; blossom by blossom, from the arrival of Marlowe somewhere about 1587, masterpieces appeared. There had never been anything like the wonderful period between the arrival of Marlowe and the death of Shakespeare in 1616, nor can there be again; for the springtime of a language comes but once.

The greatest triumphs were in dramatic poetry, involving the special use of language as part of a larger social context, including also the 'languages' of music, gesture, spectacle, the 'traffic of the stage'. Looking at the brilliance and boldness of the experiment which produced this drama, the audacity of the men who presented it, it is not hard to understand why Elizabethan poetic drama began with Tamburlaine the shepherd storming his way to a throne. The Elizabethan actor, with his jests and swordsmanship his lute and dancing, his vaulting and tumbling and stately triumphs, his hazards of poverty and prison showed 'the very age and body of the time, his form and pressure'.

In setting out my findings, my first hope has been to interest not only the student, but also the common reader.

M. C. BRADBROOK

ABBREVIATION

E.E.T.S.	Publications of the Early English Text Society.
M.S.	E. K. Chambers, *The Medieval Stage*, 2 vols. Oxford 1903.
E.S.	E. K. Chambers, *The Elizabethan Stage*, 4 vols. Oxford, 1923.
M.S.C.	Malone Society Collections, ed. W. W. Greg. Oxford 1907-.
M.S.R.	Malone Society Reprints. Oxford 1907-.
Hillebrand	H. N. Hillebrand, *The Child Actors, University of Illinois Studies in Language and Literature XI*, Illinois, 1926.
Nichols	John Nichols, *Progresses and Public Processions of Queen Elizabeth*, 2 vols, 1788. (In this work, the items are paged separately.)
P.M.L.A.	Publications of the Modern Language Association of America, Baltimore 1885-.

To
EDITH EVANS
and the memory of her
friend and mine
JUDITH WILSON

NOTES ON THE BADGES
AND ARMORIAL BEARINGS

William Hunnis applied for his arms in 1568; they could not be claimed in right of his descent but of his present position in honourable society. His crest (not shown) is a man's head with an arrow piercing his cheeks diagonally from right to left. The arms and particulars of the grant are given in his biography by C. C. Stopes.

Shakespeare's arms were granted to his father in 1596.

Burbage's arms are recorded in a visitation of 1634. They were probably simply adopted by custom—perhaps as an adaptation of the arms of the famous inn? The boar supplied also a pun on his name.

Alleyn claimed to be descended through his mother from the Towneleys of Lancashire, but there is no evidence of this. Strictly he had no right to impale Henslowe, since his wife was Henslowe's stepdaughter only; moreover, Henslowe's arms look like a bold adaptation of the royal arms. The arms of Dulwich College are differenced from Alleyn's.

The players' badge, worn on a pewter arm-shield, or on a brooch in the hat, was formed from his lord's cognisance or badge. This was never his lord's arms, but might sometimes be adapted from the crest. Some lords had more than one badge; the Lord Chamberlain's was a flying swan. The Lord Admiral's badge was a white lion charged with a blue crescent on his shoulder. The badge was personal to the head of a family, while the arms might be borne by all members of the family (suitably differenced): retainers wore the badge, and Summer Lords would sell mock-badges to their 'followers'.

It is perhaps worth noting that the badge of Richard III, who supplied Burbage's first famous part, was a boar; and that Shakespeare in his tragedy made much play upon it. So Burbage may have been influenced by this, also, in his choice of arms.

PLAYERS'
ARMS

1. Arms of Shakespeare   2. Alleyn impaling Henslowe
3. Burbage   4. Hunnis of the Chapel

LORDS' ARMS
AND BADGES

5. Badge of the Queen's Men   6. Arms of the Earl of
Nottingham, Lord High Admiral   7. Arms of Baron
Hunsdon, Lord Chamberlain   8. Badge of Leicester

ACKNOWLEDGEMENTS

THE writing of this book was begun in America, with the help of generous grants from the Folger Shakespeare Library, Washington, and the Henry E. Huntington Library, San Marino, California. To the Directors and staffs of these two libraries my most grateful thanks are due. Some of the material in Chapters II and III appeared in an article in the *Huntington Library Quarterly* for February 1961, and much of that in Chapter X in an article in *Studies in English Literature* for Spring 1961, published by the Rice University, Houston, Texas. Part of the material for Chapter XI was given as a paper at the Eighth Annual South-Central Renaissance Conference, in March 1959, and appeared in the *Rice Institute Pamphlet* for July 1960.

I am very grateful to my friends Helen Cam for kindly reading the manuscript, and Rupert and Kathleen Bliss, in whose home part of it was written.

M. C. B.

PART ONE

Players and Society

CHAPTER I

FROM MINSTREL TO COMEDIAN
The Actor's Art, 1300-1572

Festive and seasonal nature of medieval plays—regional differences—minstrels and heralds—changing ideas and habits in the late fifteenth century—retainers and strollers—royal entertainment under Henry VIII—the theatre of the Hall—the early Tudor interlude — effects of the Reformation — propaganda and censorship — growth of professionalism — position under Edward VI, Mary and in the early part of the reign of Elizabeth.

THE public theatres, established in England in the second half of the reign of Elizabeth Tudor, depended on an open audience in London. Although the full extent of dramatic activity is only now being revealed, there would have been no Elizabethan drama if players had remained strollers. Rooted in pastime, plays became a cultivated and selected growth, depending on the coalescence of poets and actors in London, where the theatre evolved as a social institution, in terms of the relationship between certain bands, calling themselves servants of the nobility, their audience and the controlling powers of Church and State.

The new theatre was no unheralded triumph of the poets, served by innovating ranters on a bare stage. At least two hundred years of scenic entertainment in English lay behind it, with their inheritance of traditional skill in mounting shows, singing, reciting. (1) As drama grew out of this wide easy flow of entertainment, professional actors were separated off and defined from the mass of 'players'. The creative leap was taken in the year 1576, when James Burbage of Leicester's Men opened the Theatre in Shoreditch—the most significant date in the history of English drama. To this date, a return will constantly be made: it is the *main* starting-point for each of the four parts of this book.

Medieval playing took many forms and was seasonal and festive. Because it was polymorphous it remained undeveloped, however complex; because it was seasonal and festive, it lacked the concentration which daily habit alone supplies. It was play; and any form of art is work. A picture of sub-dramatic entertainment emerges from the local records of the fourteenth and fifteenth century; pastime and game, folk custom, mumming, shows, disguising, pageants, culminated in the civic theatre of the provincial Mystery Plays, and the metropolitan Royal Entries. Today when the arts of display and production challenge the pre-eminence of the playwright, the power of sub-dramatic forms becomes clear.

What happened in the theatre of the Hall—whether a Lord's Hall or a College Hall—is harder to establish. There are few details of performances there, and fewer of the rewards bestowed, so that the status of performers is hard to define. Visiting 'minstrels', 'histriones' or 'lusores' might provide anything from harping to interludes, as 'plays' or 'games' mean anything from a sack race to a Mystery. At the great festivals, household servants or youthful gentlemen might make their Offering in the Hall. From the more learned of these groups, the literary drama began; but only with the founding of the London theatre was the profession of Actor or Comedian established, while the printing-press gave an independent poetic life to the plays, enabling them to survive the destruction of the theatre which bred them.

Medieval man, if secular or religious only in the sense of Chaucer's monk, led a life of action rather than thoughts; his drama was accordingly one of action and display. Gorgeously arrayed in borrowed vestments, players vaunted themselves on gaily painted pageants or scaffolds; hell belched flames, while the devil 'pomped' in feathers; angels censed and threw roses; the banners of Pilate and Herod miraculously dipped in salute as their Captive was haled into the judgment hall. Drawn upon a hurdle to her martyrdom, St Apollonia had her teeth torn out with a three-foot pair of pincers. Atrocities, dependent sometimes on conjuring tricks, were only one sub-department of the marvellous; King Arthur's frequent and often gratified wish that he might see a marvel before he sat down to feast probably represents the kind of cue which a great lord was expected to give for the entry of some 'unexpected' pageant.

Drama grew directly from a heightened sense of daily life, whether in the Trinity House at Hull where Noah was presented with his plumb-line, or when Alice Perrers, mistress of Edward III, appeared at a tournament as the Lady of the Sun. (2) From the royal court, through the guild plays of the great towns to the village merriment, each had his own form of dramatic festivity—out of doors in Spring and Midsummer, within the Hall at Christmas.

Machinery was costly, and expensive properties appeared again and again, while accompanying speeches might vary for person and occasion. Pageantry of castles and ships, fountains and arbours, flowers that grew up with a turn of a winch and opened to reveal a singing child, trumpeting angels with practicable joints belonged only to great cities; as weeping Madonnas, bleeding crucifixes, bowing Gods in glory belonged only to great churches.

Mystery plays in English can be dated from the third quarter of the fourteenth century; they appeared in Chaucer's lifetime, though not with especial strength in Chaucer's city of London. They belonged to the great religious cities of the prosperous Midlands and north-eastern counties, to York, Coventry, Lincoln, Chester. At Beverley, the guildsmen sat in a wooden 'castle' to see their plays, the civic equivalent of the throne or dais. From 1416 Coventry had its Hock Tuesday martial and historical show, as well as its Mystery plays, presumably with the Church's blessing, (3) but as early as 1352 the Bishop of Exeter was prohibiting lewd plays 'in theatro nostro civitatis'. These were perhaps only town sports on the 'platea' or enclosed green 'place'. For those in the yet remoter west, the Cornish rounds would have provided sites both for 'guary' miracles and for wrestling; at Tintagel, where the great circle lies between churchyard and castle, this double function is powerfully suggested. The lower or castle gate leads to the auditorium, the churchyard gate to the performers' segment.

Humble groups developed seasonal ritual into local pastime; folk drama was the product of the centuries 1200–1500. The processional bringing in of May, with a dance, mock bridal, weddings with rush rings at Midsummer and a night in the greenwood led to the choosing of a Summer Lord and Lady, to ridings and plays of Robin Hood, morris dances and mock fights. At Christmas, St George and the Dragon pranced into the Hall where tenants were feasted by their lord. There were also harvest feasts. In 1244 Bishop Grosseteste complained of clergy who 'make plays that are called miracles, and others called the bringing in of May or Autumn' and banished such plays from his diocese. He also forbade minstrels to be seen or heard in monasteries, but himself entertained a noble harper in his chamber. The social obligations of a great lord spiritual, no less than his superior entertainment, might be urged in mitigation of inconsistency. In the fifteenth century his cathedral city of Lincoln was to become the home of the 'Hegge' plays and of the *Castle of Perseverance*; while at Oxford, one of the College Lords of Misrule mockingly took the title of Robert Grosseteste.

By this time, especially in the richer and more thickly populated regions of the south and the south-east, successful town plays were carried round to neighbouring towns where 'gatherings' were made and feasts held. In the fifteenth century there were such plays at Reading and all along the South Coast—Lydd, New Romney, Hythe, Rucking, Folkestone. New Romney's play was of the Passion, but others may have been secular, as in Grosseteste's days. Lost plays of Sir Eglamour and Degrebell given at St Albans in June 1443, and of 'a knight named Florence' at Bermondsey in the same year, were presumably open-air performances by town players. In 1498 at Dublin, the dumb shows included King Arthur and the Nine Worthies as well as biblical subjects. The secular inclusion of shepherds and midwives in the Mystery plays survives even in the most skilled and costly performance, the sacred Offering—for many guilds carried offertory lights in the procession and the pageants were sometimes known as Corpus Christi Lights.

Guild Pageants circled through the City, stopping before the houses of chief merchants, who paid handsomely for the privilege; town players travelled to neighbouring places carrying their play and shaking their money-box. It was natural also that in the playing season, household servants of the great should visit others in their region, and at Christmas came the boy bishops from the cathedral schools and the song schools of great abbeys. There was competition for good players and in 1473 Sir John Paston complained of the defection of a servant whom he had kept for two years to play 'St George, and Robin Hood and the Sheriff of Nottingham' (4)—a winter and a summer play.

A different pattern prevailed in the far north country, with its great fortified castles, where lords temporal or spiritual held their court in almost royal state, isolated among rough country, with small scattered villages, lonely farms and peel towers hidden in the folds of the hills or on the moorland. The Palatine Bishop of Durham, in whose lands the King's writ did not run, entertained *histriones* of the king in 1300 and 1302; during the Scottish campaign of 1333-5 he received the player troupes of various lords who had evidently accompanied their leaders to war, 'in his party and quarrel defensively arrayed'. *Histriones* of the 'king of Scots' —Balliol, the Pretender—were also entertained. The singing boys of the Chapel Royal went to France in the war of 1544.

This oldest form of service was still found in Elizabeth's reign; in 1586 his players accompanied the Earl of Leicester when he set out to command the Queen's forces in the Netherlands. (5)

Among the tenantry, ballads and northern jigs were popular; and these were to develop into the song-and-dance acts of the Elizabethan public stage. This region was also the home and natural setting for many legends of Arthur, which in the late fifteenth and early sixteenth century became attached to the country round Penrith, maintaining the supremacy of the traditional British hero Gawain, as well as recent heroes like Harry Hotspur. Here the traditional form of entertainer, the minstrel, lingered longest; though the town of Kendal was famous for its play.

The term 'minstrel', used loosely to cover all kinds of professional entertainer, covered also the widest range of eminence and infamy, from sworn servants of the King (minstrels of honour) to gipsy rogues and jugglers, ballad singers and blind fiddlers at a country fair. At the end of the thirteenth century Thomas de Cabham, sub-dean of Salisbury, divided *histriones* into three classes, based on types of performance; the first those who transform their bodies by gestures and leaping, either naked or wearing horrible masks; others, those who tell scurrilous tales; the third—and these alone were tolerable—being musicians and reciters of history. (5a)

Heralds and their allies the minstrels were necessary to a great household; they recited the praises of their lord and his forebears, consoled him in misfortune, celebrated his triumphs, made mock of his enemies. Display, proclamation, challenge were common to heralds and to dramatic shows. Scores of minstrels, including four Kings of the Minstrels, flocked to the Pentecostal feast and tournament of Edward I in 1306. The nineteen minstrels of Edward III received a fee of 12d. a day in war, and 20s. a year in peace; they would enjoy their manchet in the Hall, and occasional rewards as well. By the reign of Edward IV they were required to attend merely for the five great feasts of the year. At other times, only two or three need be in attendance; and their number had dropped to eight in all. The Great Household itself moved round from one royal seat to another, and while the English climate would oblige all minstrels of any standing to attend their lord and eat his bread in the winter season, hopes of reward and restlessness might send them abroad in the summer.

From the fourteenth to the sixteenth century minstrelsy was in steady decline, while local playing was on the increase. As music became more complex, poetry more courtly, society more literate, and as the spectacular standard of ceremonial entertainment was raised, accomplished players attached themselves in other capacities to their lords' households, and became singing men of his chapel, secretaries or chaplains. The term minstrel, confined to the baser kind of performer, became a contemptuous term, which indeed it had sometimes been in Langland's day.

The reign of Edward IV may be taken as the dividing-line; in 1469 he founded a Guild of Minstrels, headed by the royal servants, because of illegal competition from peasants and rude artificers. The musical aspect now predominated over others. The Guild regulated town minstrels, and minstrels of honour: it still survives as the Musicians' Company of London. Its headquarters was the chapel of the Virgin within St Paul's. From very early times the northern minstrels had had their own court at Chester, where the family of de Dutton licensed them annually at the Midsummer Fair. In 1457 the town waits of Coventry were forbidden to visit 'abbots and priors' beyond a ten-mile circuit of the city. These town waits would have been tradesmen, who wore the city badge on their arms. Waits were distinguished from minstrels in the royal accounts, their duty being merely to 'pipe the watch' from Michaelmas to Shrove Tuesday, but elsewhere the terms were interchangeable.

PLAYERS AND SOCIETY

In the mid-sixteenth century one minstrel guild was organized in the south and two in the north, presumably to try to regulate the growing number of strollers and keep them out; these were at Canterbury, York and Beverley. In 1555 the last-named forbade millers, shepherds and husbandmen to act as minstrels outside their own parish. By Elizabeth's time, Thomas Whythorn, music master to Archbishop Parker, could declare that minstrels who 'sold their voices' were no longer worthy of the ancient title and should be called rogues or beggars; John Stockwood could complain in the pulpit of Paul's of 'idle loitering fiddlers and minstrels, with whom we of the country are as much troubled as you are with players', a series of insults to the Earl of Oxford's Men described them as fiddlers or minstrels, (6) and Thomas Newton quoted the proverb 'To live a Minstrel's life' as meaning 'nicely, idly and altogether in a manner upon other men's cost'.

It is difficult to tell whether their 'mirths' included mimes or dumb shows in illustration of the recited tale, as well as jigs and other elementary dialogue forms; whether most minstrels travelled in troupes; or exactly what, beyond their wandering life and the tradition of clerical anathema, they bequeathed to the common players of Elizabeth's day. Besides the pitiably feeble rhymes of the blind John Audelay, the poorest fiddler might carry the noble ballad of Chevy Chase.

At least three other classes of player may be distinguished in the late fourteenth and the fifteenth century; civic performers of the great towns, where it is probable clerical and lay efforts united; interlude players of the great households; and 'lads of the parish' who, perhaps assisted by the sexton or other literate character, produced their seasonal Offerings. By Elizabethan times, the second group had largely absorbed the function of the first, but its members were recruited from the third.

The north country was hospitable to liveried players of

interludes. Records of Selby Abbey show that from about
1450 the players of Yorkist lords began to visit there. In the
years before Bosworth Field there appear men belonging to
the Dukes of York and Gloucester, the Earls of Northumberland and Westmorland, Lord Lovell, Sir James Tyrrell, Sir
Edward Hastings, Sir James Harrington, Sir John Conyers.
At Maxstoke Priory, records give a similar picture. In the
late fifteenth century, players of more than fifty lords have
been recorded; but these may not all have been interlude
players. From this time they were rivalling the 'poor fellowship of the minstrels', and were joined, as it would seem, by
town players. Economic distress may have driven some poor
men to the roads; the artisans in *Histriomastix* take to the
strollers' life because 'trades serve no turns', as in the black
twenties of this century the unemployed Durham miners
in their desperate need went out into the countryside with
their ancient sword dance in the hope of earning their
bread.

The problem of retainers, that is of men who wore the
livery of some household without rendering regular service,
troubled the early years of the Tudor monarchy; it seems
probable that gentlemen would 'entertain' players, as Stow
puts it, if they seemed likely to reflect credit, while the men
would gain protection from a livery, and aspire to social
pretensions beyond those of town players. This could and
almost certainly did lead to the multiplication of small
groups of country players whose standards were little above
those of the minstrels and fiddlers with whom they disputed
the Hall of a country mayor or the favours of a fair-time
crowd. With bear-wards, jugglers and fencers they were an
offence to the eye of the Tudor magistrate; several Elizabethan writers have left unflattering portraits of this
group. (7)

The value of this widespread activity in creating a
potential audience, and enlarging the field from which
performers might be drawn, does not lessen the need for a

metropolitan centre to all this dramatic activity. From all parts of the country there was an inflow of talent. In skill and splendour the city of London must always have been pre-eminent, (8) and the tradition spectacular. Raherus, the *mimus* of Henry I, is said to have magnified the fame of his new priory of St Bartholomew by means of some feigned miracles, which were no doubt feats of conjuring. The Edwards were all patrons of the spectacular tourney and the minstrel; and the rich Livery Companies of London began to celebrate the presence of God's vicegerent in their midst with even more splendour than the great cathedral cities made their Offering to God. From the reign of Richard II the Court became more settled at Westminster. From about 1384 a guild of parish clerks performed Mystery plays at Skinners' Well in summertime, whence it became known as Clerkenwell. Thomas Heywood, an Elizabethan inhabitant of the district, records the tradition and the royal attendance of Edward IV; but these plays were unimportant compared with such Royal Entries as those which greeted Richard II and his successors or, later, the Midsummer Watch at which the Guilds marched by the light of hundreds of cressets, through streets decorated with sweet flowers and green boughs, to the music of trumpeters. (9)

The tragic counterpart to this summer festivity came at the execution of Farrell, a follower of Robert the Bruce, who was led through Cheapside in mockery, dressed as a Summer Lord, with a garland of leaves on his head, to his death beside the Tower; Bruce himself was in mockery described as a Summer Lord. (10) Perhaps memory of such scenes lingers in Shakespeare's *Henry VI*, when the vengeful Margaret crowns Richard of York with a paper crown and stands him on a molehill before stabbing him to death, 'to right our gentle hearted king'.

That king, like other Lancastrians and Yorkists, delighted in shows; Lydgate's mummings for Henry VI and for the City companies, dating from about 1430, survive and were evidently long remembered; for the figures of Lydgate and Henry VI appeared as presenters in the Induction to Richard Tarlton's play of the Seven Deadly Sins some hundred and fifty years later. (11) Richard III is the first king to be known as the patron of a troupe of players, and under the Tudors spectacle increased both in Court and City; but at first in the old multiform style. Pageants of ships, castles, arbours were wheeled along, filled with singing children; or lovely ladies armed with gingerbread, comfits and rosewater repelled the attack of knights. For a coronation or a triumph, the fountains ran with wine. Both in City and Court, the wedding festivities of Prince Arthur and Katherine of Aragon marked a new level of splendour; the King's troupe of four interlude players, headed by John English, in 1503 took a play to Scotland for the wedding of Princess Margaret to the Scottish King.

Perhaps these royal players were still expected to be capable of musical performance or feats of activity, as their Elizabethan descendants certainly were; but simple dialogues, interludes and debates for dramatic performance were already beginning to circulate among the troupes of three, four or five men, who in the services of great lords were giving themselves principally to such performance, and who were moving out in ever wider circles from the service of the Hall.

The distinction between perambulating and strolling is a fine one. A circuit of twelve miles constituted the legal verge of the royal Court; in the north, where distances were greater, players might have thought little of thirty miles. As the lord's men moved out, to gain the admiration and rewards their fine clothes and fine title might win in the countryside, so country players hastened to Court with their offerings. In the early sixteenth century, lord's men and town's players alike were received by the King; before 1509, Henry VII had rewarded not only the men of the Lords of Oxford, Northumberland and Buckingham, but players from London, Essex, Mile End, Wycombe, Wimborne Minster and 'the players of Kingston towards the building of the church steeple'.

Though they might have been entertained, it is unlikely that their plays were actually attended by royalty. Henry's magnificent son himself maintained two troupes, one under English and the other under Sly, making eight men in all. These played at Court and also before the City companies; the Drapers record the name of Hinstock as the leading King's player in the thirties, and from the Elizabethan play of *Sir Thomas More*, the name of another, Mason, can be gathered. More had served as a page in the household of the Cardinal Archbishop of Canterbury, John Morton, who entertained the poet Medwall; this brilliant and learned group wrote and acted farces. Henry VIII's court was rivalled by that of Cardinal Wolsey, and it is 'My Lord Cardinal's players' who come to make their offering of service to the City Sheriff in the play of *Sir Thomas More*. (12)

Besides taking part in tourneys of unparalleled magnificence, or in Christmas mumming and disguising, appearing suddenly in the Queen's chamber disguised as Robin Hood, or in the Cardinal's Hall with a troupe of masquers to court and flirt after the new Italian guise, King Henry encouraged merrymaking among his subjects. He 'knighted' the chief archer of the city band; rode thirty miles to see a play, unrecognized; summoned the boys of St Paul's, who in 1527 put on a play in French and Latin, directed against the 'heretic Luther' for the benefit of the King and the French Ambassador. Christmas was the great season for Revels, led by Lords of Misrule. Both the King and the Lord Mayor had such lords for the better ordering their sports.

In Henry's reign the pattern of Tudor entertainment was fully established. Humble players were already so numerous as to rouse the suspicions of the City Fathers, who in this same year (1527) licensed a stage performance for the benefit of All Hallows Church, but as two years later, in permitting one for the benefit of St Catherine Creechurch, stipulated that no other is to be allowed. (13)

The most magnificent court entertainments came from the Gentlemen and Children of the Chapel Royal under their master William Cornish, who controlled them from 1509 to 1523. They ousted both the King's interlude players and the musicians of the Chamber. Rivalled by the performers of Wolsey's Chapel, perhaps by Lord Oxford's, their dramatic interludes can be imagined from the descriptions given, although no text of Cornish has survived. Nurtured in the splendour of Catholic ritual, pomp was familiar to the players. The account books show how gorgeously these interludes were produced; music, pageantry and costuming outweighed the slight allegorical themes.

Roughly, for the first half of the sixteenth century the theatre of the Hall predominated, where traditional arts mixed with sharp and novel controversy, and dialogue was eventually to challenge display. This, however, was not only the Hall of the great lord, but also of the school, college, or lawyer's Inn. The Interlude developed as part of a feast; its grace and sprightly sharpness depended on the script. Learning was lightly worn by the generation of Erasmus and More, though the plays were often debates of scholastic questions which elsewhere the students might tackle in all solemnity. Sometimes they were made to appear to spring from extempore discussion, as in Medwall's *Fulgens and Lucres* (1497), which starts with a discussion between two servants and turns into a play on the theme 'Wherein consists true honour and nobility?'

The sudden intrusion of players with a cry of 'Room' from the Vice, the apparent irruption of members of the audience into the play, aided the real improvisation to which players must often have been driven, and for which Sir Thomas More was celebrated. It was the common fate of plays given at feasts to be interrupted by spectators' change of plan; and hired players might be turned off and on again like gramophone records. (14) Nevertheless, the kind of attention that can be given in a closed building is always more concentrated than is possible in the open air; sharp debating-points must have been followed keenly by trained listeners. Spectacle became a secondary matter; though gorgeous garments were the players' chief resource, and a change of garment was often the climax to a play, the simple forerunner of the transformation scene. Players became skilful at incorporating convenient features of the Hall, such as the fireplace or the minstrel's gallery, into their action; but Interludes could be staged anywhere, put on cheaply, and, as printers often noted, played by four or five men. Strollers could thus carry round not 'their play' but a whole repertory. In the Elizabethan play the Lord Cardinal's players offer Sir Thomas More the choice of six Interludes (some of which survive), and he chooses *The Marriage of Wit and Wisdom*. Such a theme betrays the origins of the Interlude, either in a school, college or learned household. Redford's famous *Wit and Science* was written for the boys of St Paul's singing school, who in the later part of Henry VIII's reign outshone the performers of the Chapel Royal itself; the most versatile and brilliant writer of interludes, the anti-clerical John Heywood, also wrote for St Paul's boys.

These interludes were eagerly sought for, handed down like worn-out garments to the humbler performers, and persisted for many years in the repertory of country strollers.

Play as offering encouraged and sometimes involved the notion of play as detraction. A neutral performance was something hardly to be understood. The Paul's play against Luther is companioned by Skelton's *Magnificyence* (1529) directed against Wolsey. Four years earlier the Cardinal had sent the lawyer John Roo to the Fleet prison for a play which he thought reflected upon himself. In a closed society, such suspicions were natural; they were most maked in the case of plays at the University. (15)

Henry VIII's break with Rowerm brought opportunity

and new risks for satirists. In the year of his marriage to Ann Boleyn a play satirizing cardinals was produced. A priest in Suffolk offered four plays to Thomas Cromwell; John Bale, another Suffolk priest, stated that he wrote Protestant Miracle plays. In 1537 the scholars of Christ's College, Cambridge, put on the Pope as Antichrist in their play of *Pammachius*, to the scandal of their Chancellor; while in Suffolk, seditious May Games were played by peasants, where 'one played Husbandry and said many things against Gentlemen, more than was in the book of the play'. A papal play given in York caused a seditious rising. In 1539 the first actor martyr, Spencer, a priest turned interlude player, was burned at Salisbury for heretical views on the sacrament, and Sherman, keeper of the Carpenters' Hall in London, was cited before their Court for procuring a play to be acted there 'in which priests were railed on and called knaves'.

In 1542 Sir Richard Morison suggested to Henry that instead of the May Game of Robin Hood and Maid Marian, anti-papal plays should be given 'to set forth and lively declare to the people's eyes the abomination and wickedness of the Bishop of Rome, the monks, friars, nuns and such like, and to declare the obedience due to the King'. But the task of nationalizing popular pastime was one before which even Henry paused. Instead he set out to control it. 1543 saw the beginning of late Tudor censorship.

As early as 1533 interludes on controversial matters had been forbidden. They must therefore have appeared in some numbers. In 1543 a heavy hand was laid on such interludes, together with 'books, ballads, rhymes and other fantasies' which dealt with the interpretation of scripture; offenders were to be tried by the Bishop or two Justices of the Peace. On the other hand, 'all and every person' might set forth plays for rebuking and reproaching of vice and setting forth of virtue.

In the city of London they were forbidden at night—and must therefore have been played. A clothworker was bound over not to produce plays in his house; in April 1543 a craftsmen's company of twenty joiners were jailed for playing on Sunday morning, and three of them committed to the Tower for a fortnight. Four men, the Lord Warden's players, who were sent to the County prison, despite their livery, like the joiners must have been guilty of an offence against order, though their play may not have been seditious. For every such charge preferred, it may be assumed that a dozen others escaped detection.

Pastime had lost its innocence; censorship had begun. A Government utterly inexperienced in problems of this kind could proceed only by trial and error. The process continued, with varying fortunes; the consequence was that casual playing became more difficult, especially in the great cities, so that a few troupes became trusted and preferred, and thus established themselves. Though the attempt to control performance hampered the Elizabethan players, it also made easier the emergence of the Great Companies who founded the Elizabethan stage.

In addition to controlling plays, it became necessary to control players; and this fitted in well enough with existing Tudor policy. The great civic theatres of the provinces, especially the Catholic north, were most dangerous and most vulnerable. They were entirely in the hands of the guilds, and the Government turned to its clerical arm for suppression. The story is by now well known; larger northern towns fought hard to preserve their plays, and the process of suppression was not complete till 1575, when the last performance was given at Chester (the year before Burbage opened his Theatre). As late as 1600, the town sought to revive them. The books were called in for censoring, and eventually censored out of existence; this process was easier than a flat prohibition; and it worked. (16) As the church images were defaced, the illuminated manuscripts thrown to chandlers, so plays fed bonfires or the worm. The Coventry men's 'storial show' was banned although they protested that it was not 'Popish'. These great provincial cities, deprived of their own plays, became the centres for common players, as the records of Coventry, Lincoln, Norwich, Shrewsbury make plain. At Shrewsbury, however, they were rivalled by local schoolboys, who gave famous performances of Whitsun plays in the Quarry, led by their master Ashton, in the early years of Elizabeth's reign; and probably in many smaller places, notably Hadstock in Suffolk, a play-loving centre.

In an age of religious tension, all social and political problems tend to formulate themselves in religious terms. The new union between Church and State was strong, but its exact balance was still precarious. Doctrinal and social interests which led to the control of plays coincided with the need to order the more restless and disorderly part of the population, and so led to the further control of players. A policy of restricting religious comment joined with a policy of keeping society static; that is, of controlling a group which *might* include players.

Wanderers on the roads had been a problem since the mid-fourteenth century, when Langland drew his picture of hermits, minstrels and 'heaps' of friars. Among these wanderers, by the end of the fifteenth century, were many disbanded soldiers who carried the protection of a lord's livery. The term 'retainer', like that of 'minstrel', extended over the widest possible social range, and might cover all from local gentry, who took the livery of a great lord, down to yeomen, tinkers and cobblers.

The connexion between retaining and vagrancy appeared when on 26 May 1545, Henry VIII announced his drastic intention of taking up for the Navy ruffians, vagabonds, masterless men, common players, who haunt the Bankside; and in the same breath once more forbade retaining other than household servants or those allowed by royal licence. The common players in question may have been gamesters, but if any masterless interluders were already on the future site of the Rose and the Globe, they would have been liable to impressment.

B   33

Wanderers were being closed out of entertainment or forced to seek the protection of a livery. Even if he no longer sought to dominate courts of law with his retainers, a large train was necessary for a nobleman's prestige. (17) Celebrated players like the Duttons could skip about from the service of one great lord to another, while some northern households, like Haughton's at Lea Hall, kept resident players in the household. The livery of a mere knight or squire would be significant only in his neighbourhood, and eventually players were accused of dropping their allegiance to their proper lord if they strayed afield and took the livery of someone more important. The tradesmen players of *Histriomastix* (1599) invent a lord for themselves, becoming Sir Oliver Owlet's Men, and offer to play in a country town, distinguishing themselves from the last set—'a couple of coney-catchers that cozen mayors and have no consort but themselves. But we are a full company, and our credit with our master known.' They abandon this town performance to play before a lord who offers a higher reward, but finds their playing so bad that he orders them to break off; and their final fate is to be taken up for soldiers, in spite of pleading the privilege of their livery. Their apparel is looted by the troops, who cry, 'Come on players, now we are the Sharers and you the hired men. . . . Look up and play the Tamburlaine. . . .'

Without the protection of their livery such strollers could have been disowned by the minstrels' guilds (but for strollers the guild form of social organization did not work well). Poor gentlemen may have been prepared to sell their protection, as it appears that they sold their livery to wealthy yeomen's sons to escape the need for military service. (18)

Although Edward VI repealed his father's Act of censorship of 1543, during his reign and that of Mary, as religious tension grew, control tightened. In 1549 plays defaming the Book of Common Prayer were banned—so they must have existed; a London currier was forbidden to put on plays in his house; while in August the king forbade any plays till All Saints, the start of the Christmas season. The Lord Mayor then arranged for any interludes given in London by 'common players' to be inspected by two deputies. In 1551 penalties were imposed, bombasted out with a long moral diatribe against such common players as 'idle persons who live by others' labour'. Plays in English were now required to be licensed by the King or six of his Privy Council; which meant in effect that they could not be licensed at all. Lord Dorset's players were licensed to perform only in his presence. In 1552, a London cooper was in trouble and was sent to the Tower. The Venetian Ambassador reported virulent anti-papal plays. High and low alike were seething.

In administrative terms, the problem was to avoid flat prohibition and find some practical way of supervision through delegation from the central power. Mary combined her father's and her brother's methods, requiring the licence of the Privy Council for plays and also forbidding any handling of scripture or religious doctrine. In practice she appears to have tolerated licensing locally by Justices of the Peace; but in 1557 plays were forbidden in London even during the Christmas season, unless licensed by the Ordinary; while the founding of the Stationers' Company in the same year attempted the control of printing.

Meanwhile players continued to give trouble—village players in Sussex, Essex, Canterbury, players in London and the northern parts. Sir Francis Leek's Men put on a seditious play in the north; they were a wandering troupe, wearing his livery, and badge on their sleeves. The leader of Protestant polemical playing, John Bale, had fled overseas: Hunnis of the Chapel Royal, imprisoned in the Tower for his share in the Throgmorton plot, shivered in rags as winter drew on.

Passions of religious controversy forced development of the common players, as they forced Government planning.

Elizabeth began her reign in the Christmas season of 1558, and the Court saw some anti-papal Antics; she started cautiously in her efforts at control with a proclamation of May 1559. As the season for playing interludes was now past till All Saints, and some that had been played were unsuitable, in future no plays were to be given either openly or privately except as approved by the Mayor, two Justices of the Peace, or the Lord Lieutenant. Anything dealing with matters of religion or Government was to be eliminated, nobles and gentlemen to be held responsible if their servants did not obey.

This proclamation formed the basis of the Elizabethan censorship, later expanded to a central check on playbooks through the Revels Office, with a local countercheck on performance through the Mayor and Justices. It is in fact the basis of control today; the Lord Chamberlain censors plays, and the local Watch Committee the conditions of performance.

Henry VIII's experiment of propaganda was briefly and unsuccessfully revived in 1589, during the Marprelate controversy with the Puritans, but it led to the closing of the theatres. Like the earlier 'troublesome times' for actors, this ensured that only the strongest survived.

Although plays given privately by privileged groups might occasionally be subject to censorship, the social risks which the Government most feared were those arising from the common people inflamed by propaganda. Control therefore increased in severity as plays were openly given, while the difficulty of enforcement mounted in proportion as players or audience were casually assembled.

So the joiners, coopers and curriers were censored out of playing—although at the Hall of the suppressed Guild of the Holy Trinity at St Botolph's, Aldersgate, plays were given from 1557—the height of Mary's Catholic revival—to 1568. In spite of the earlier prohibition upon performance at night, in 1543 and 1553 some of these plays were given at late hours; at St Olave's Silver Street, on 29 July, 1557, 'a stage-play of a goodly matter' began at eight in the evening and ended at midnight 'with a good song'. (19) The prohibition of nocturnals in 'houses, court-yards or gardens' was repeated in 1569, and again as late as November 1584.

The official tendency to restrict and limit players was sharply confirmed by the great Act for Restraining Vaga-bonds of 1572. This required licensing of all troupes, and confined the power to noblemen only, or to Justices of the Peace. The latter would presumably have licensed any of the old town or village players who wished to travel with their play. But the day of such players was over, though in North-wich in Cheshire in 1575/6 the town waits were licensed to play Comedies and Interludes and Tragedies. The Chelms-ford players, who had been wont to hire out their costumes to neighbouring towns, sold off their stock in 1574; as Brain-tree did in 1579. Once, the author of *Ralph Roister Doister* himself had provided them with a play. Bungay, in play-loving Suffolk, followed in 1591. In 1597, when the Act was renewed with amendments, the Justices lost their power to license, while the nobles, for better security must each put hand and seal to the authorization of players. By now town players had presumably withered away. (20)

The effect of the Act of 1572 was to define the actors' status, restrict the number of licensed troupes, and so by a process of concentrating ability to foster the growth of professionalism, while at the same time it confirmed the old status of the lord and his men. This might otherwise have disappeared, for an entirely different form of organization was growing up. The object of the Act was to stop poor strollers from pestering the country. The result was a growth of corporate bodies who by the end of Elizabeth's reign had evolved into the Common Players of Shoreditch, and Bank-side. Their stability, their relatively fixed station, enabled them to fulfil the hopes of Sir Richard Morison in a far grander way than he could have imagined possible, and in

Shakespeare's history cycle to present, by way of pastime, all the glories of the State.

In the course of two centuries playing in England had evolved from its heterogenous beginnings to a recognized art. The heralds and minstrels, with their traditional skills of proclamation and display, aiming at praise or contempt; the craftsmen with their carpentry, gilding and colours; the clash and shock and brilliant pageantry of the tournament; the harpers, singers, tumblers, gymnasts; the conjurers with their terrifying tricks and marvellous transformations; all contributed to the art of the Theatre. The players themselves represented the heralds and minstrels; the liveried household servants; the provincial craftsmen; and the humble 'lads of the parish' with a kettle for a helmet and a wooden sword. For many of them were the sons of such men.

All this merrymaking had been drawn together by poets and dramatists of the great houses, the young men of Oxford, Cambridge and the Inns who supplied the interludes, the comedies, histories and tragedies. If traditional sports and traditional Offerings had not been given new form by the debaters, and turned to the handling of vital controversial issues, there might have been an Elizabethan theatre, but there would have been no Elizabethan drama. The interlude, product of the New Learning, sired that drama, though its power, scope and richness derived largely from the great and diversified popular shows and pastime. Interludes themselves were not made to be read but to be performed; Elizabethan drama was likewise an embodied art, and existed for performance. To treat it as book-art is to do it great violence. By a 'play' it is probable that no Elizabethan would have meant the script or 'book', but always an *event*, the play-in-being, the enacted mime in which players and audience shared. This deep and natural immersion in performance, this assumption of a common activity, was their most precious inheritance from the theatre of the Middle Ages.

CHAPTER II

THE NEW ESTATE

Social Status of the Common Player in London
1559-1603
The Rise of Leicester's Men and the Founding
of the Theatre

Social opposition to players, especially strollers—the value of the servingman's livery—opposition in the City of London—conflicts between central and local government—trouble in the provinces—rise of Leicester's Men—use of inn-yards for acting —the Patent for Leicester's Men—their building of the Theatre —further developments inside and outside the City—activities of Henslowe—social establishment of the actor's profession—its full recognition in the last years of Elizabeth
and the first years of James I.

THE two succeeding chapters follow the main stem of Elizabethan dramatic development; the evolution of the leading troupes of Common Players, their settlement in London, and their triumph over the opposition which their success evoked. This was so strong as several times to threaten the demolition of their wooden galleries and gaily painted scaffoldage, leaving them only the forlorn shell of an empty ring. By skill, audacity and persistence, the actors overcame the fears and social prejudice of powerful and well-entrenched resistance.

Under the protective shield of their lord's badge, invoking a declining, obsolescent form of service, which was in their case sometimes little better than a legal fiction, the players established themselves as purveyors of a commodity for which the general public was prepared regularly to put down its cash. They did not aspire to 'honour's lofty reach' or sink to the level of country hedger and thresher but

> *Your patience yet we crave awhile till we have trimmed*
> *   our stall;*
> *Then young and old come and behold our wares and buy*
> *   them all.*
> *Then if our wares shall seem to you well woven, good and*
> *   fine,*
> *We hope we shall your custom have again another time.* (1)

Players aspired to the condition of merchants and citizens; to attain it, they masqueraded as members of the gentlemanly profession of serving men. By their enemies, they were constantly confounded with rogues and vagabonds, thieves and cheaters who lived at Fortune's alms. It was the men to whose condition they aspired who provided the strongest opposition. The merchants were their steadiest opponents; while the moral claim that plays taught virtue made players into rivals of the only licensed instructors, the preachers of the Word. Every attempt to justify players on didactic grounds was met by the retort that plays were the devil's sermons—a hideous mockery or antitype of true instruction. (2) The rhetoric and showmanship of preacher and actor are not entirely dissimilar, and this natural rivalry left the player at a severe disadvantage, for all authority and prestige lay with his opponent.

His difficulty sprang from his lack of any fixed status or recognized place in the commonweal; his occupation was in its present form not traditional. Having no place in the scheme of things, he had no place in society. The establishment of two playhouses, the Theatre and the Curtain, in 1576 and 1577 was a turning-point in the struggle; shared with other purveyors of pastime, such as fencers and bearbaiters, they were the outward and visible sign of the common players' right. The public ring or fenced 'platea' outside the City walls, familiar enough in the provinces, had in the City of London been converted to the private property of the common player, owned or leased. It was almost a form of Enclosure, comparable to the enclosure of the common fields, and even more profitable; and for its greater glory, given the Roman title of Theatre, at which the godly and learned were inclined to raise an eyebrow.

The war upon plays and the war upon players were not quite the same thing. At moments of crisis, the central Government might put down plays without necessarily feeling hostile to players; extreme ascetics, such as Rainolds of Oxford, would ban not only public acting but all academic exercises and 'morals teaching education' as well.

The Government aimed at preserving the peace, by regulating and, if necessary, suppressing inflammatory public comment on risky subjects. The City's steadfast attempts to put down players sprang from a variety of feelings. Those acknowledged were: Protestant aversion from idolatry and images; danger from pugnacity in the audience; and the infection of plague. But in addition certain prejudices, based on social conservatism, operated against a new and hitherto unrecognized form of employment, whose position was ambiguous, while its profits were infuriating.

In the early part of Elizabeth's reign, merriment and interlude were not differentiated yet from games and festivities, three-men songs, jigs and feats of activity. Dramatic art as an independent skill emerged but slowly from the cocoon of 'playing'; the emergence of the art followed the emergence of a new class of men, performing a recognized social function. This is the basis of the Elizabethan struggle. The position was won by, and conceded to, two or three Great Companies, who achieved a local habitation and a name in the capital. Following Leicester's Men in the mid-seventies, the Queen's Men in the eighties, the two Great Companies of the Lord Admiral and the Lord Chamberlain finally took the lead in the nineties. (3) For polemical purposes these Great Companies could still be confused with the crowd of pitiable vagabonds who roamed the countryside, their packs filled by a few tattered gaudy garments and a half-dozen thumbed old interludes. In practice, they established themselves as a new estate—one of the most difficult achievements in a society which demanded that traditional form at least should be adhered to; which poured new wine into old bottles and supplied long pedigrees for its new nobility.

Class consciousness had never been more acute than it was under the Tudors, with new chances of rapid rise and fall. The remedy for social evils was generally held to consist in the firm maintenance of things as they were. All should keep to traditional occupations: the Catechism could be wrested to mean that

> *In this world there cannot be*
> *More great abomination*
> *To thy Lord God, than is in the*
> *Forsaking thy vocation*

and so keep
> *The landlord with his term,*
> *The ploughman with his ferme,*
> *The knight with his fee,*
> *The merchant with his ware.*
> *Then should increase the health*
> *Of the commonwealth.* (4)

The City merchants whose opposition to the players was most unrelenting, and whose fine new houses so prominently displayed their own superfluous wealth, themselves did not always observe traditional formulations, but this only sharpened their disapproval of upstarts like the common players.

In such a society, their lord's badge was socially as well as legally of great value to the men. Theoretically, like the boys' troupes, they were giving London performances as rehearsals for their Christmas Offering at Court; any attack on them was an attack on the Queen's 'solace'. The vital point was that players did not receive houseroom or wage off their lord; and that admission to their rehearsals was not free.

The writer of that nostalgic and old-fashioned pamphlet, *A Health to the Gentlemanly Profession of Serving Men* (1598) depicts an idyllic society in which poor gentlemen trained up to service were in all senses the companions of their masters. Having a small patrimony, they did not depend on wages but on the rewards that came their way from their master and his friends—the good marriage that might be arranged, the rent-free farm in old age. Lords despised money and seldom used it, living 'of their own', hunting with a large retinue in the carefree manner of Lear with his hundred knights.

Servingmen's only maintainance consisted in liberality, for their wages was never able in any age to defray their necessary charges and expenses. But I would not have you misconster this Liberality, that it was bestowed on them in mere commiseration, pity and charity, as them of ability do upon impotent beggars; but the servant by his duty and diligence, did merit and deserve it, though it was over and above his covenant and bargain.   (D2 v)

By this time, the writer says, the master despises the servingman—no trained gentleman, but some clown who serves without wages to avoid military service; or else 'covenants they keep and perform as artificers do with their apprentices and workmen with their labourers; but preferment over and above get they none'. The indignity of a fixed wage is clear. Thomas Whythorn, when he became a servingman, felt this degrading for a musician.

In their lack of any wages at all from their lord, players bettered the most gentlemanly tradition. They seem to have established a rough scale for their occasional performances in private. £6, 13s. 4d. was the customary reward for a court performance in the early part of Elizabeth's reign, which if Her Majesty were especially pleased, she might double or treble; in 1575 the reward begins to jump and within a year or so is established at £10, where it remained throughout her reign. Forty shillings is the top price for provincial plays, and ten shillings more common. Forty shillings was the boost to the box office supplied by the Essex faction when they got Shakespeare's company to put on the old play of *Richard II* at the Globe on 7 February 1601. (5)

Players' reception in the country depended largely on whose livery they wore, and rewards were proportional to the grandeur of their lord, though gatherings no doubt depended on merit. In a provincial city, the Mayor after giving permission for a performance would bestow his reward, to which the bystanders would add what they pleased; but the Lord Mayor of London and the City Fathers, who put on their own highly expensive Shows on Simon and Jude's Day, and on great public occasions, were by no means disposed to reward common players. Aldermen and members of the Common Council might, however, command performances in their houses; and it would seem that sometimes these performances were what we should call 'public'—that is, anyone was admitted, and the players took up a gathering. Any large hall, garden, or courtyard would have served players; the records make it clear that performances in London were by no means confined to inn-yards. (6) Profit making by individual citizens would not be at all incompatible with collective denunciation of players.

The City records speak for themselves. Plays were first flatly forbidden, outdoor or indoors, in 1542. Then they were allowed only in the Livery Halls, the private houses of Aldermen, or the open street. They were forbidden before three o'clock, forbidden after five o'clock, forbidden on Sundays, forbidden in Lent, forbidden in Cheapside. They were to be played only in open streets and not in close and secret places. Prentices and journeymen are forbidden to go to plays. At least five times plays are forbidden for plague. The City made three determined general attempts to put down plays —in 1574-6, 1580-4 and 1597-1600. Yet after each defeat, the players returned. Their own ingenuity and persistence and the strength of public appetite are the only explanations.

The economic motive emerges clearly in this series of prohibitions, coupled with an attempt to keep the players to the traditional rôle of serving men. In London in 1565 plays were forbidden 'where any money shall be demanded or paid for the sight or hearing'. In 1574 the profits made by the children of Paul's was one of the objections brought against them by the City Fathers—such small players, such enormous profits! As late as November 1584 the City protested to the Privy Council:

It hath not been used nor thought meet heretofor that players should have or should make their living on the art of playing . . . but that men for their living using other honest and lawful arts or retained in honest services have by companies learned some interludes for some increase to their profit by other men's pleasures in vacant times of recreation. (*M.S.C.* I, 2, 172)

The *quête* of the folk players was tolerable, but to live permanently by such means was intolerable and dishonest. As they had done before, the City Fathers demanded that players should appear only at weddings or other festivities 'without public or common collection of money or of the auditors or beholders thereof'.

Village players who went round shaking their money-box became for the time strolling players; now, this custom appeared to have so extended that some men were living in a state of perpetual holiday. As late as 1591 it could still be observed that formerly even royal players appeared from All Hallows till Twelfth Night only 'and these men had other trades to live of'. At Christmas also servants would give shows 'without making to be players to go abroad for gain' and artisans would play for recreation of their labours without collecting money. (7)

Firm persistence in public standards clearly obsolete could lead only to discomfiture, but domestic rebellion could at least be quelled. It seems that schoolmasters had joined in the competition for public patronage; for in March 1574 the Merchant Taylors' company observed that when boys from their school played in the Livery Hall

at our common plays and such like exercises which be commonly exposed to be seen for money, every lewd person thinketh himself (for his penny) worthy of the chief and most commodious place.

(*E.S.* II, 75)

The Merchant Taylors were the boys' patrons and lords, but had been thrust aside in their own Hall and not given the seats of honour as Chief Spectators, which traditionally were their right. No more plays were to be allowed in consequence. This was not pure City pomposity, (8) simply the assertion of the ancient social form of Drama as the private 'Offering' to a superior from his servants or dependents.

Tumults had damaged the building also; and the Merchants added that concourse

bringeth the youth to such an impudent familiarity with their betters that often times great contempt of masters, parents and magistrates followeth thereof.

Society demanded that all men should owe allegiance to a lord, or to a master, from whom they received paternal and authoritative supervision. (9) An ordinary man was expected to have some one place where he belonged and where he earned his living honestly, because only so could he receive this paternal supervision. Settlement was the great Elizabethan panacea for all social ills; it meant stability. Hence the scandal of a wandering life. Players fulfilled none of these requirements. They were without fixed habitation and were subject to a bewildering variety of control. Socially the whole problem of the actors in the seventies and eighties turned on the question of who should control them, and in what respects; for by these ligaments of control and responsibility they eventually became knit into the community.

For some time, however, they found themselves between the crossfire of central and local government. Henry VIII issued a letter enabling one of his own jesters Thomas Brandon to 'crash' the City and become free of the Leather-sellers (10), but no one else was capable of such boldness, though Hunnis of the Chapel Royal insinuated himself by marrying the widow of a Grocer. Noblemen might demand extraordinary privileges for their players; the Lord Mayor of London has the precedence of an Earl and could say 'No' to Pembroke or Worcester on occasion.

The moral objections of the City were therefore based on the fact that Playing was not Work, but Idleness. To be given entirely to this way of life was to be guilty of Idleness, to promote it in others. Social duty required not only that the labourer should work for all in the sweat of his brow, but that he should work without respite. Lords might enjoy some recreation, but artificers should not need so much. 'That in the captain's but a choleric word, which in the soldier is flat blasphemy.'

To demand rewards for this idle way of living was to be guilty of a kind of dishonesty, cheating or filching money gained by labour of others. Acting was not recognized as a commodity. Entertainments should be free and spontaneous; so players were freely compared both with thieves and with whores. (Even after they had achieved success, a mocking pamphleteer in *Ratsei's Ghost* (1604) could put them under the protection of a highwayman, who knights the chief player as Sir Simon Two-Shares-and-a-Half!)

Finally, as both City and Court were convinced, to be without fixed habitation and membership of a local community was to be suspect. In an age familiar with displaced persons and large-scale unemployment these social problems seem commonplace and the responsibility to lie with the community; but to the Elizabethan magistrate, idleness was guilt and vagrancy was crime; players were judged guilty by association, and the best of them confounded with the worst.

Everyone agreed that players should be controlled, and most of these concerned were prepared to do it themselves. The conflict between the Court and the City of London, most acute between 1574 and 1584, produced a series of experiments out of which in the end a working compromise emerged. When, a decade later, in 1597-1600, the two seemed united in a desire to reduce playing, none of their ferocious orders for the tearing down of scaffolds had any consequences. The bark of the Elizabethan Government was very much worse than its bite, when the regulating of large numbers of society was involved, since it lacked any power capable of dealing with more than a handful of offenders. In short, there was neither standing army nor professional police. Consequently the Acts of the Privy Council often seem to indicate a target which they hope will be approached, rather than an order which they fully expect to be carried out. (11)

If the City Fathers had both economic and moral objections to players, they had a much more immediate apprehension of the danger of riotous assemblies. The Privy Council were given to snapping at them for their weakness in enforcing proscriptions; the Lord Mayor in his turn would threaten the Justices of the Peace for Middlesex. (12) In the weakness of coercive power lay the players' opportunity; nor did they lack the gentlemanly boldness conferred by their livery.

In 1580 the young lawyers of the Inner Temple were engaged in a fight with some of Lord Oxford's men, including Lawrence Dutton, one of the family of 'Chameleons'. Next year members of Gray's Inn made an onslaught on Lord Berkeley's players, whose lord came to their defence and wrote to the Lord Mayor that they had been set upon and should be released. Their misdemeanour had been to play on Sunday; but if set free, they would depart.

On other occasions the Lord Mayor would find himself flatly disobeyed, as by James Burbage who stood upon his lord's protection; or by Lord Strange's Men, when, warned by the Lord Mayor of general inhibition, they yet 'in very contemptuous manner departing from me, went to the Cross Keys and played that afternoon'. (13) 'Contempt' is the fault urged against players even by friends such as Henry Chettle. In the later years of the century, Worcester's Men, the third company, striving to rival the two leading troupes, were consequently particularly ill behaved, both in town and country. In the provinces, a defiant attitude was more frequent; the Mayor of Norwich would give players a reward to depart without playing; they would take the money and play for a week. He would produce a letter from the Privy Council; they would flourish their patent.

Although the Council were prepared to support players in London, where they provided entertainment for the Court, on other occasions severity prevailed. In October 1575, the Vice-Chancellor of Cambridge University made a plea against 'bad persons . . . wandering about the country' and was told to beware of 'light and decayed persons who for *filthy lucre* are minded . . . to devise and set up in open places shows . . . of unhonest games'; he was to forbid open shows within five miles. In consequence of this, the University was less troubled for many years afterwards, except for the disturbances provided by their own plays. In 1584, further disturbances at Oxford caused the Queen to speak sharply to Leicester the Chancellor, and he, who in his youth had played the part of a Christmas Prince at the Inner Temple sports, and whose players had supplied the royal entertainment for a decade, wrote

as I . . . think the prohibition of common stage players very requisite, so would I not have it meant thereby that tragedies, comedies and exercises of learning . . . should be forbidden. (14)

The toleration of common plays was a matter of time and place, and at the University the danger of turbulence was too great; further reasons included care for the students' health, the need to save them spending their small exhibitions on such follies, and the need to avoid 'lewd and evil sports'.

In 1592 the Cambridge prohibition was renewed after a renewed complaint signed by Legge, the author of *Richardus Tertius*, among others. The year before, Gager, chief champion of academic plays at Oxford, could write that he was concerned only to defend the dignity of his college and the efforts of the towardly young men, his friends; as for plays, 'I can forebear, and think of them as they are'. He agreed with his academic opponent that to play for money made players infamous. Amateurs were not involved in this infamy, denounced by St Augustine and by the schoolmen; but Rainolds, Gager's opponent, who himself in youth had acted in *Palamon and Arcite* before the Queen, continued to denounce every kind of play on moral grounds and with all the lack of charity that moral grounds confer. The players continued likewise to visit the Universities, where they were given some small reward to go away peaceably without playing, or where they acted privately. *Hamlet* and *Volpone* must have been so given. Meanwhile the drama of the schools, so venturous and experimental in the first half of the century, declined and withered away to Christmas shows and other sub-dramatic forms.

Wherever provoked, common players showed their spirit. At Norwich in June 1583, one Wynsdon tried to get into the Queen's Men's performance without paying, and upset the takings. Pursued by the stage duke in full costume (it was Bentley) and by Singer and Tarlton, he fled. His servant hit the 'Duke' on the head with a stone; luckily it was a servant of Sir William Paston and not a player who stabbed and killed Wynsdon. More luckily, the story seems never to have reached London and the players' clerical opponents there, who would certainly have made the most of it.

By 9 July of that year the Queen's Men were at Cambridge and the Vice-Chancellor must have been relieved that the University was down for the Long Vacation.

Yet considering all chances, the record of grave disturbances at plays in the later sixteenth century is negligible, in relation to the number of performances given. Perhaps the City Fathers did not realize the calming effect of an admission charge. Those who have paid their penny want their pennyworth. In the sixties and seventies fear of sedition and 'busy rumour' made it preferable that plays should be given in the open street, whatever hindrance to traffic the traffic of the stage might impose. For in 'close and secret place' performances might have reached that depth of pointedness and caustic freedom customary at the University and Inns of Court. It was part of the oath of every freeman of the city that he should report any conventicles and secret meetings to the Lord Mayor.

In writing the famous scene in *Sir Thomas More* against the evils of rioting, Shakespeare (if it were he), in depicting the plight of the poor Flemings sent plodding to the coast for transportation, may well have been prompted by the sad and similar fate of poor players, sent to trudge the roads for ill-behaviour not their own. His keen sense of the horrors of civil disorder must have been sharpened by the direct consequences for his company of any breach of the Queen's peace at the playhouse.

Like the Flemings, players remained sojourners; others could indulge in conduct which would have been fatal to them. When, in the Christmas sports of 1594, the students of Gray's Inn could not by reason of tumults go forward with their own play, they called in the common players to put on *The Comedy of Errors*. Next night they amused themselves by trying for witchcraft one of their number, disguised as a conjuror, alleging that he had caused their disorders and then brought in to their disgrace 'a sort of base and common fellows'. These common fellows in all probability included Richard Burbage and William Shakespeare. Only a jest; but a sharp one.

PLAYERS AND SOCIETY

When Elizabeth came to the throne in 1558 she inherited from her sister the four interlude players who were paid servants; their names continue in the household accounts till 1585, but their acting if continued must have been for private amusement only. She had also lutanists and musicians of her chamber, gentlemen and singing boys of her Chapel. Companies of trumpeters, jugglers, a fool, a minstrel and a bear-ward toured the country in her livery. All were part of the old household, the rambling, casual, motley company, descended from the Great Household of medieval times, which had eaten together in Hall of the royal bread, and of which the inferior part had 'gone out of court' to travel.

Her entertainment, however, was largely provided from the households of her nobles whose privilege it was to amuse her. The greatest of her subjects was Leicester; his star rose with her accession. During the reign of Mary, imprisoned in the Tower for his part in the reign of his sister-in-law Jane Gray, Robert Dudley had been in no position to require household entertainers; but in 1559 he was writing to the President of the North to allow his men to play in Yorkshire. When he wished to entertain his sovereign they would of course be summoned from trudging the roads and would appear with the Bear and Ragged Staff on their sleeves to swell his train and support his dignity. Not till the seventies did they become the dominant London group; they provided the model for all later troupes.

In 1565, Leicester was licensed to retain a hundred persons, yet it is doubtful if the players had any formal standing in his household. In these early days, companies sometimes played together; the better the player the more likely he was to change services as he pleased—the gifted Duttons changed their livery so often that they were nicknamed 'The Chameleons'. But Leicester's Men could complain of a cobbler who spoke evil words of the Bear and Ragged Staff, and Tarlton found it ill to jest with a man who wore on his sleeve Lord Clinton's badge of a Salamander.

52

THE NEW ESTATE

It seems that, as Stow reports, divers great men would 'entertain' companies of players into their service; that is, they would bestow a suit of livery on any group of players who seemed likely to add to their credit. These could have been aspiring groups of craftsmen. When they opened the Theatre, Leicester's group consisted of five men. There is no evidence that they used Leicester House. When as prelude to the Act for the punishment of vagabonds an order against retainers was proclaimed in 1572, directed against 'masterless men, not using any lawful merchandise, craft or mystery' and including practisers of 'subtle, crafty and unlawful Games or Plays' such as fortune telling, physiognomy, juggling, also pedlars, tinkers, petty chapmen, 'fencers, bear-wards, common players in interludes and minstrels, not belonging to any Baron or honourable person of greater degree', Leicester's men, at this time six in number, appealed to their lord for protection. Had they resided in his great house, just outside the City, they need not have begged

... that you will now vouchsafe to retain us as your household servants and daily waiters, not that we mean to crave any further stipend or benefit at your lordship's hands but our liveries as we have had, and also your Honour's licence to certify that we are your household servants when we shall have occasion to travel among our friends as we do usually once a year and as other noblemen's players do and have done in times past. (*M.S.C.* I, 4 and 5, 348-9)

A little quatrain praying for their Lord wound up the petition, similar perhaps to the prayer for the Queen which wound up a public performance.

> *Long may your lordship live in peace,*
> *A peer of noble peers,*
> *In health, wealth and prosperity,*
> *Redoubling Nestor's years.*

The patent, sought by Burbage, Perkin, Laneham, Johnson, Wilson and Clark, would protect these men individually as well as collectively. By the process known as 'exemplification' any one of them could carry his privileges with him, and extend them to cover a group which he joined. (15) On the other hand, it bound more firmly together a strong fellowship, such as Leicester's Men; the tie between the men was stronger than the one binding each to his lord. Responsibility for their stock of plays and garments, for paying the hired men and musicians, the landlord of their house or inn, and later of finding clothes and lodging for their boy-players, rested upon the troupe.

It is probable that by 1572 they were already playing at the Cross Keys in Gracechurch Street, with which Burbage was certainly later associated. 'Taverns, inns and victualling houses' are mentioned as early as November 1565 as places where 'money is paid or demanded for hearing plays'. Two years later John Brayne, a grocer and Burbage's brother-in-law, expended £8, 10s. on scaffolding for plays at the Red Lion in Stepney. Burbage was a joiner and knew all about scaffolding.

The inn would provide an audience ready assembled; it could make a profit from selling refreshments to the playgoers. The Bell Inn hired out properties for court shows. Players could deposit their wardrobe and make a fixed financial arrangement with the innkeeper, to play regularly on certain days. Some joined their tenants; Tarlton, and another famous clown, John Shanks, began as innkeepers; Alleyn was an innkeeper's son.

Whether for these reasons, or simply that their yards were larger than the space any other citizen could offer, the innkeepers gradually captured this trade of housing the players (although as late as April 1600 a stationer was trying to build a theatre in Nightingale Lane, East Smithfield). (16)

By March 1574 it was recognized that some of the companies belonging to noblemen were not only able but flourishing, and it occurred to someone at Court, always looking for new ways of skimming the profits from trade, that a patent for licensing playing places in London would be a useful and rewarding way of control. In reply to a polite request from the Lord Chamberlain, the Lord Mayor wrote a refusal to the Court. The power to restrict assembly was vital to the control of the City and could not be delegated. Moreover, the City collected considerable sums for poor relief by granting the privilege of playing within their walls; and this power they intended to retain.

Those who contribute to the poor relief cannot themselves be considered beggars; though it seems from *Histriomastix* that even broken players might still be dunned by the Constable for this tax on performance.

The City, however, could not really be mollified even by subsidy, and hedged its permission to players with many restrictions. Hence the magnificent riposte of 10 May 1574, when Letters Patent under the Great Seal of England were granted to James Burbage, John Perkyn, John Laneham, William Johnson and Robert Wilson, the Earl of Leicester's Men.

to use, exercise and occupy the art and faculty of playing comedies tragedies interludes stage plays and such other like as they have already used and studied or hereafter shall use and study as well for the recreation of our loving subjects as for our solace and pleasure . . . as also to use and occupy all such instruments as they have already practised . . . to shew publish exercise and occupy to their best commodity . . . as well within our City of London and liberties of the same as also within the liberties and freedoms of any our cities towns boroughs etc as without the same . . . any act statute proclamation or commandment . . . to the contrary notwithstanding . . . provided the said comedies tragedies interludes and stage plays be by the Master of our Revels (for the time being) before seen and allowed and that the same be not published or shewen in the time of common prayer or in the time of great and common plague in our said City of London. (17)

This was the first social gesture of recognition towards the art of the stage; a unique privilege never repeated. The

Patent overrode the traditional right of the City to control what happened within its boundaries, and may have been issued as a forcing bid to bring the City Fathers to reason. Leicester's Men had been given in effect a Patent of Monopoly. By putting them under the Master of the Revels as censor, they were brought within the orbit of the Royal Household.

The City could retaliate only by laying down minute regulations requiring all plays and players to be licensed by the City Chamberlain, as well as all playing places; which on 6 December was duly done, not without great complaint of affrays and quarrels, incontinency in inns, heiresses allured to secret contracts, withdrawals from divine service, unthrifty waste of the money of poor and fond persons, accidents from the collapse of staging or from gunpowder used in plays. (18) The decree specifically exempts performances given for festivity in the houses of the Lord Mayor and Aldermen. This duplicate Order in effect nullified the Patent, as far as London was concerned, since the City was prepared to enforce it.

Emboldened by the support of the great, the players took the next and decisive step. On 13 May 1576 James Burbage of Leicester's Men signed the lease of a plot in Holywell in the parish of St Leonard's Shoreditch, outside the City walls, on which the first public playhouse was built. The history of the London stage had begun.

The grounds of the old Benedictine nunnery of St John's lay north-west of Bishopsgate, running along both sides of Holywell Street, which was parallel to the City wall. The Theatre stood on the north side, where the main convent building had been; the following year it was joined by the Curtain, a smaller house built on the south side, in what had been the nuns' curtene, or close. The Curtain was probably built by an actors' syndicate, and was used as an overflow house; by 1585 it was under joint management with the Theatre and at least two of the Chamberlain's Men owned shares in it later. There was probably a joint storage for wardrobe and properties somewhere in the old buildings. After a quarrel with the ground landlord of the Theatre in 1597, Burbage's company retreated there, and when in 1598 the scaffolds of the Theatre were taken down and re-erected in 1599 on the Surrey side to form the seating of the Globe, the little Curtain remained and was still standing thirty years after its more famous companion had vanished.

Four London inns were also regularly used for acting between 1575 and 1596. On the great arterial road leading up from London Bridge to Bishopsgate, the north-east gate of the City, the Bell and the Cross Keys lay in the south part (Gracechurch Street), and the Bull to the north. To the west, on Ludgate Hill, the Belsavage challenged the boys of St Paul's and of the Chapel at Blackfriars. The Boar's Head beyond Aldgate was perhaps converted to a theatre later. Tarlton and therefore possibly the rest of his first company, Sussex's Men, played at the Bull, the Bell and the Belsavage. When in 1596 players were finally driven from the inns, Burbage tried to gain a footing at the Blackfriars. He bought the old fencing school, but was stopped from using it by his own lord, a tenant there.

The system of payment was apparently the same at the theatres, the inns and the bear-baiting ring. Money was divided daily among the players and the 'housekeeper'. At the entrance a penny was collected of all comers, which went to the players. Another penny was collected at the foot of the steps leading up to the scaffold seating and a third for a quiet standing. (19) This money at first went to the landlord, but afterwards was shared between landlord and players on an equal basis. The lords who sat on the stage or in the lords' room came through the players' entrance, and paid the actors sixpence for their stools. By 1589 Lyly gives the price at St Paul's as fourpence and at the Theatre as twopence.

Stockwood in his sermon of 24 August 1578, reckoned there were eight ordinary places for playing in and about the

City (that is, common players' places) by which he reckoned, playing once a week, the companies would get £2,000 a year. He adds that although players are allowed to play only once a week they play two or three times. Plays at the Cross Keys were given on Wednesdays and Saturdays. Lord Strange's Men were playing six days a week at the Rose for eighteen weeks in 1591.

Groundlings would have been as profitable to the actors as the galleries at first, if the galleries' extra penny went to the landlord. Greatest security with greatest profit was ensured if the actors owned their playing place themselves; especially if the number of playing days was limited and the place used by other entertainers. Burbage's war with John Brayne, his financial backer, and with his ground landlord was long and vehement. Henslowe, a money lender, moved into the show business, developed all its branches. His stepdaughter married the great actor Edward Alleyn, and together they laid the foundations for the Admiral's Men.

The City Fathers worked hard to control the number and hours of performances in the places still within their walls. The traditional days for plays had been Sunday and saint's days; the Queen herself often commanded a performance on the Lord's Day, but Sabbatarianism made Sundays intolerable. Plays on weekdays were almost equally intolerable since they withdrew workers from the godly exercise of profitable employment. The prohibition of plays on Sunday, first met with in the mid-century, was still being reiterated in the last years of Elizabeth's reign. In 1594 their Lord promised for the Chamberlain's Men, performing at the Cross Keys, that they would end by five o'clock, use no drums or trumpets to advertise their show, and that they would contribute to poor relief. Inn-yards would be most convenient for winter performances, during the season from All Hallows to Shrovetide; for 'nocturnals'; and for shows put on by special request as part of a Feast. The theatres in the fields would enjoy their season in spring.

Instead of appearing at the door with 'Wilt please you to have a fit of our mirth?' players would summon an audience to wait upon them with sound of drum and trumpet, with posted play-bill and hoisted flag, and perhaps for a new play, with a procession. (20)

Henry Chettle recorded the growing alarm of citizens at the withdrawal of trade from the gaming places and bowling alleys in which they had an interest. The companies steadily grew in size; by 1594 the Lord Chamberlain's men consisted of ten 'sharers' and the Lord Admiral's of eight. The 'sharers', those named in the licence, held the stock, took the risks, met expenses and shared profits.

Henslowe first moved over to the Surrey side, and in 1587 opened the Rose, built in the garden of an Inn of that name, where the innkeeper supplied refreshments. In addition to managing a theatre, lending money to players and commissioning playwrights, he dealt in properties; and in December 1597 he paid £8 for a boy, whom he bought from a strolling player. By 1592 Lord Strange's Men, including Edward Alleyn, could petition the Privy Council for leave to open at the Rose although it was August and plague had closed the theatres since June, because the great size of their company made travelling impossible. They add that this will also be a help to the poor watermen who gain their living by rowing the audience over to the Bankside; and a petition from the watermen, headed by that toiling sculler, Philip Henslowe, is enclosed. In consequence the company, which had been exiled to Newington Butts, was allowed to come back.

By 1595 the city Alnager, Francis Langley, had opened the Swan in the old Beargarden, a little to the west of the Rose, to the disgust of the Lord Mayor, and doubtless that of Henslowe too, lessee of the Royal Game of Bearbaiting. The Swan 'the new stage or Theatre (as they call it)' (21) was the most gorgeous of all playing places; but here, by acting *The Isle of Dogs*, Pembroke's Men in 1597 drew down a general inhibition of playing. Two years later, the Globe completed the Bankside group. It stood east of the Rose, and for nine years was the only playing place of Shakespeare's and Burbage's company.

By this time Alleyn had virtually retired from acting (he sold his stock to the Admiral's Men for £50 in 1597), but he continued to play an active part in his father-in-law Henslowe's projects. So, when their rivals transferred to the Bankside, Alleyn and Henslowe met this competition by striking out in a new direction. They recrossed the river to build the Fortune Theatre in the Liberty of Finsbury, a little to the west of the old Theatre district, nearer both to the Revels Office in Clerkenwell and to the fashionable houses of West London. Its square brick frame—other theatres were circular—perhaps recalled the shape of the Hall theatres.

Alleyn began his campaign by securing the recommendation of his lord, Nottingham, to local Justices of the Peace, pleading the Rose was dangerously 'decayed' and—disregarding his friends the watermen—that crossing the river was 'noisome' in winter. The nobler inhabitants of Finsbury, headed by Lord Willoughby, at once protested to the Privy Council, just as, four years before, when Burbage tried to secure the Blackfriars, dwellers in the Liberty, headed by Burbage's own lord, had protested. They did not want the noise and thronging of the play within their quarters.

Sternly and morally the Council forbade 'public and vain' building of theatres of which there were already too many; but other local inhabitants, including some Justices, were induced by Alleyn to plead for him on the grounds of handsome subsidies for poor relief. A small group of the players' friends on the Council discovered that the Queen delighted in Alleyn's acting 'whereof of late he hath made discontinuance', adding that another playhouse had recently been pulled down. This, of course, was the house of Alleyn's rivals, the Theatre. So Alleyn's fame and a little manipulation of the facts pushed permission through in April 1600.

A full and stormy meeting followed, from which a much-amended document emerged, tidying up the situation. Two houses only were to be tolerated, one on the Bankside and one in Middlesex. The northern one was the Fortune, and the rivals' Curtain was ordered to be demolished or converted. The Admiral's Men were to play only at the Fortune, the Chamberlain's only at the Globe (22); Alleyn had thus confined his rivals to the worse side of the river and avoided all mention of his own 'decayed' house there, the Rose, which he had no intention of demolishing; while the rival Swan fell into disuse, and served only for fencing matches and occasional plays. Performance in any common Inn was again forbidden (so it had probably restarted), and players were limited to two performances a week. The Justices of the Peace and the Lord Mayor were told that enforcement depended on their efforts, without which the Council would have laboured in vain. Of course it had.

The immediate result was that the boys' private theatres were reopened and by 1602 the Earl of Oxford had persuaded the Queen to tolerate a third men's troupe, his own men combined with Worcester's. The Council therefore assigned to them the Boar's Head to prevent their 'changing their place at their own disposition, which is as disorderly and offensive as the former offence of many houses'. By May 1603 Henslowe had inveigled them over to the decayed Rose, and was trying to control them himself; by 1604, when they received a new patent as Queen Anne's Men, their usual playing places were said to be the condemned Curtain and the Boar's Head. By 1606, continuing at the Curtain, they had also moved into the Red Bull, a new theatre in St John's Street, Clerkenwell. On the other hand the City appear to have gained some control over playhouses outside the walls.

Doubtless many other temporary and obscure playing places in the neighbourhood have perished without trace; in 1595 and 1597 the Lord Mayor spoke of the Theatre, the Bankside 'and all other playing places in or about the City'—meaning presumably the inns, gardens and courts. In the mid-sixteenth century plays were given as far out as Islington; and in times of plague the archery ring at Newington Butts was used, though it probably offered no more than a booth within a fenced 'place'.

Fashions in theatres rose and fell; the most ruinous and weatherbeaten old structure might be reopened for some casual performance. All main theatres were used for playing fencer's prizes; contests of wit—such as Wilson's challenge to all comers at the Swan or that between Taylor the Water Poet and a defaulting opponent at the Hope—imply that individuals would sometimes hire the stage. At the Theatre in 1582 there was 'a scurvy play set out all by one Virgin,* which proved a fyemarten without voice' and Heywood wrote a prologue and epilogue for 'a young witty lad playing the part of Richard III at the Red Bull' to encourage him.

Not only did the 'gorgeous playing place erected in the fields' give the players a fixed habitation; in spite of the special provision of the Lord's Room as symbol of their patron's natural right, it conferred a new status. These were no longer Common but City Players; soon they were claiming the academic titles of Comedians or Tragedians. 'Some term them Comedians, othersome Players, many Pleasers, but I, Monsters', exclaimed William Rankins. There was much in a name.

Relying on the support of the general public, players had risen to be employers of labour. They had their apprentices. Kempe could describe himself as a 'grave Alderman of the playhouse'—in a play. The Theatre constituted the players' Livery Hall or something very like it. Later, Dekker went so

---

* A surname (see Lyly, *Pappe with a Hatchet* B2 r); this was a masculine player.

far as to compare it with the Royal Exchange, the most magnificent edifice of mercantile greatness.

Social responsibilities accumulated. Players had to keep the road in repair as well as contributing to the relief of the poor. As soon as they became firmly established, the Court began to take its pickings; the Office of the Revels, reorganized in 1581 under the energetic Edmund Tilney, gained wide powers over players in general, which were gradually asserted by Tilney through his power to license plays, in effect a tax on production. He also steadily raised his fee to 5s. a week when the houses were open and 7s. for new plays.

Between their many masters, whose edicts often conflicted, the players pursued their audacious career. The structure which finally emerged was that playbooks were licensed by the Master of the Revels (the City's attempts to get a share in this never succeeded); playhouses were first licensed by the local authority, with some later interventions from the Privy Council; the players' lords were free to use their influence to help their servants, whose incorporation depended on the patronage given them. The death of a lord dissolved his players, until they could be taken over by his heir or find another patron. Yet the patriarchal significance of their livery must have counted for less in the world of affairs as time went on; in 1594 a printer spoke of 'Ed. Alleyn's company', not the Admiral's; in 1598 Heywood could be both sworn servant to the Lord Admiral and indentured servant bound to Philip Henslowe. A share in the company could be bought and sold like any other commodity; it could also be bequeathed, partitioned, or held jointly by more than one person. (23)

Before the turn of the century at least one player had taken up the general challenge of contempt and become a Gentleman. William Shakespeare's acquisition of coat armour was thought a goodly jest by the players themselves, but 'Not without Right' is exactly the motto which the situation seemed to call for. Other players simply appropriated well-known bearings.

The official location of the players, first noticed in 1600, was grandly endorsed when in 1603 James I issued his Letters Patent to Shakespeare and eight fellows, constituting them the King's Men.

In addition to these, mentioned by name, 'the rest of their associates' were permitted also

freely to use and exercise the art and faculty of playing Comedies Tragedies Histories Interludes Morals Pastorals Stage Plays and such others like . . . to shew and exercise publicly to their best commodity . . . as well within their now usual house called the Globe within our County of Surrey as also within any town halls or Moote halls or other convenient places within the liberties and freedom of any other City University Town or Borough . . . (24)

Moreover, it is requested 'to allow them such former. Courtesies as hath been given to men of their place and quality'.

Their place and quality! Such a phrase sounds almost respectful. It recognizes their dignity and the value of their art. Under James the privilege of licensing players was, theoretically at least, restricted to members of the royal family. Though in the country districts other players continued to travel much as before.

In 1608 the King's Men fulfilled the plan they had nursed for a dozen years, and for the winter season moved indoors to the Blackfriars. The days of the old open theatre were passing; yet one more was to be erected, when from the demolished timbers of the Bear Ring, Henslowe built the Hope, retaining a movable stage for the better display of the bears.

The whole spilling and seething mass of public sports still flowed in and out of the same buildings; Alleyn was joint Master of the Royal Game, and the wealth by which he achieved gentility lay not in his own acting but in the marshy

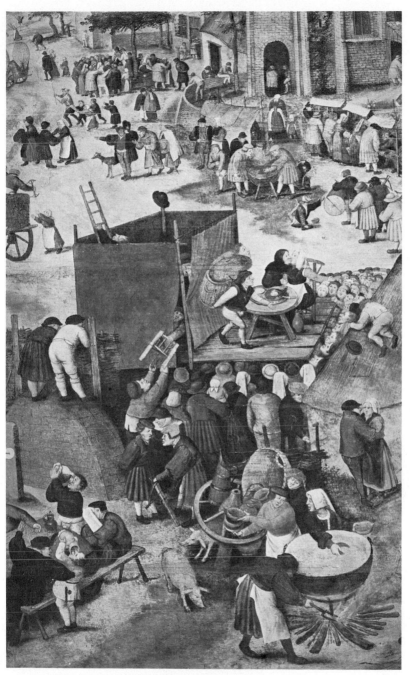

A Fairground Play
Detail from *A Village Fête*, 1632
By Pieter Brueghel the Younger
1564-1637/8

Poetry as Offering
Gascoigne presenting his *Tale of Hemetes
the Hermit* to Queen Elizabeth
as a New Year's Gift, 1575/6

Edward Alleyn
From the painting at Dulwich College
Painter unknown

Richard Burbage
From the portrait at Dulwich College
Reputed a self-portrait

piles of the Rose and the torn fur and snapping jaws of the Bear Ring.

For the King's Men, the Lord's Room and its scutcheon no longer dominated the stage; in 1610 Jonson describes its dark recesses as the usual haunt of 'the shop's foreman or some such gay spark' with his 'pusill'. Dekker's Gull prefers to 'the stage's suburbs' a seat on the stage itself.

No, those boxes, by the iniquity of custom, conspiracy of waiting women and gentlemen ushers, that there sweat together, and the covetousness of sharers, are contemptibly thrust into the rear.

(*E.S.* IV, 366)

Yet such is the rigidity of social thinking that as late as 1615 it was still possible for the author of *The Character of a Common Player* to taunt the actor with his dependence on public support, as something both deceptive and improper.

Howsoever he pretends to have a royal master or mistress, his wages and dependence prove him to be a servant of the people. When he doth hold conference upon the stage; and should look directly in his fellows' face; he turns about his voice into the assembly for applause sake like a Trumpeter in the fields, that shifts places to get an echo.

(*E.S.* IV, 256)

In the same year the Master of the Revels, Sir George Buc, in his Treatise of the third University, printed with Stow's *Annales*, mentions London's qualifications for the teaching of language, poetry and music:

That most ancient kind of poetry, the dramatic, is so lively expressed and represented upon the public stages and theatres of this city, as Rome in the age of her pomp and glory never saw it better performed (I mean in respect of the Action and Art, not the cost and sumptuousness).

But it is clear that he thinks of players as being guided and instructed by his own Office; it is clear too that his local

habitation, not theirs, is what qualifies their art as part of the 'third university'.

I might add hereunto for a corollary of this discourse, the Art of Revels, which requireth knowledge in grammar, rhetoric, logic, philosophy, history, music, mathematics and in other arts (and all more than I understand, I confess) and hath a settled place within this city ... (25)

Seven years later still, Henry Peacham, writing in his *Compleat Gentleman* (1622) 'of nobility in general' says:

Touching Mechanical Arts and Artists, whosoever labour for their livelihood and gain, have no share at all in Nobility or Gentry; as Painters, Stage Players, Tumblers, ordinary Fidlers, Inn keepers, Fencers, Jugglers, Mountebanks, Bear-wards and the like; (except the custom of the country determine the contrary) ... where I said the custom of the country I intend thus; by the law of Mahomet, the Grand Signior or Great Turk himself is bound to exercise some manual trade or occupation (for none must be idle).

(Ed. G. S. Gordon, Oxford 1906, pp. 12-3)

Here it would appear that while players are removed from gentility, they are also saved from the stigma of Idleness. Their commodity has been recognized as equal to that of a painter, their industry to that of an inn-keeper, even by an authority on social precedence.

The present chapter has followed the fortunes of the London players as they appear from the records. In the next chapter, the literary battles which arose from the social situation will be discussed. This involves returning to the year 1576, and the founding of the theatres, and retracing the sequence of events already considered, to see effects and consequences as they were shown (often very distortedly) in literature of defence and attack.

SOCIAL STATUS OF THE COMMON PLAYER

Attack and Defence
1577-1615
and the Rise of the Player-Poets

The attack by the clergy—Northbrook, Stockwood, Gosson—Mundy and Rankins—the players' scurrilous replies—the City renews its attack—formation of the Queen's Men—the Marprelate controversy—new literary attacks by the dramatist Robert Greene, especially on Shakespeare—Chettle's answer: a general defence, and exposure of the City's economic motives for opposition—the debate renewed in the War of the Theatres —*Hamlet* and the players—Heywood's *Apology for Actors* and the reply—the case of Father Leak.

THE founding of the Theatre and the Curtain in 1576 immediately sent up the temperature of the opposition, and the Church turned on its heat; or, as it would appear, the City Fathers appealed to their clerical mercenaries. The City sermon at Paul's Cross was preached on three occasions in 1578 and 1579 by John Stockwood, master of the Skinners' School at Tonbridge, in eloquent and obviously inspired denunciation of plays. (1) The publication of John Northbrooke, a Bristol divine (1577), was followed by that of the renegade player and playwright, Stephen Gosson (1579), by Anthony Mundy's pseudonymous *Second and Third Blast of Retreat from Plays* (1580), by Gosson's second work (1582), by Philip Stubbes (1583) and William Rankins (1587). From these works, particularly from that of Gosson, who as Lodge observed in his *Defence* knew what he was talking about, something can be learned of the social prejudice threatening the players.

The accusations were familiar; this admonitory repression was the reaction to a setback, and had little practical effect. Players were accused of that capital crime in Puritan eyes, Idleness. They were drones and caterpillars of the commonwealth, in no way distinguished from dancers and tumblers ('dumb players'), gamesters, fiddlers, minstrels, fencers. The collapse of a scaffold at a bear-baiting in Paris Garden on Sunday 13 January 1583 was used by the Rev. John Field, father of the future actor and poet, as an instance of God's wrath against plays.*

In the writings of divines, as in the eyes of the Government, it was principally the sins of the audience which were aimed at, and their conversion from ungodly pastime which was sought. In the course of the argument, attention was drawn to that part of the provoking group which proved most articulate in protest and defiance—the common players.

Later treatises are therefore directed exclusively against the men's dramatic companies; for neither the choristers of St Paul's nor of Blackfriars (protected by the royal livery) were touched. (2) The common stages were singled out as being exceptionally dangerous and exceptionally successful. Moral argument is sometimes reinforced by mundane considerations. It is not Liberality, but Prodigality, declares Northbrooke, unconsciously recalling a Paul's interlude

to bestow money and goods in such sort as it [is] spent, either in banketting, feasting, rewards to players of interludes, dicing and dauncing etc for the which no great fame or memory can remain to the spenders or receivers thereof.   (Ii r)

---

* A hundred years later, Milton showed Samson, in player's livery, divinely led to pull down the pillars of a very Elizabethan playhouse on the chief spectators.

Hamlet gave Polonius the answer to that remark.

As well as being the first, Northbrooke is by far the most learned of the opponents. Stuffed with quotations that range from the Fathers to Chaucer's denunciation of dice-playing, and Sebastian Brant's *Ship of Fools*, his work was reprinted a number of times, providing an arsenal for all his successors. The broad reproof of pastimes reaches from diceplay, against which he writes an 'invective', to dancing, against which he contents himself with a treatise. Although plays and players are the first objects of attack Northbrooke allows moderate recreation; he would permit

Scholars to make Orations, to play good and honest Comedies, to play at tennis and such like etc.   (M2 r)

But with considerable force he makes the point that large and rich stipends should not be given to church musicians, while preachers of the Word are paid 'very little or in a manner nothing', and observes

If Christian people do run unto the church as to a stage play, where they may be delighted with piping and singing (and do thereby absent themselves from hearing the word of God preached) in this case we must rather abstain from a thing not necessary, than to suffer their pleasure to be cockered with destruction of their souls.
                                        (M1 v)

The stage is for him 'a spectacle and school for all wickedness and vice to be learned in'—in fact, the school of Satan; the Theatre and the Curtain are therefore to be dissolved and put down by authority, like the brothel houses and stews (I2 r). In a long ironic tirade, he asks those who wish to learn all manner of sins and wickedness to come to the play.

To see what reward there is given to those Crocodiles . . . if you will learn how to be false, and deceive your husbands, or husbands their wives, how to play the harlots, to obtain anyone's love, how to ravish, how to beguile, how to betray, to flatter, lie, swear, foreswear, how to allure to whoredom, how to murther, how to poison, how to disobey and to rebel against Princes, to consume treasures prodigally, to move to lusts, to ransack and spoil cities and towns, to be idle and blaspheme, to sing filthy songs of love, to speak filthy, to be proud, how to mock scoff and deride any nation, like unto Genesius Aralatensis etc shall not you learn then at such interludes how to practice them?

(K1 r and v)

This earnest work, in the form of a dialogue between Youth and Age, has at least the merit of conviction. Youth is converted from his 'naughty idle plays and pastimes' and 'wily wanton life'; both agree that the players who so much frequent 'this most noble and most honourable city of London' are not tolerable or sufferable, and that the Theatre and Curtain should be pulled down.

Stockwood was backed not only by the City but by the Earl of Huntingdon, President of the Council of the North, brother-in-law of Leicester and Warwick, a noted supporter of Puritan preachers. (3) In his Bartholomew Day Sermon of 24 August 1578, he also attacks the Theatre and the Curtain by name, complaining of the bawdiness of interludes and coupling them with bear-baiting, bull-baiting, silver games, dicing, carding, tabling, dancing and drinking (D5 v). The Lord Mayor is exhorted to put down profanation of the Lord's Day when there is 'flocking and thronging to bawdy plays by thousands' (F6 v). The profits made by players, which he estimates in all at £2,000 a year, appal him; perhaps these figures were supplied for him by his masters. In his sermon of 10 May 1579 he has more to say about the iniquity of country pastimes (4) and admonishes nobles and gentlemen not to entertain

in the country such a train to follow you with long poles in their necks nor in the City to wait upon you with long blades by their sides, with slashing and cutting and ruffianly quarrelling, and for never so little a word speaking, imitating the speech of the Devil to our saviour Christ: If thou be a man of thy hands, come meet me in Smithfield.

(N1 v)

The smoother Gosson, a student of Oxford and pupil of Rainolds at Corpus, who had come down without his degree, shows himself a very Proteus in his attack, and appeals to every possible kind of listener. In his *School of Abuse*, he is modestly self-depreciatory to Philip Sidney in his opening dedication, and broadly flattering to the City Fathers in his closing one: 'You are the masters of free men.' He is delicately polite to the City Gentlewomen, whom he begs to refrain from plays where even *their* virtue will not protect them. He confesses his own fault in writing plays but 'I burnt one candle to seek another and lost both my time and my travail when I had done' (C7 v), somewhat ingenuously suggesting that

they that never step from the university for love of knowledge, seeing but slender offences and small abuses within their own walls will never believe . . . such horrible monsters in playing places. (B3 v)

The play-acting scholar who did not succeed in London is clearly hoping to provoke a witty controversy on a subject of general interest, which might bring him into notice and favour. He raises the old charge

We have infinite poets, and pipers, and such peevish cattle among us in England, that live by merry begging, maintained by alms, and privily encroach upon every man's purse. (B1 r)

At the same time he admits the skill of the players and warns the City

how many nets soever there be laid to take them, or hooks to choke them, they have ink in their bowels to darken the water; and sleights in their budgets, to dry up the arm of every magistrate. If their letters of commendation were once stayed, it were easy for you to overthrow them. (E7 v, E8 r)

71

Similarly, while inveighing against them as beggars, he can accuse the players of ostentation and expense, though in his rôle of candid and judicious observer he allows

It is well known, that some of them are sober, discreet, properly learned honest householders and citizens well thought of among their neighbours at home, though the pride of their shadows (I mean those hangbyes whom they succour with stipend) cause them to be somewhat ill talked of abroad.   (C5 r and v)

He transfers his wrath to the hired men

which stand at the reversion of vi.s. by the week [wages of a crafts-man], jet under gentlemen's noses in suits of silk, exercising themselves to prating on the stage, and common scffiong when they come abroad, where they look askance over the shoulder at every man, of whom the Sunday before they begged an alms.   (C5 r)

He half expects an attack, and even poses some imaginary objections of an 'arch-player' to his case. Sure enough it came and Gosson had started the controversy he was clearly hoping for, though all his suppleness and inviting candour gained him nothing but the scorn of Sidney.

In Gosson's *Defence*, printed later that year, players have become 'the worst and most dangerousest people in the world'—for a familiar reason:

> *Cet animal est très mechant:*
> *Quand on l'attaque, il se défend.*

From beggars, they have sunk to thieves; 'a thief is a shrewd member in a commonwealth; he empties our bags by force; these ransack our purses by permission' (pp. 87-8). The 'pleasant invective' has been replaced by snarling admonition.

In his second full-scale work, *Plays Confuted in Five Acts*, Gosson takes up a much more holy and authoritarian attitude. We must suspect even the smallest pleasures; plays are idolatry. He is smarting under attack and complains that both eloquence and favour are against him; the open reprehension given on the stage he now considers in all cases unchristian, and its 'scoffing and jeering' is most severely censured. He objects to players impersonating men above their station, a curious social taboo which is echoed later by Rankins:

For a mean person to take on him the title of a prince, with counterfeit port and train, is by outward signs to shew themselves otherwise than they are, and so within the compass of a lie. (E5 r)

and wrests the catechism, in common with most of his generation, to say

we are commanded by God to abide in the same calling wherein we were called, which is our ordinary vocation in a commonweal . . . if private men be suffered to forsake their calling because they desire to walk gentleman like in satin and velvet, with a buckler at their heels, proportion is so broken, unity dissolved, harmony confounded, that the whole body must be dismembered and the prince or the head cannot choose but sicken. (G6 v, G7 r)

Take but degree away, untune that string and hark what discord follows, as one of the players was later to observe.

Yet his account of the players' origins suggests that some players might plead the stage as their natural calling— and that some of the players had begun to take boy apprentices. (5)

Most of the players have been either men of occupations, which they have forsaken to live by playing, or common minstrels, or trained up from their childhood to this abominable exercise, and have now no other way to get their living. (G6 v)

This provided no excuse in the eyes of such a reformed sinner as Gosson, now a schoolmaster in the country. Sarcastically and in paradox he terms them 'the Gentlemen Players of the City of London'—the gentlemen citizens being something of an anomaly, how contemptible are these antics to aspire to the one condition as well as the other. Such as have left their occupations are warned to return, the rest to ask forgiveness for their illspent life and endeavour in future to live within compass.

Let them not look to live by plays, the little thrift that follows their great gain is a manifest token that God hath cursed it; that which is gotten over the devil's back is spent under his belly, it comes running and departs flying with the wings of an Eagle in the air. (5a)

(G7 r)

Uncased, like the vice in their plays, these 'gentlemen' would appear beggars or thieves; but in their masquerade they seemed to every schoolmaster and divine—and to at least one poet—to be usurping his own function. Outraged by their profits, the City saw the players as a horrible parody of a guild, while the players' defence that their drama was profitable to the spirit and instructed in virtue was a red rag to all their learned opponents. When Northbrooke approaches it, the number of his purely vituperative adjectives, such as *filthy*, rises in a steep curve. Gosson is equally indignant that they should usurp his office of schooling:

Sometimes you shall see nothing but the adventures of an amorous knight, passing from country to country for the love of his lady, encountering many a terrible monster made of brown paper, and at his return, is so wonderfully changed as he cannot be known but by some posy in his tablet, or by a broken ring or a handkercher or a piece of a cockleshell, what learn you by that? When the soul of your plays is either mere trifles, or Italian bawdry, or wooing of gentlewomen, what are we taught? (C6 r)

Players distort history, amplifying it 'where the drums might walk or the pen ruffle'. They cut it down when it has too many characters, and where it has no pomp, they stretch it out to make it serve. All the familiar transformations are invoked; plays are the devil's sermons, playhouses schools of vice and lust. Wandering players are compared by Northbrooke to those ancient enemies, the wandering friars, and Stubbes roars

> O blasphemy intolerable! are filthy plays and bawdy interludes comparable to the word of God, the food of life and life itself? . . . the devil is equipollent with the Lord . . . [yet] you shall have them flock thither thick and threefold, when the church of God shall be bare and empty. (N4 r and v)

Anthony Mundy who pseudonymously supported (6) Gosson with the *Second and Third Blast of Retreat from Plays* was in the employment of the City for their pageants. His work was probably commissioned; it was decorated with a handsome copy of the City arms, the cross and dagger, and he goes so far as openly to criticize the players' lords:

> Since the retaining of these caterpillars, the credit of noblemen hath decayed, and they are thought to be covetous by permitting their servants, which cannot live of themselves, and whom for nearness they will not maintain, to live at the devotion of alms of other men, passing from country to country, from one Gentlemen's house to another, offering their service, which is a kind of beggary. . . . For commonly the goodwill men bear to their lords, makes them draw the string of their purses to extend their liberality to them; where otherwise they would not. (pp. 75-6)

Naturally these 'drones, which will not labour to bring in, but live of the painful gatherers' are to be 'thrust out of the beehive of a Christian commonwealth' (p. 152). This argument could hardly be pursued after the Queen herself had acquired a troupe of players; so in 1583 Stubbes is content once more to call them 'buzzing dronets' adding 'Go they never so brave, yet are they counted and taken for beggars. And is it not true? Live they not upon begging of everyone that comes?' (M.I.r.) Thomas Newton, the editor of Seneca's plays and a friend of Hunnis of the Chapel, in his translation of Danaeus' *A Treatise Touching Dice Play and Prophane*

Gaming (1586) ventures on what now would seem the obvious defence:

Augustine forbiddeth us to bestow any money for the seeing of stage plays and interludes: or to give anything unto the players therein, and yet these kind of persons do, after a sort, let out their labour unto us, and their industry many times is laudable.   (E6 r)

That Playing could be Industry was a paradox which would not for many years gain general acceptance. (7) Idleness was vizarded as Honest Recreation and Deceitful Diligence as Good Husbandry in the monstrous revels of the Devil's Chapel of Adultery at Holywell.

For William Rankins, the last and most heated of the Elizabethan Puritan opponents, the Queen's livery was no protection and the Queen's example no precedent. To those who object to his speaking against men

that are privileged by a Prince, nay, sworn servants to the anointed, allowed by magistrates and commended by many, I easily answer, Most men liked the masking of apes in Egypt whose golden coats could not cover their brutish state . . . nor can the coat of a mighty and puissant Prince privilege a subject to wander into error, and to build their habitations under the cedars of Saba. Princes are as gods and may command, subjects inferior creatures and must not offend. . . . The Prince must be pleased, therefore the subjects be diseased. For that is poison to some which is medicinable to other and of a particular good may spring a general evil. (8)

The social differentiation of morals could hardly be more unequivocally put.

The players did not directly reply to this attack; Gosson reports that they had offered large rewards to anyone in the Universities who would enter upon their defence; but fortunately for them no one did. They lost little by the suppression of Lodge's weak and generalized answer (9) for on the level of theoretic debate they stood no chance at all. The cards were in their opponent's hands. When they put on the lost *Play of Plays and Pastimes*—which sounds like a hasty revamping of *Wit and Science*—Delight is separated from Life by Zeal. To answer them, Gosson had merely to distinguish between Delight Spiritual and Delight Carnal; scholastic reasoning was not designed to explore new facts, but for the logical ordering of a traditional body of knowledge, based on a limited set of authorities. There was no way of escape from the closed circle of accepted assumption, only endless manipulations and deploying of the familiar instance from the Bible and the Fathers.

The players retorted against their opponents in their own way—the traditional ridicule of pastime, as practised at South Kyme or Wells. (10) Clowns, who would on occasion crack a daring jest at the expense of their lord's enemies, would be unlikely to spare Gosson, and from his previous association with them would have all the intimate knowledge needed to barb their bitterest jests.

A scurrilous little work of which he complains, *Strange Newes out of Affrick*, probably presented him as some kind of fabulous monster; perhaps he was put on the stage in this form. His low birth and foreign extraction (his father being a joiner of Dutch origin) were evidently jested at. Perhaps he found it prudent to retreat to the country; Lodge calls him 'an owl in an ivy bush' a phrase for an absconding debtor. In 1584 he was in Rome [perhaps, like Mundy, as a spy]; by the next year he was ordained and preaching in London, and by 1600, just after the Theatre had been demolished the Rev. Stephen Gosson was inducted to the wealthy nearby parish church of St Botolph's, Bishopsgate. He lived to beg charity for some of his flock from Ned Alleyn's foundation at Dulwich, and to bequeath his wealth to his brother William, who led with talent and success the royal drummers of King James.

Whatever scurrilities were indulged in by the players would seem fair retort in a controversy where their opponents not only held but abused every advantage. 'Beware therefore,

77

you masquing players, you painted sepulcres, you double dealing ambodexters' admonishes Stubbes; yet the divines were expert at loading their arguments, assuming their conclusions and exemplifying what they denounced. Gosson based his first treatise only on 'prophane writers, natural reason and common experience', but when Lodge replied in the same terms, accused him of ignoring Holy Writ. Northbrooke and Stubbes say that it is blasphemy for players to handle sacred subjects and profanity for them to ignore such subjects. The unmeasured fury with which later the players are accused of backbiting, of uncharitable and unchristian detraction, is equalled only by the ease with which these divines slip into theatrical terms, talk of plays confuted in five acts, or write allegorical masks of the Marriage of Pride and Lust in the Chapel of Adultery in Holywell. Three of the opponents had been either actors or playwrights and the fourth was to become a dramatist some years later. The convert's hysterical note sounds in their voices; Gosson, in his stress of the almost irresistible enchantments of the theatre betrays all the fury of a writer scorned.

Backing the chorus of protest with administrative action, the City appears to have made some attempt totally to suppress plays in the years 1580-4. They issued a flat prohibition, always a sign of weakness, if only because it was impossible to enforce. The element of contempt as well as disapprobation appears in the Lord Mayor's description of players to the Lord Chancellor with 'tumblers and such like' as 'a very superfluous sort of men'. Neither the players nor their lords were lacking dexterity; Gosson had dedicated his second work to Sidney's father-in-law, Walsingham, and it was Walsingham who made the next move, as Stow records, in his first mention of the Common Players.

Comedians and stage players of former time were very poor and ignorant in respect of these of this time; but being now grown very skilful and exquisite Actors for all matters, they were entertained into the service of divers great lords; out of which Companies, there were twelve of the best chosen, and at the request of Sir Francis Walsingham they were sworn the Queen's servants, and were allowed wages and liveries as Grooms of the Chamber; and until this year 1583 the Queen had no players.   *Annales* (ed. 1631), 698

In spite of her four interlude players, she had no players in the new sense; and the new men in fact received no wages. They were on the same footing in the royal household as in other households; moreover, they had no formal patent or warrant, and were perhaps not fully incorporated, but remained in their old troupes. Robert Wilson, who was chosen, went to the Netherlands with Leicester's Men in 1586. It may be that the Queen's protection was sought for, by exemplification, in all the several companies to which her Grooms of the Chamber belonged.

Wilson and Tarlton are two chosen players mentioned by name in the *Annales* for their power of extempore wit. In this, it may be imagined, lay the players' chief weapon. But they were not without friends. Sir Philip Sidney stood godfather to Tarlton's child; when Sidney was dead, from his own deathbed Tarlton appealed to Walsingham to protect this child.

Plague added to the difficulties of these years, and the theatres remained closed for some time. Preachers were always ready to see plague as the punishment for plays. The collapse of staging at the Beargarden on a Sunday in January 1583, with the riots of Whitmonday 1584, must have stiffened the opposition's case; and when in November 1584 the players sought to move the Privy Council to gain admission to the City inns for the Christmas season, on the usual plea that they needed to rehearse for Court Revels, they were bold enough to add a draft summary for the regulations governing them and a suggestion of the conditions which they would observe. To have the players dictating their own terms through the Privy Council was more than the City could tolerate, and the Lord Mayor returned a sharp refutation; his own summary of the situation as it had been worked out ten years before, when the last great flare-up had occurred, on the issue of the Patent to Leicester's Men; and his comments. Every company that was summoned to Court now called themselves the Queen's Players, and thus claimed to play in the City. The City Fathers hoped by tolerating twice-weekly performances by the Queen's Men at two specified inns to prohibit all other players. (11) The remedies proposed state that plays shall be allowed only in private houses and without public assembly; or if more be required, that players shall stick to the restrictions of 1574; that the Queen's Men only be tolerated, and most important, that they be not allowed to divide.

It was unseemly, in the view of the Lord Mayor, that plays intended for the Queen should be first 'commonly played in open stages before all the basest assemblies in London and Middlesex'; besides the risk of infecting the Court with plague.

It is an uncharitable demand against the safety of the Queen's subjects and per consequens of her person, for the gain of a few, who if they were not her Majesty's servants should by their profession be rogues, to esteem fifty [deaths] a week so small a number as to be the cause of tolerating the adventure of infection.   (*M.S.C.* I, 2, 173)

The crisis of 1574-6 had ended not only with the opening of the Theatre by Leicester's Men but with the emergence of three other Great Companies, the Admiral's (first mentioned in 1574), Lord Pembroke's (1574-6) and Lord Strange's (1576-7). The crisis of 1582-4 produced the Queen's Men, bringing the players still nearer to control by the Crown, and a reorganization of the Revels Office (Tilney succeeded in 1579 and pushed through his reforms in 1581); while the Men were strengthened by the eclipse of the boys' theatres.

This second struggle provoked several ineffectual orders

for the tearing down of scaffolds; and on 26 February 1585 a committee was set up in Parliament to consider a bill against 'Idleness and Incontinent life and for the punishment of rogues and vagabond's which may have been aimed at the players. Giles Fletcher the elder, brother of the Bishop of London and shortly to be City Remembrancer, was a member of this committee; but no bill was drawn. (12)

The Puritans, on paper, won the scolding match; the real victory, as before, went to the Players. Tarlton's *Tragical Treatise* is the only player's Defence of Poetry; and Tarlton was a somewhat inconsistent tactician. While Stubbes denounced the Maypole as a stinking idol, the clown's advice was 'to pull down the church and set up the alehouse'. (13)

The general attack on the Puritan Martin Marprelate was an irresistible chance for players to retort upon their 'precise' opponents under cover of assisting the Church and standing for clerical orthodoxy. In 1589, Lyly, Nashe and the players in general threw themselves into the controversy on the side of the Bishops and in *The May Game of Martinism* adopted the coarse licence of rural sports, which called down a general inhibition; but this was a mild form of restraint, compared with the savage sentences that could be inflicted for libel. (14) While the bulwarks of royal favour and popular demand still held, plays were safe; the silken flag continued to wave, and the trumpets to play up merrily. The players showed their social orthodoxy by putting on *The Play of the Cards*, in which four parasitical knaves rob the four principal estates of the realm—soldiers, scholars, merchants and husbandmen. Almost it was forbidden

because it was somewhat too plain, and indeed the old saying is sooth boord is no boord, but a counsellor [Sir Francis Walsingham] would allow it, saying, They that do that they should not, should hear what they would not. (15)

Finally when in March 1592 a feeler was put out by

the Office of the Revels to see if the City companies would be prepared to pay Tilney a substantial annuity for suppressing plays, they simply said it was too dangerous a precedent, and they would not start paying annuities to any Court official. (16) The enforcement of any such matter would have fallen upon themselves, and evidently they recognized by now that it was impracticable. This inadvertent tribute by their old enemies is the strongest witness of the players' success.

In this same year of 1592 there came another attack—from within the citadel—witnessing to the fact that the eighties had seen the rise of Elizabethan drama, as distinct from the Elizabethan theatre. By the mid-eighties the Queen's Men were demonstrating the dignity of their art, as the building of the playhouses had done a decade earlier; but more significantly, young men from the University were following the earlier path of Stephen Gosson. Lodge, son of a Lord Mayor, Lyly, grandson of the famous grammarian of St Paul's, the brilliant Nashe, and above all, Christopher Marlowe, had given a new dimension to poetry and new magnificence to the stage.

From being dependent upon plays which seeped down to them from the academic performers, Common Players had risen to heights whence they could commission a tragical discourse, or a stately comedy. The medleys which Gosson described were out of fashion. The most popular writer of comedies was Robert Greene, witty, shiftless, popular Bohemian poet, known to all London for his 'jolly red peak' of hair and his gay reckless goodfellowship. He was at loggerheads with such staid pedants as Dr Gabriel Harvey; but he could write himself 'in artibus magister' and felt the wide social difference between himself and his employers and boon companions, the players. Every craft was guarded by privileges, and the art of writing plays, as Greene felt, was reserved for men of learning. Hence the last and greatest usurpation of the upstart players was to produce a poet of their own, a man who, however skilled and well mannered, had *not* enjoyed the privilege of spending his youthful years as an out-at-elbows poor scholar.

Seen as the last step in the advancement of the common player, Shakespeare's claims were bold ones, and the splenetic indignation of Robert Greene was an expression of general social prejudice which would have been perfectly intelligible to his contemporaries. Greene, like Gosson, dramatically abjured his dramatic connexions, his recklessness and 'atheism', and in a highly emotional series of repentances he denounced his popular coneycatching pamphlets and all other profane work. He told his own story several times in guise of a romantic tale.

Never Too Late (1590) describes how one Francisco 'yet living in England and therefore I will shadow his name', when reduced to such poverty that he had pawned his clothes, fell in with a company of players, who invited him to write Comedies, Tragedies or Pastorals. They promised to reward him largely for his pains, if he could 'perform anything worth the stage', and his first comedy succeeded so well that 'happy were the actors that could get any of his works, he grew so exquisite in that faculty'. Eventually, of course, he fell into evil ways and ended wretchedly.

The narrator when asked for his judgment of plays, players and playmakers, says that some who have been 'too lavish against that faculty have for their satirical invectives been well canvassed' (I3 v)—that is, they have been staged by the players; he will venture to give his opinion only on condition that what he is about to say in confidence will not be repeated to anybody. With this brief salute to Gosson and Mundy, he proceeds to talk about the ancient Romans. This is of course simply a way of discussing the current situation; the Elizabethans were as ready to see themselves 'shadowed' under Roman terms as they were to see the Romans 'shadowed' in Elizabethan costume upon their painted scenes. In *The School of Abuse*, Gosson used Ovid's *Art of*

Love to describe the playhouses. The term 'Roman' gave to prejudice and presupposition the authority and precedence of the ancients—the very name Theatre, given to 'the gorgeous playing place erected in the fields' was, as Stockwood saw, an example of this converting emotions into reason, a rhetorical 'augmentation'. At first the comedies might be presented in 'Rome' by such as More in London:

under the covert of such pleasant comical events, aimed at the overthrow of many vanities that then reigned in the City . . . so highly were comedies esteemed in those days that men of great honour and grave account were the actors . . . rewarding the author with rich rewards. . . . Thus continued that faculty famous, till covetousness crept into the quality, that mean men greedy of gains grew to practising the acting of such plays, and in the Theatre presented their Comedies but only to such as rewarded them well for their pains; when thus Comedians grew to be mercenaries, then men of acount left to practice such pastimes, and disdained to have their honour blemished with the stain of such base and vile gains; insomuch that both tragedies and comedies grew of less account, in Rome, in that the free sight of such sports was taken away by covetous desire; yet the people (who are delighted with such novelties and pastimes) made great resort, paid largely and highly rewarded their doings, in so much that the actors by continual use grew not only excellent but rich and insolent. (I4 r)

Put in contemporary and more colourless terms, Greene says that common players have attained wealth, security and independence through popular support; they have been able to raise their charges; and at the same time, their increasing skill has led to a decline in amateur acting—a statement borne out by the decline of acting at the Universities in the last part of the sixteenth century.

Greene goes on to tell a few stories of how Cicero snubbed Roscius, and how the actors 'excel in pride as they excel in excellency'. He finds no inconsistency between his hero's ready acceptance of payment from the common players for writing, and his denunciation of their covetousness in seeking rewards; concluding that plays are necessary in a commonwealth for the suppressing of vanity, 'the play-makers being worthy of honour for their art, and the players deserving both praise and profit, as long as they wax neither covetous nor insolent'.

This from Greene, who had sold *Orlando Furioso* to the Queen's Men and then, when they went on tour, sold it again to the Admiral's Men, must have raised ironic cheers in the tiring house.

In his posthumous *Groats-Worth of Wit* (1592), the same tale is retold, the hero now being transparently named Roberto. In his destitution, Roberto encounters a player:

'A player' quoth Roberto 'I took you rather for a gentleman of great living; if by outward habit men should be censured, I tell you, you would be taken for a substantial man.' 'So I am where I dwell' (quoth the player) reputed able at my proper cost to build a windmill. What though the world once went hard with me when I was fain to carry my playing Fardle a footback; Tempora mutantur, I am sure you know the meaning of it better than I; but thus I conster it; it is other-wise now; for my very share in playing apparel will not be sold for two hundred pounds. (D3 v)

Greene objects that the player's voice 'is nothing gracious' but he replies that he is famous as Delphrigus and the King of Fairies.

The twelve labours of Hercules have I terribly thundered on the Stage, and played three scenes of the Devil in the Highway to Heaven.

(D4 v)

As Roberto clearly stands for Robert Greene, it would be natural to assume that this rich player would combine recognizable traits with libellous imputation, hitting both particular and general. When he turns out to be also 'a country author, passing at a Moral', it may be that the reader was expected to recognize one who had also started in the country, and had come to be the object of Greene's attack in the postscript to the same work. William Shakespeare is the most likely candidate for the player with the ungracious voice, boasted author of *The Moral of Man's Wit* and *The Dialogue of Dives* who

for seven years was absolute interpreter of the puppets. But now my Almanack is out of date.

> *The people make no estimation*
> *Of morals teaching education*

Was not this pretty for a plain rime extempore? If ye will, ye shall have more. (D3 v)

This is caricature, not portrait—stock caricature, for some of the features are borrowed from Nashe (17); but Shakespeare is the only player-poet singled out by Greene, as he later appeals to the scholars Nashe, Marlowe and Peele to leave playmaking and to the two who have written against plays (i.e. Gosson and Mundy) not to return. London players are but puppets, antics, apes, buckram gentlemen, painted monsters, fit only for the fairground of a country town.

Greene's attack led to the apology from his printer, Henry Chettle, giving Shakespeare amends. But in *Kind Hart's Dream* (1592) Chettle did more than apologize for Greene; he answered him. His plea for pastimes combines the Dream Vision (a recognized form for 'glancing' comment) with the satiric one of a Packet of News. This plea is not given the form of a logical argument, but comes from within the world of fiction, in imaginative terms. Kind Hart, the itinerant tooth drawer, evidently a famous figure at London fairs, falls asleep in a tavern and in his dream 'discovers the false hearts of them that wake to commit mischief'.

Five lately deceased representatives of arts and pastime, 'not obscure but not honourable' appear, to give letters for 'Piers Penniless' Post'. The grave physician Dr Burcot, who had saved the Queen's life when she was ill of the smallpox, protests against quacks and mountebanks, to Kind Hart's great delight. (18) The wandering ballad singer Anthony Now-now, the villainous conjuror William Cuckow, the famous clown Richard Tarlton, and Robert Greene, all plead for their rights.

The old ballad singer complains of lewd songs, illegally printed, sung at fairs by gangs who are in league with pick-pockets, especially a troupe called Barnses Boys, who, led by a plumber, are travelling the countryside round Bishop's Stortford. It is vile that 'boys of able strength and agreeable capacity should be suffered to wrest from the miserable aged the last refuge in their life (beggary excepted) the poor help of ballad singing'. They make twenty shillings a day while he, who had always delighted in godly songs and will not sing such bawdy pieces as *The Ballad of Watkin's Ale* or *Friar Foxtail*, must pawn his fiddle and trust to Psalm 32 and Job's patience for a poor belly-pinching pittance.

This plea, discriminating the rights of the humblest of entertainers, is skilfully placed to cover the entrance of Tarlton, to whom is entrusted the main defence of the City Actors.

His defence consists of the shockingly low revelation that behind all the moral indignation of the Puritan citizen against the players there lies a powerful economic motive. Playhouses remove valuable custom from the more dis-reputable rival entertainments of the city, imperilling the wealth of their landlords. This point had in fact been more briefly made by Nashe in *Piers Penniless His Supplication*, where he praises the 'stately scene' and 'honourable representation' of true tragedies, and remarks that the trades hindered by actors are those of rival entertainers—Vintners, Alewives, Victuallers (F4 v). Chettle picks up and expands Nashe's point, but through his figure of Tarlton makes his points lightly and mockingly, as perhaps they were put in the theatre. 'Greene's' letter, addressed to Nashe, is a piteous recantation of his real postscript in *A Groats-Worth of Wit*, and an appeal against those who after his death are speaking ill of him, the envious spite of Gabriel Harvey in particular. Nashe is encouraged to defend his dead friend as well as himself—though 'Greene' recognizes that perhaps little encouragement is needed. These pleas fit in perfectly with Chettle's handsome apology to Shakespeare, and the refusal to apologize to Marlowe, who was guilty of the fault commonest among players, Contempt. Chettle's work has a single purpose—which is to refute Greene.

Its fantasy, both unpretentious and humane, is much more than the first evidence of Shakespeare's emergence as a dramatist of wit and reputation, of courtly behaviour, well-provided with friends. Its defence of the whole art of entertainment, though put in the humblest form, probably represents the kind of reply which the players had given in their extempore jests.

Although an academic debate on plays continued with unabated vigour at Oxford, it did not continue in the City. During the War of the Theatres between men and boys' companies at the end of the century, poet and player once more 'went to cuffs in the question' upon the topic which Greene had already raised—whether the learned poet had the right to feel superior to his employers, the common players. Shakespeare, who earlier had jested at country players, now took the City players' part. So, in that tragedy where his mind made its greatest creative leap, players appear in their own person—the Tragedians of the City, as Hamlet learns with surprise, are come to Elsinore.

How comes it that they travel? Their residence, both in reputation and profit, was better both ways.

(2, 2, 352-4)

But there have been disturbances; and there are rivals, who despise 'the common stages—so they call them'—who write for the eyrie of children. The first play scene in *Hamlet*, as it reflects upon the actors' art, can be studied line by line; Hamlet's final injunction to Polonius—and to the players—

shows the ticklish social balance between player and lord, with the possibility of contempt on both sides.

HAMLET:

Good my lord, will you see the players well bestowed? Do you hear; let them be well used; for they are the abstracts and brief chronicles of the time; after your death, you were better have a bad epitaph than their ill report while you live.

POLONIUS:

My lord, I will use them according to their desert.

HAMLET:

God's bodykins, man, much better. Use every man after his desert and who should scape whipping? (2, 2, 553-63)

But after this recollection of 'the statute', he remembers also to warn the players

Follow that lord; and look you mock him not. (2, 2, 577)

The noble patronage of Hamlet, as Shakespeare showed it, held up a flattering mirror to Nature; the Nine Worthies of *Love's Labour's Lost* and the craftsmen players of *A Midsummer Night's Dream*, drawn in mockery without malice, could proceed only from a secure and fully professional position. In greater or lesser degree Shakespeare's constant reflexions upon the stage colour, all his work down to the final masques and the final meditation upon illusion and transience in the great speeches of Prospero.

It was another poet-playwright, a man of the theatre and of temper not unlike Shakespeare, who shortly before Shakespeare's death ventured to publish the first *Apology for Actors* (1612). Thomas Heywood's work, written perhaps in 1607, is largely a rhetorical plea for the antiquity and good standing of the actor, addressed to the removal of social prejudice. Bearing an epistle to 'his good friends and fellows, the City Actors', it was dedicated to his former lord, the Earl of Worcester—though by now he was one of Queen Anne's Men.

Handsomely printed, and introduced with the pomp of Greek and Latin verses of commendation, it includes also tributes from Heywood's fellow actors—Perkins, Beeston, Pallant from Worcester's Men, John Taylor from Sussex's. There is also one from his friend John Webster, who provides the best of all comments on the detractors:

> Let their ignorance condemn the spring
> Because 'tis merry. . . .   (a2 v)

The opposition are boldly described as hypocrites—the clerks' abusive name for the actor. Perkins says

> Still when I come to plays I love to sit
> Where all may see me in a public place
> Even in the stage's front, and not to get
> Into a nook and hookwink there my face
>
>   (a3 r)

as some detractors do. Webster hints at the purchase of 'letters of commendation': of Heywood he says

> You give them Authority to play
> Even whilst the hottest plague of Envy reigns,
> Nor for this warrent shall they dearly pay.
>
>   (a2 r)

This authority comes from the ancient dignity of actors, who are established in blood by tracing their pedigree and dignity from Roman times. The stupendous rewards of Roscius (£6, 13s. 4d. a day), the decline of the stage when the 'precise' Marcus Aurelius (like James I) fancied himself mocked in a comedy, provided each contemporary reader with a Mirror, in which his own time was enlarged beyond life-size, augmented to imperial state.

Heywood's poetic justification of Melpomene is very near to the defence of plays in *Hamlet*; plays present a clarified image both of virtue and of scorn, so that they inspire noble minds to noble deeds. In a tirade which exactly reverses

Northbrooke's, Heywood demands if the spectators would learn all manner of virtues? If so, they are to be found in plays. Vice, which can be accepted tacitly and passed over as it lies cradled in the mould of nature and hidden by habit, becomes in plays truly seen, and can be first repudiated then, because only then is it recognized.

> *A play's a true transparent christal mirror*
> *To shew good minds their mirth, the bad their terror.*

(a3 v)

Heywood's description of the great Roman theatres owes nothing (as his opponent points out) to the Ancients, but is an enlarged and celestial vision of the only Theatre he knew, a 'cloud-capped' dream in which the successive stages of its evolution were traced.

The first Roman theatre, as Heywood saw it, was

in the manner of a semicircle or half-moon, whose galleries and degrees were reared from the ground, their stairs high, in the midst of which did arise the stage, beside, such a convenient distance from the earth, that the audience assembled might easily behold the whole project without impediment . . . not being roofed but lying open to all weathers.

(D2 r)

Later the outside of the stage was hung with linen cloth, and the inside with curtains. A later form had two movable stages which could be joined or used for separate scenes to be played simultaneously. (19) Pompey's theatre, built of stone, seated four thousand people; and finally the glories of the fifth theatre, built by Julius Caesar, are described.

The bases, columns, pillars and pyramides were all of hewed marble, the coverings of the stage, which we call the heavens (where upon any occasion their Gods descended) were geometrically supported by a giant-like Atlas, whom the poets for his Astrology feign to bear Heaven on his shoulders, in which an artificial sun and moon of extraordinary aspect and brightness had their diurnal and nocturnal motions. . . .

(D2 v)

91

Here also were shown the spheres which made 'a sweet and ravishing harmony', the elements and planets in their degrees, the stars both fixed and wandering, the signs of the zodiac, the zones and the poles, 'the perfect model of the firmament, the whole frame of the heavens, with all the grounds of astronomical conjecture'.

In the principal galleries were special remote, selected and chosen seats for the Emperor, patres conscripti . . . all other rooms were free for the plebs or multitude. . . . From the roof grew a loover or turret, of an exceeding altitude, from which an ensign of silk waved continuously. (D3 r)

This splendid vision of a more than earthly Globe Theatre (was Atlas really carved on the stage posts there?) pushed comparison between microcosm and macrocosm to its utmost limits. In the Theatre of the Universe, the players' Lord looks on from His room at the spectacle of all creation.

> *If then the world a Theatre present,*
> *As by the roundness it appears most fit,*
> *Built with star-galleries of high ascent,*
> *In which Jehove doth as spectator sit,*
> *And chief determiner t'applaud the best,*
> *And their endeavours crown with more than merit,*
> *But by their evil actions dooms the rest*
> *To end disgrac't, whilst others life inherit.* (a4 v)

This was a return to the Great Theatre of the Mysteries, in which God the Father had visibly sat enthroned and had visibly dealt doom at the end of the play.

There is no need to stress the difference between the simplicity of Heywood's view and the complexity of Shakespeare's. (20) Descending to more mundane facts, Heywood candidly admits that the theatre is open to abuse, but dissociates himself from the scurrilities of the boys' theatres, and, piously recalling the names of his predecessors, protests:

Many amongst us, I know, to be of substance, of government, of sober lives and temperate carriages, housekeepers and contributory to all duties enjoined them, equally with them that are ranked with the most bountiful. (E3 r)

Some three years later he was answered by I. G. (evidently a cleric, but not one of the 'sectists . . . sour and rank' who had been challenged) in a mixture of pedantic literalism and moral fury, supported by the thirty-eight-year-old arguments of Northbrooke, Gosson and Stubbes. Nothing had been learnt and nothing forgotten. The achievements of Marlowe, Shakespeare, Jonson were entirely ignored. With heavy sarcasm, Heywood is termed 'Master Actor' (he was no graduate). His expressions of humility and insufficiency are mockingly appropriated word for word; then the thunder follows.

God only gave authority of public instruction and correction but to two sorts of men; to his ecclesiastical ministers and temporal magistrates . . . God requireth no such thing at their hands, that they should take it upon them; but it is the devil's craft, that will sometimes change himself into an angel of light . . . God gave authority to instruct and preach, to correct and anathematize, only to the Apostles and to their successors and not to Players; for it is unlawful to cast pearls before swine.

(A Refutation of the Apology for Actors (1615), pp. 57-58)

It is an added insult that since

they find such sweet gains to maintain their idle life . . . they give their whole industry . . . now at last, by giving two hours' vain babbling for as many hours' gathering of money, some of them become rich in the commonwealth. (p. 4)

Vindictively, I. G. advocates the lash for strollers, if not for the City Actors. Even the universities are 'branded with infamy' and their actors denounced for preferring 'an ounce of vainglory, ostentation and strutting on the stage, to a pound of learning'.

The belated appearance in print of a set and formal defence evoked all the old prejudices and the old assumptions in a much embittered form. Though the arguments are still Northbrooke's, the tone is that of Gosson at his worst. No better proof could be desired of the rigidity of social modes of thought. But Heywood's *Apology* stands, a modest witness of the confidence which the years had brought to the Common Players; they knew themselves an ornament to the City, famous all over Europe, and they knew too that they had done much to enrich the language. Heywood, speaking as poet and player, does so, as he says, for greater men than himself.

> Our English tongue, which hath been the most harsh, uneven and broken language in the world . . . is now by this secondary means of playing, continually refined, every writer striving in himself to add a new flourish unto it; so that in process . . . it is grown to a most perfect and composed language, and many excellent works and elaborate Poems writ in the same, that many nations grow enamoured of our tongue (before despised). (F3 r)

Lest it be thought that the Puritans were singular in their attitude, it is worth remembering the case of Father Leak, a Catholic priest imprisoned for his faith in the Clink, adjoining the theatres of the Bankside, during the year 1618. Father Leak became a regular attender at plays, his confinement evidently being a lax one. This year, the Archpriest of England issued a general prohibition for priests to attend common plays. Father Leak stood upon his defence, alleged his right to attend, and questioned the Archpriest's right to issue the prohibition. A lengthy rebuke was administered to him, it was pointed out how unsuitable in a sufferer for the faith was such company as that of the playhouse, and how he was free to attend any private plays in gentlemen's houses. The argument incorporates most of those brought by the Puritans against plays; but the upshot of the matter was that to prevent 'contention' the prohibition was withdrawn, and the imprisoned priest permitted once more to seek the scandalous consolation of public stages. (21)

Some of the distinctions drawn are interesting; he

doth not forbid to go to any stage plays, but to go to play or plays, acted by common players on common stages . . . you . . . may go to a stage play or plays either in the Inns of Court, when the revels are, or in the King's or Queen's Court, or in the universities, or in any noble-man's or gentleman's house, although the said plays be performed by common stage players, because stages in these places cannot come under the name of common stages.   (Fol. 110)

The audience consists 'most of young gallants and Pro-testants (for no true Puritan will endure to be present at plays)'. The young of both sexes go but 'neither matron nor grave nor sage man is there seen' (Fol. 144). When Father Leak urged that there was no greater scandal in common plays for manner or matter than 'those that be Collegial', he was corrected*: no one will agree if

the odds between the composers of the one and the composers of the other be indifferetly nconsidered . . . a common stage player [is] one that professeth himself a player and lives by the gain thereof, as by his trade or occupation, a taxation too unworthy to be laid on the actors of scholastic or collegial plays who are commonly youths of best parentage among the company and of noblest towardness.
                                                        (Fol. 78)

The writer appears to be somewhat out of touch with affairs, as he goes on to say that *histriones* not only cannot be admitted to holy orders, but cannot accuse or bear witness in court 'even by the law of our own country, as I have been informed'! The medieval canon on which this is based is quoted by Northbrooke (K2 v).

---

* In 1617, the scandal of Sunday morris dances in churchyards of Catholic Lancashire led to the issue of the 'Book of Sports', where dancing—not interludes—was allowed to churchgoers.

CHAPTER IV

THE CREATION OF THE COMMON AUDIENCE

Spectacle and 'activities' in the theatre—casual notion of performance—distractions in the inn-yards—rival attraction of the Chief Spectator—general fear of assemblies, especially of riots by London prentices—pickpockets in the theatre—the effect of the clown's jig on the audience—emotional effect of English histories—of comedies—of the dancing of Kempe—unifying effect of history play—compared with courtly games—effects of regular attendance—fears of the magistrates—lack of power to control a crowd—disturbances in the provinces—unifying effect of Marlowe's plays.

IT should by now be clear that the Elizabethan theatre was no isolated phenomenon, a closed trade performing its mysteries before a passive set of onlookers, but continuous with the life of the times, one branch of the flourishing tree of sports and pastimes. Drama was mixed up in the public mind with the athletics of fencing, with bear-baiting, dancing on the ropes and other activities; and even, in prohibitions, with football. The nobler forms of pastime, triumphs, tourneys and guild shows, were closely allied with heraldic display and with the arts of music. In the earlier part of Elizabeth's reign, common players were acting in Morals and interludes which drifted down to them from the declamatory and rhetorical drama of the schools, still closely linked with debate; these performances probably had the same relation to the original, in social standing, as the ballad had to the courtly romance in medieval times.

In the seventies, spectacle, with song, is still, in courtly entertainment, the most prominent interest. The single curiously garbed actor who played the minstrel at Kenilworth displayed his musical talent, as the patent to Leicester's Men had warranted. Offerings were literally given in the Paul's play of *Liberality and Prodigality* where Prodigality ends a song with three gamesters by showering the audience with 'buttercups'. In Wilson's *Cobbler's Prophecy* Ceres casts comfits to the audience; a foreigner, von Wedel, describes a show at the Theatre in 1584, in which bear-baiting, horse-baiting and bull-baiting led up to an interlude, which was followed by a fireworks display, when a huge rose opened to shower fireworks, white bread, pears and apples on the spectators, who scrambled for the prizes. (1)

The theatre of the Elizabethans, in its social atmosphere, was less like the modern theatre than it was like a funfair. Indeed, George Gascoigne terms the performances at Belsavage Inn 'worthy jests' of 'Belsavage fair'. Merriment, jigs and toys followed the performance: songs, dumb shows, fights, clowns' acts were interlaced.

When Leicester's Men visited the court of Denmark in 1586 they were described as singers and dancers; Robert Browne of Worcester's Men, who toured the continent for thirty years with other English actors, jumped and performed activities. A mixed bill seems to have been popular in Gosson's day, and the principle of the 'medley' or 'gallimaufry' play was fully understood.

For the eye, beside the beauty of the houses and the Stages, he (the Devil) sendeth in gearish apparel, masks, vaulting, tumbling, dancing of jigs, galliards, moriscoes, hobby-horses; shewing of juggling casts, nothing forgot, that might serve to set out the matter with pomp, or ravish the beholders with variety of pleasure.

Plays Confuted (E1 r) (2)

The taste for such entertainment was universal. 'Sundry feats of activity' were shown before the Queen by Lord Strange's Men in 1582; 'feats of activity' were seen again in 1587, 'sundry feats of tumbling, activity and matachines' [sword dancing] in 1588. At the other end of the social scale 'activities of youth, activities of age' were the usual offering of country mummers to their audience.

Three, four or five plays in one were a popular form; Tarlton's *Play of the Seven Deadly Sins* was of this kind. The clown's vaudeville act remained a separate feature of plays till Caroline times, and so did the afterpiece with animal-baiting, such as the favourite spectacle of an ape tied on a pony's back, while the pony was baited by dogs. (3)

Plays competed with many forms of entertainment, from bear-baiting to sermons. Their gradual evolution from miscellaneous gambols to poetic drama depended partly on the specialization of the performers; partly on the arrival of new writers for the stage; but partly also on the concentration of the plays in fixed places, and on the establishment of a routine. Christmas saw plays in the City inns whenever the actors could wring permission from the City Fathers; inn-yards were more convenient for the audience in winter time. The setting must have given an exuberant but domestic flavour to performance. Companies would still appear any-where on command, of course, to give a taste of their quality —this was in conformity with the old tradition of occasional, holiday pastime; but regular performances create a regular audience; this produces a quite different kind of attention and response with more trained and expert attention to the actors. The simplest would have been trained at sermons to be edified by much they imperfectly understood. Yet in an open air, daylight theatre, attention must be less exclusively given to the stage, and more to the complete concourse. At an inn, there must also have been some coming and going throughout the performance. Inns and taverns were even more notorious centres of tumult than playhouses; in their chambers, city maidens were lured into 'privy contracts' and coneycatchers worked their tricks, their movements covered by the bustle and activity all around. Ready supplies of food and drink warmed up performances on a chilly afternoon;

and inns had other entertainments within their fairground—'noises' of musicians, singers of three-man songs, shows of dwarfs, freaks and monsters in private rooms; and resident prostitutes. On the Bankside the popular Rose Theatre was actually built in the garden of an inn, and the proprietor supplied refreshments. The Red Bull also sounds as if it might have been once an inn. The Fortune had a taphouse attached.

Whether at inn or theatre, the audience's mood would naturally be one of pastime; they had no duty to attend to the performers, being involved in the give and take which was their part of the show, slipping out for refreshment or dodging the shower of fireworks. Their opponents constantly accused the audience of wishing not only to see but to be seen, and those who sat in the Lord's Room in the early days were certainly part of the show, as the gallants on the stage were later. In Court performances, eyes would be as much on the Queen as on the spectacle, while her Chair of State displayed her to all. (4)

The presence of a Chief Spectator would imply yet another kind of attention. The play would be directed toward him in compliment; or occasionally, in malice, as when the Cambridge students brought in the Mayor of the town to hear himself mocked in *Club Law*. This happens in the play scene in *Hamlet*. The King, Queen and all the Court would have expected a play celebrating the royal accession and marriage, ending perhaps with the descent of Juno, Hymen or Concord. A tragedy would be tolerable only by contrast (like *The Misfortunes of Arthur*, offered to Elizabeth by the students of Gray's Inn). Instead of this, a most unseemly tale was offered and Claudius was perfectly within the tradition when, as Chief Spectator, he inflicted the deepest snub by rising, calling for lights and walking out. He need not be played in panic. Elizabeth once behaved in the same fashion, (5) when she was affronted by a scurrilous piece of anti-papal buffoonery.

On the other hand, if pleased, the Queen might bandy words with a player as she did with the Lady of the Lake at Kenilworth; Shakespeare's noble audiences in *Love's Labour's Lost* and *Midsummer Night's Dream* are likewise following precedent, and the more supple performers may have wooed their audience by ready-made jokes, offering them the chance to triumph in repartee, as mummers would play with loaded dice which ensured that the Prince should win.

In the common theatre, the audience gradually realized that the offering was addressed to them all; that each was a Chief Spectator. It must have been an intoxicating feeling for the humbler men to hear the obsequious prologue or epilogue addressed to him—spoken perhaps by a mimic Duke or Prince (6); to feel himself entitled to resentment or applause as lord of the show. This feeling must gradually have prevailed over the joys of common pastime, and turned the play from a joint frolic into a performance. To adopt the attitude of Chief Spectator in the Jacobean theatre would have been anachronistic. Dekker's gentlemanly gull, who exacts his full sixpennyworth of notoriety, takes leave in the middle of the play; but even the gull uses this deep snub only when he thinks he has been personally glanced at.

The Elizabethan opposition made the double charge that plays taught bawdry, trickery and baseness; and that the audience did not attend to the plays, but were engaged in bawdry, trickery and baseness of their own. Gosson denied that 'any filthiness indeed is committed within the compass of that ground', but says that assignations are given, and whores advertise themselves. The players may resent the notion that they are

Lords of this misrule or the very schoolmasters of these abuses; though the best clerks be of that opinion, they hear not me say so. . . . Were not players the mean to make such assemblies . . . such multitudes would hardly be drawn into so narrow room. They seek not to hurt, but desire to please; they have purged their comedies of wanton speeches, yet the corn which they sell is full of cockle.

The School of Abuse (C3 v and C4 r)

Stockwood denounces

Flocks of as wild youths of both sexes, resorting to interludes, where both by lively gesture and voices there are allurements unto whoredom.

Sermon of 24 *August* 1578 (I8 r)

The audience, according to Gosson

generally take up a wonderful laughter and shout all together with one voice, when they see some notable cosenage practised, or some sly conveyance of bawdry brought out of Italy.

Plays Confuted (C8 v)

and are not slow to play back such scenes. Their behaviour is worthy of Ovid's pen; and Gosson adapts Ovid's description of the Theatre to the modern event:

You shall see such heaving and shoving, such itching and shouldering, to sit by women; such care for their garments, that they be not trod on; such eyes to their laps, that no chips light in them; such pillows to their backs, that they take no hurt; such masking in their ears, I know not what; such giving them pippins to pass the time; such playing at foot saunt without cards; such tickling, such toying, such smiling, such winking, such manning them home when the sports are ended, that it is a right comedy. *The School of Abuse* (C1 v)

Stubbes carries this one stage further when he follows the playgoers home where 'in secret conclave (covertly) they play the Sodomites or worse'. Gosson candidly admits that 'there comes to plays of all sorts, old and young; it is hard to say that all offend, yet'—he recovers himself—'I promise you I will swear for none' (*Plays Confuted*, F3 r).

Greene, in his repentant account of Roberto the Archplaymaking-poet describes his tavern company, and Henry Crosse adapts this to an account of the common audience.

His company were lightly the lewdest persons in the land, apt for pilfery, perjury, forgery, or any villainy. Of these he knew the casts to cog at cards, cozen at Dice; by these he learnt the legerdemaines of nips, foists, coneycatchers, cross-biters, lifts, high lawyers, and all the rabble of that unclean generation of vipers.

Groats Worth of Wit (D4 v)

Now the common haunters are for the most part the lewdest persons in the land, apt for pilfery, perjury, forgery, or any roguery, the very scum rascality and baggage of the people, thieves, cutpurses, shifters, coseners; briefly an unclean generation and spawn of vipers.

Virtue's Commonwealth (Q1 r)

The preacher did not scorn to borrow from the playmaker in such a cause; while the City Fathers had a set description which they used regularly in their complaints of the audience. (7) Like the players, the audience was defined exclusively in terms of its lowest elements, and the image became fixed.

Fear of plague and fear of tumults are the two chief apprehensions of the City. Fear of plague was strengthened by the sense that God would not leave unpunished the wickedness of listening to players rather than preachers; 'What availeth it to have sweet houses and stinking souls?' asked Stockwood, while in 1569 the Lord Mayor could in the same breath forbid playing in open places and command the removal of filth and ordure from the street. Orders for the closing of the playhouse in time of plague were issued by the Privy Council, and this was the most serious hazard which the player had to face. (8)

'Tumults and outrages' were the commonest complaints not only of City Fathers and of country magistrates, but of poets and players themselves. The danger of any open

assembly has already been discussed; it is suggested by
Thomas Churchyard in his *Rebuke to Rebellion* (1588):

> *At Maypole mirth or at some marriage feast,*
> *Or in a fair, where people swarm like bees,*
> *These stinging wasps but new come out of nest,*
> *Do fly for life, and so together greese,*
> *Like little mites or maggots in a cheese.*
>
> (Nichols, II, 61)

Secret assemblies were on the other hand equally dangerous; so that whether the players appeared in public or
private they provoked suspicion. The one kind of assembly
was likely to be riotous and the other seditious. Henry
Crosse mentions

> especially these nocturnal and night plays, at unseasonable and undue
> times; more greater evils must necessarily proceed of them, because
> they not only hide and cover the thief, but also entice servants out of
> their master's houses, whereby opportunity is offered to loose fellows,
> to effect many wicked stratagems. *Virtue's Commonwealth* (W 1 v)

In fact, the City of London's fear of tumults is at first
directed towards controlling prentices, rather than the
criminal element in the audience. The aldermen were
naturally preoccupied with the young men for whom they
were personally responsible. As early as 1549 they ordered
that youths were to be kept indoors between ten at night and
four in the morning from May till Michaelmas and were
not to be allowed any May Games. Prentices, servants,
children and journeymen were at various times forbidden to
go to the play.

Prentices and servingmen were natural enemies; the few
serious disturbances at the theatres seem to have been caused
by prentices—those of 1584, 1592 and 1597; the prentice
holidays, Shrove Tuesday and May Day, sometimes produced attacks on playhouses and bawdyhouses.

On Whit Monday 1584, according to the Recorder of

the City, one Challis alias Grostock saw a prentice lying asleep on the grass in the sunshine, near to the Theatre, perhaps sprawled on his back with his mouth open. At all events, unable to resist, he 'did turn upon the toe upon the belly of the said prentice'. He then called the prentice a rascal and others said prentices were but the scum of the world. A riot ensued which two days later was revived inside the Curtain theatre by a servingman Brown, who attacked some prentices, hoping under cover of the tumult to loot and rifle more freely. Five hundred assembled the first day and a thousand the second.

Tarlton's News out of Purgatory (1590) opens with a similar scene; the narrator says:

Upon Whitsun Monday last, I would needs to the Theatre to a play: where, when I came, I found such concourse of unruly people that I thought it better solitary to walk in the fields

(Ed. Halliwell (1844), p. 54)

where falling asleep (like the unlucky prentice) he dreams of the ghost of Dick Tarlton.

The clown's audience must have been amongst the most unruly, and hence, in *Kind Hart's Dream* (1592) Chettle makes Tarlton plead with the young people of the City

either to abstain altogether from plays or at their coming hither to use themselves after a more quiet order.

In a place so civil as this city is esteemed, it is more than barbarously rude to see the shameful disorder and routs that sometimes in such public meetings are used. The beginners are neither gentlemen nor citizens nor any of both their servants, but some lewd mates that long for innovation, and when they see advantage that either serving men or prentices are most in number, they will be of either side, though indeed they are of no side, but men beside all honesty, willing to make booty of cloaks, hats, purses or whatsoever they can lay hold on in a hurly burly. (E4 r and v)

Since the audience would come attired in its holiday best,

lifters might hope for hats, gloves or chains worth their attention. Greene, in his unregenerate days, tells how the attraction of the clown's jig ruined a cutpurse's chance. A young beginner, working in the easy freedom of the Bull yard during the Christmas holiday, took a purse and stepped out into the stables to examine it. Finding nothing but gaming counters in it, he went back, to spy a master cutpurse with his drab, who acted as receiver; he stationed himself between them, to note their style.

In a short time, the deed was performed, but how, the young nip could not easily discern; only he felt him shift his hand towards his trug, to convey the purse to her; but she, being somewhat mindful of the play, because a merriment was then on the stage, gave no regard; whereby, thinking he had pulled her by the coat, he twitched the young nip by the cloak, who, taking advantage of this offer put down his hand and received the purse of him.

Third part of Coneycatching, 1592 (Bodley Head reprint, pp. 37-8)

The young nip passed on his own useless takings to the drab and sauntered off. That deep fascination which diverted the drab from her duty would make the play a specially profitable assembly. Notorious cutpurses were well known in the theatre, and could be picked out from the stage by their 'hawks eyes for their prey' and their 'villainous hanging look' as they would 'thrust and leer'. (9) The most famous, Cutting Dick, hero of a lost play, was also depicted in jigs.

In the course of his dance from London to Norwich in 1599, Will Kempe found himself accompanied by two London cutpurses, who were taken among the market-day crowds at Burntwood. They pretended to have a bet on his performance but

The officers bringing them to my inn, I justly denied their acquaintance, saving that I remembered one of them to be a noted cutpurse, such a man as we tie to a post on our stage for all people to wonder at, when at a play they are taken pilfering.

Kempe's Nine Days Wonder, p. 9

The penalty for cutting a purse was hanging; Kempe's anecdote would suggest that those taken were not always given in custody, or not immediately. To secure a cutpurse redhanded would not have been easy without risking the kind of hurley-burley which was the players' deepest fear; in 1612, the magistrates ordered the total suppression of jigs, owing to uproar at the Fortune Theatre where 'diverse cutpurses and other lewd and illdisposed persons in great multitudes do resort thither at the end of every play, many times causing tumults and outrages'.

This sounds as if they edged in when the gatherers had left their stations, and mingled with the crowd as all pressed together through the narrow passages to the exit.

> For as we see at all the playhouse doors,
> When ended is the play the dance, and song,
> A thousand townsmen, gentlemen and whores,
> Porters and serving men together throng.
>
> John Davies, *Epigrams*, 1595

The clown's jig must have given the cutpurse his best opportunity. These were at their height in the nineties and continued at the popular theatres north of the river till well into the seventeenth century. The year after the magistrates' inhibition, Dekker observes

I have often seen after the finishing of some worthy Tragedy or Catastrophe in the open theatres, that the scene after the epilogue hath been more black (about a nasty bawdy jig) than the most horrid scene in the play was; the stinkards speaking all things, yet no man understanding anything; a mutiny being among them, yet none in danger; no tumult, yet no quietness; no mischief begotten and yet mischief born; the swiftness of such a torrent, the more it overwhelms, breeding the more pleasure.

Strange Horse Race (*Works*, ed. Grosart, 1885, 3, 340)

But the magistrates evidently were not convinced of the absence of danger; and what had caused the suppression of jigs could undoubtedly have caused the suppression of plays.

Hopeful defenders of the stage urged that actors exposed the tricks of cutpurses, and also of other cheats; Heywood in his *Apology* perhaps went rather far in suggesting that the clown's drunken act was a warning to drunkards. But by the time Nashe wrote *Piers Penniless* in 1592, he could distinguish between different kinds of prentice in the audience; and there was indeed a wide gulf between the young goldsmith or mercer who might rise to be Lord Mayor, with a brother at the Inns of Court, and the poorer kind of handicraftsmen.

Whereas some petitioners of the Council against them object they corrupt the youth of the city, and withdraw prentices from their work; they heartily wish they might be troubled with none of their youth nor their prentices for some of them (I mean the ruder handicrafts servants) never come abroad but they are in danger of undoing.

Piers Penniless (ed. of 1595, F4 r)

Nashe justifies plays as the resort during 'the afternoon, the idlest part of the day' of men that are their own masters 'as Gentlemen of the Court, of the Inns of Court, and a number of captains and soldiers about London'. It is preferable to gaming, whoring or drinking. Here too, the broken spend-thrift who can find 'a play for him to go to for his penny' shall be saved from melancholy thoughts and treasonous plots.

Regular settled habits of performance would have made for order; the street performance, like that in a private house or at Christmas in the Hall was only too sure to be attended with tumults. The records of the Inns of Court and the royal Court itself are full of scenes of tumult, and swaggering of gentlemen seems to have been more dangerous than excitement of the stinkards. While the crowd at common theatres probably did not contain a much higher proportion of ruffians than any other London crowd, it would inevitably be in an excitable mood. Both opponents and defenders of the stage describe the deep impression which action could produce. Puttenham in his *Art of Poetry* (ii. viii) says 'the common people, who rejoice much' in plays, are attentive to 'matter' as well as 'shews'. Heywood knew the Londoner responded to a patriotic appeal from 'brave Talbot, the terror of the French', Edward III, or Henry V.

What English blood seeing the person of any bold English presented and doth not hug his fame and hunny at his valour, pursuing him in his enterprise with his best wishes and as being wrapt in contemplation, offers to him in his heart all prosperous performance, as if the performer were the man personated? so bewitching a thing is lively and well spirited action, that it hath power to new mould the hearts of the spectators. . .   Heywood, *Apology* (B4 v)

'Bewitching' and 'enchanting' are the very adjectives used by Gosson to describe the perilous power of the theatre, where the crowd, seeing Bacchus wooing Ariadne, are driven to sympathetic transports.

The beholders rose up, every man stood on tiptoe and seemed to hover over the prey, when they sware, the company sware, when they departed to bed, the company presently was set on fire, they that were married posted home to their wives; they that were single vowed very solemnly, to be wedded.   *Plays Confuted* (G5 r)

Comedies make our delight exceed, for at them many times we laugh so extremely, that striving to bridle ourselves, we cannot . . .
                                                                    (F5 r)

Not content with tickling the outward senses, the play will 'by the privy entries of the ear slip down into the heart and with gunshot of affection gaul the mind where reason and virtue should rule the rost'. Women, being governed by affections more than by reason, were far more exposed by their natural susceptibilities to danger in the playhouse. Massinger illustrates the difference between the sexes in his

Roman Actor, where an old man remains unconverted by *The Cure of Avarice,* performed for his benefit, but the Empress falls in love with the leading actor.

In real life, the greatest tribute to an actor which the age witnessed was the passion of emulation roused by Will Kempe in his nine-days' dance from London to Norwich. Two country lasses joined his dance; one kept up with him for a mile after a young man had ignominiously fallen out of the attempt; the other lass danced with him for an hour in his chamber. At Rockland, the innkeeper dressed in his best to welcome the great man and cried out

'O Kempe, dear Master Kempe, you are even as welcome as . . . as . . . as . . .' and so stammering he began to study for a fit comparison 'thou art even as welcome as the Queen's best greyhound'.   (p. 18)

He too ventured to accompany Kempe forward, but 'good true fat-belly', collapsed after two fields' length and called Kempe back for a farewell:

'Dancer' quoth he, 'if thou dance a God's name, God speed thee! I cannot follow thee a foot further; but adieu, good dancer; God speed thee, if thou dance a God's name.'   (p. 19)

Kempe was graced by an official reception at Norwich by the Mayor (accompanied by the City Waits), was made free of the Merchant Venturers and also received a handsome reward. His story shows the tremendous power of the clowns, particularly among the unsophisticated. In this susceptible state any crowd could quickly turn riotous—the danger lay in bringing them near the flash point.

The basis of folk plays, including many of the clowns' acts, is most frequently a fight or a mock fight. The only surviving Robin Hood May Game is made up largely of fights. (10) In Kenilworth's 'storial shew', the muster men followed their drill display by depicting a battle. To witness a mock fight paradoxically enough has a calming effect on the audience. By their taste for such shows, whether it were two clowns slinging custard, or brave Talbot defying the French, Elizabethan audiences discharged their belligerence. The English history play must have been one of the great means of unifying the spectators and creating an audience out of a throng.

At the Court, the art of 'commoning', of using shows and games, music and poetry and dance as a means of intercourse had long been familiar. As John Stevens puts it in *Music and Poetry in the Early Tudor Court*:

The element of communication was not paramount. The courtly ritual, whether 'in earnest or in game', existed chiefly for the benefit of those who conducted it. In these formal games the king and the court *performed* the allegory of love.   (p. 169)

Idealizing natural relationships, the delicate artifice of 'the game of love' at Court heightened and restrained the feelings of those who took part; the mock-fights of villagers, whether they were setting up a straw Jack o' Lent as a cock-shy, or bestowing 'Easter smacks' upon one another, were also a form of intercourse. To start a fight is still a well-recognized form of effecting an introduction among small boys. These seasonal and holiday sports were acceptable because their times were fixed. Theatres offered a perpetual holiday. Yet by raising the simple celebrations to a form of art comparable to that which courtiers had long enjoyed in 'the game of love', the history play gave to the common people in a free and ennobled form the means to express their instincts of community.

Henslowe's accounts, which were made up day by day, imply that his theatres were seldom unused. The growth of the companies, and the presence of the hired men, who had to earn their six shillings a week, suggest daily performance, but it cannot be assumed. It is likely that the choristers played only once a week. But regularity of performance is more important than frequency in creating an audience. It would appear from a prohibition of December 1581 that sometimes plays were even given in the forenoons. The Lord Chamberlain, appealing at the beginning of the winter season of 1594 for leave that his Men should play at the Cross Keys, writes:

they have undertaken to me that, where heretofore they began not their Plays till towards four o'clock, they will now begin at two, and have done between four and five, and will not use any drums or trumpets at all for the calling of people together. . . .

(*E.S.* IV, 316)

an obliging offer which meant that the players were once more ready to intrude upon the hours for Evening Prayer.

The speed with which a crowd assembled, and their own lack of any means of control, explains the apprehensions of the City Fathers. It must be assumed that Elizabethan magistrates were neither tyrants nor milksops, but responsible and able men, guilty only of that universal weakness, the habit of thinking along familiar lines, acting according to precedent and treating anything unfamiliar as suspicious. The comparatively sudden emergence of such a phenomenon as the mixed theatrical crowd, bubbling with excitement, produced a natural reaction of alarm and alertness.

City prejudices lie plainly on the surface of their documents, as when the Recorder, reporting the affray of Whit Monday 1584 remarks

and some there were little better than rogues that took upon them the names of gentlemen and said the prentices were but the scum of the world. . . .   (*E.S.* IV, 297)

but he had imprisoned his prentices as well as the servingmen; and then had been faced with a riot of other prentices, attempting to get their fellows out of custody.

The leading actor in the Queen's troupe co-operated in carrying out orders, but James Burbage refused to come to the City court

he sent me word that he was my Lord of Hunsdon's man, and that he would not come at me, but he would in the morning ride to my lord,

and even after seeing Hunsdon's hand to the order suppressing plays—it had been reluctantly set down—Burbage refused to be bound.

The magistrates were prepared to be severe; and the central government, when it intervened, was drastic. This is illustrated by an episode of 29 June 1595 recounted by Stow. Unruly youths started throwing stones at the warders of Tower Street, urged on by an old soldier with a trumpet. They were arrested by the Sheriffs, but disorder grew; the Lord Mayor rode to the spot, and because the City Sword was borne before him, narrowly himself escaped a clash with the royal warders from the Tower. On 4 July the Queen appointed a Provost Marshal, with the power to hang offenders, since order was not yet restored. Five of the unruly youths were convicted of high treason; they were hanged, drawn and quartered on Tower Hill on 24 July.

London crowds had long been notorious; Froissart had remarked 'The Englishmen are the perilousest people of the world, and most outrageousest if they be up, and specially the Londoners.' (11) Sir William Walworth's summary treatment of Wat Tyler was a shining example to every Lord Mayor. And London, as everyone recognized, had developed a large criminal class. Among the regular complaints of the City, it was alleged that plays, even if not turbulent, offered an excellent rendezvous for criminals to meet and lay their plans. It might be felt that taverns or bowling alleys, or possibly a sermon, would serve the same purpose, but the *potential* risk of assemblies and the indirect risks, if exaggerated by prejudice, need not therefore be dismissed as entirely imaginary.

As it must be assumed that the prohibition of any practice indicates that it is fairly widespread and frequent, and repeated prohibition that it is increasingly so, it must be assumed that for every disturbance serious enough to provoke savage repression there were many lesser tumults and affrays that went unrecorded; for every cutpurse who was taken there were a number who went free.

The Elizabethan notion of what constituted order was in itself different from that of today. Seventeen people were crushed to death at a distribution of alms in Leadenhall in 1601—a mishap with many precedents. When the Queen was witnessing a play in Oxford in 1566, the collapse of a wall killed several people; but after sending her officers to help, she ordered the play to proceed. The most obvious evidence of disturbance in the theatre is the cost of repairs to the fabric. Henslowe opened the Rose in 1587 and by 1592 he had to pay £108 for repairs, including repainting the stage and mending the roof. Three years later he spent almost exactly as much again for 'painting and doing it about with elm boards and other reparations'—the last presumably to enclose the space beneath the stage—at that level where Professor Hotson would insert his glass windows for a semi-basement tiring house! Somebody's elbow or fist would have been through those windows the first day.

Eight years later the cost of erecting the brick-built Fortune Theatre was fixed in the contract at £440 and its painting cost a further £80; repairs amounted to £120 annually, or almost a quarter of the original cost. Although a wooden and plaster building open to the weather would certainly need repainting, the expense of these repairs must represent rough usage by other forces than those of wind and rain. It cannot be assumed that there was no alternative to uproar on the one hand and attentiveness on the other.

Alfred Harbage has rightly protested (12) against the imputation of lawlessness which an uncritical reading of the City's complaints might suggest; but he seems to think that assemblies so respectable as to be positively tame have suffered from slanderous imputations: and his account of the resources for quelling trouble furnishes a classical case of understatement:

Elizabethans had a very real fear of the potentialities of a crowd—any crowd. They were less used to crowds than we are, less adept at policing them. (p. 14)

But

Were Shakespeare's Londoners truly such galvanic creatures? Imagine if you will some London carter plodding beside his oxen on the road to Hackney, some London housewife sewing a fine seam, some London mason patiently, skilfully pointing the stones of Bridge Gate . . .

The behaviour of individuals is no guarantee for the behaviour of a crowd; it may again be recalled that the Tudor Government had no means of quelling uproar. Kett's Rebellion, which started at a stage play in 1549, (13) showed that a city like Norwich, faced with a rising that started in 'bruits and rumours' might find itself at the mercy of Robin Hood's justice for six weeks before local forces could be assembled.

After the theatre riots of 1592, the Privy Council's orders for a 'Midsummer watch' of householders furnish a pitiable example of their meagre resources. Local justices are to tell the constable and most substantial housekeepers in their neighbourhood to lock up servants and prentices overnight, and keep a watch themselves with any weapons they may have. (14) Apart from the constables, with one or two sheriff's officers and marshal's men, order had to be kept by citizens; as for the watch—'every man knows what belongs to a watch'.

If this were so in London, the country districts were even less well provided. Sometimes players might hope for a quiet performance; Robert Willis's description of *The Cradle of Security* which he saw as a child at Gloucester somewhere about 1570 must have been peaceful. It was 'the Mayor's play', the official showing, and the Mayor and Aldermen came to see it. The little boy stood between his father's knees, as he sat upon one of the benches 'where we saw and heard very well'. Seventy years later, as an old man, Willis could say 'This sight took such impression on me, that when I came towards man's estate, it was as fresh in my memory, as if I had seen it newly acted.' (15)

Yet fear of disturbance might provoke magistrates into rewarding players 'to rid the town of them' as the Barnstaple accounts bluntly declare. At Marlborough in 1600, players had to contribute 3s. towards repairing windows and a table in the Town Hall (repairing the table alone cost the town 10s.). At Southampton in 1623 it was decided that plays were so 'hurtful, troublesome and inconvenient' in breaking up furniture in the court room, that stage players and interlude players were to be admitted to the Town Hall no more. No one appears to have been jailed or charged as a result of these affairs. When the King's players visited Ludlow in November 1627, some five or six Shropshire lads who had evidently been to the fair, inflamed with drink, violently broke into the performance, beating the sergeant who was called to keep the peace, hauling and dragging him along the street, while with flaming torches they thrust away the players, who attempted a rescue. This was at ten or eleven at night. (16)

The more rascally the players, the more likely they were to be in league with ruffians and pickpockets. In *Bartholomew Fair*, Jonson shows a puppet master working in collaboration with a cutpurse; Chettle also describes some of the fair gangs.

As with the players, so with the audience—there came all sorts to the play, as Gosson observed, and as the Privy Council more than twenty years later was to prove. In May 1602 they apparently ordered the Lord Mayor to round up vagrants from ordinaries, bowling alleys, bawdy houses, theatres and ship them for Flanders—the expedient Henry VIII had threatened to clear the Bankside in 1545. (17) The manœuvre was hopelessly bungled; it was asserted that the bowling alleys were combed and 'all the playhouses beset in one day' but after a week the total haul included

Gentlemen and servingmen, lawyers, clerks, countrymen with law causes, ay the Queen's men, knights, and as it was credibly reported, one Earl. (18)

This serves to show that the City was unable to carry out a fully prepared piece of work at the Theatre; their chance of dealing with a sudden emergency may be measured by this failure.

The first audience was the clown's audience, who were accustomed to exchange witticisms with the actors and to see themselves as part of the show. Perhaps assembly is a better word than audience for such a gathering. With the emergence of the Great Companies and the establishment of the theatres, the new audience also emerged, although clowns with their jigs and their improvised personal scurrilities were still part of the tradition. It was they who replied with coarse home thrusts to the Puritan attack. It was they who took so full revenge for past injuries in the Martin Marprelate merriments that it led to the closing of the theatres. (19)

The combined art of the new actors and the new poets first created a truly theatrical audience. Marlowe, interpreted by Alleyn, based his triumph on the rejection of

> *jigging veins of rhyming mother wits*
> *And such conceits as clownage keeps in pay.*

Clowning and the simple didacticism of 'morals teaching education' vanished together, as the image of the shepherd-conqueror emerged to charm the whole auditory; though Marlowe readmitted the clowns to *Dr Faustus*, Alleyn became Master of the Royal Game, and Nashe in his *Isle of*

Dogs repeated the scurrilities of the previous decade, perhaps with the same kind of animal show as the worming and purging of Martin the Ape; so in 1597 the theatres closed once more.

Yet, in the meantime, London had built up a theatrical tradition which was stable, and which supported half a dozen dramatic poets as well as the Great Companies for whom they wrote. Foreigners were impressed by the splendour of the theatres, by the dignity of the audience and even by the elegance of the prostitutes. It was long before the general fears subsided. As tradesmen, schoolmasters and clergy saw in the players potential rivals of their work, so this new phenomenon of the theatrical audience acted as a focus for social fear. City magistrates feared their prentices would get out of hand, their daughters be inveigled into secret contracts; statesmen feared sedition, or busy meddling with matters of state and religion; preachers feared bawdry and filthiness; players themselves feared riot and spoil, with their disastrous consequences. The 'quaking prologue' rubbed colour into his cheeks; poets alternately stormed at the audience and wooed it. Shakespeare's most eloquent word on the subject comes when he identifies himself with this many-headed monster of whom he is servant:

> *O for my sake, do you with fortune chide,*
> *The guilty goddess of my harmful deeds,*
> *That did not better for my life provide*
> *Than public means, which public manners breeds.*
>
> (Sonnet 111)

From these harmful deeds his name had received a brand, as of a convicted criminal. No doubt the leading poet of the Lord Chamberlain's Men had been told by some starched Precisian that players were in the Statute for rogues and vagabonds. Yet if he had not been stung by the insults of the pulpit on the one hand, and confronted by the wary hawk-eyed look of some noted cutpurse from the galleries on the other, it might not have occurred to him to give Falstaff that cool justification of purse taking:

> *Why, Hal, 'tis my vocation, Hal; 'tis no sin for a man to labour in his vocation.*
>
> (King Henry IV, Part I, I, 2, 116)

The part played by actors in the creation of the common audience can be surmised only indirectly; the part played by the poets can be studied. To transform their social 'commoning' or intercourse to attentive watchfulness at the theatre meant a shift of social habit in the audience; to transform their art from the narrative to the dramatic form was a more exacting test for the poets, for the shift of focus and the loss of many traditional ways of doing things must have been severely felt. This literary revolution went unrecognized by contemporaries, who were preoccupied with different questions of language. It may seem small recognition now so abruptly to condense and reduce in a single chapter what took place between the courtly 'commonings' of Chaucer's age and the dramatic 'traffic' of Shakespeare's. The story of the poets' contribution, as told in the next chapter, will however conclude this first part of the book—that dealing with the development of the main stem of dramatic art in Elizabethan times, the common stages of London.

CHAPTER V

THE POET'S ART AND THE PLAYER'S QUALITY

The Integration of Drama and the Rise of Tragedy

Transition from medieval narrative to drama as dominant form—
Chaucer's method of involving his audience—Lydgate's disguisings—Cornish 'guary' plays—morality plays—interludes—
inability to establish nature of dramatic illusion—antic shows—
the medley and the later interludes—Marlowe's solution—
development of single character parts illustrated by the Vice,
Kyd's Hieronimo, and Shakespeare's King Richard III—
persistence of some features of the medieval 'courtly
game' in entertainments of Elizabeth.

ELIZABETHANS might be excused for being uncertain
about the status of players, since they were very uncertain about the nature of plays. It was only in the
late 1580s that full poetic drama enjoyed a golden sunrise.
Alongside the transformation of the Minstrel into the
Comedian, a transformation in the social presentation of
literature replaced narrative by drama. Elizabethan drama
was created on the common stages, by fusing the art of orator
or presenter with that of the mime, so turning a recital
accompanied by gesture and costume display into a complete
action, bodied forth, with the player's 'whole function suited
with forms to his conceit'.

This change, which began with the guild plays, was completed with the plays of Kyd, Marlowe and the early Shakespeare. It was a search for literary form, which should
capture and display the social relations between player and
audience as they shared together the imaginative acts which
the poet had conceived for them.

The dominant form of Chaucer's day was narrative, where the only actor was the poet; Chaucer in a little pulpit, declaiming his verses, was making his Offering in person. A subtle art of leading the audience out from the world of everyday into the world of imagination developed in his Inductions or Dream Visions, which were also used to draw the audience into the poet's story.

In the prologue to *The Legend of Good Women*, Chaucer makes the Queen both his chief spectator and the centre of his vision. Love commands

> *When the book is made, give it the Queen*
> *On my behalf, at Eltham or at Shene—*

as later poets were to make their Offering to Elizabeth. *The Book of the Duchess* is an offering of consolation to Chaucer's bereaved Lord, John of Gaunt. The greatest of his Inductions shows the pilgrims assembling at Southwark, not far from the site of the future Globe, with every brilliant detail picked out as if by a Presenter; they are recognizable often by their garb alone. The stories unfold with battles between the churls, as between the clowns in a play.

The subtlety of Chaucer's perspective was quite lost to the Elizabethans, who looked on him with a mixture of veneration and indulgence, as some honest old countryman with frieze jerkin and homely speech might be received in fine company. (1) They relearnt from Petrarch what Chaucer already had expressed with a fineness quite beyond them, an elegance which was not achieved again in English till the time of Pope.

None of Chaucer's successors was able to command the delicate perspective by which he could take himself and his listeners out of the world of everyday and into the Garden of the Rose. Narrative forms stiffened and grew literary in the worst sense: but the combination of recited verse and spectacular display which the guild plays supplied was used by Chaucer's disciple Lydgate. His 'disguisings', Christmas shows both for the King and the City, were highly spectacular; the verses, instead of being spoken by the actors, were recited by the poet, as presenter. In a curious account of staging which Lydgate gives in his *Troy Book* (ostensibly of course a description of the ancient stage), the poet recited a tragic story while actors wearing vizards came out of a tent and played it 'in the midst' of the theatre; the theatre was semicircular, and the poet stood in a small raised pulpit. (2) This must represent his own method of presenting his disguisings.

The Poet as Presenter wore a special garb; a child so dressed greeted Elizabeth in her Coronation Entry; and Hunnis so dressed welcomed her to Kenilworth. Perhaps in Shakespeare's *Pericles*, Gower still wore this traditional garb as he came 'to sing a song, that old was sung'.

The play as 'Song' or 'Tale' with acted accompaniment (or the pageant-figure, with a label on his breast proclaiming his name for the literate, and a presenter to introduce him), needed integration. A curious variant on Lydgate's fantasy is recorded from the remote Cornish west as late as 1602 by Richard Carew.

The guary miracle, in English a miracle play, is a kind of interlude compiled in Cornish out of some scripture history, with that grossness, which accompanied the Romans' *Vetus Comedia*. For representing it, they raise an earthern amphitheatre, in some open field, having the diameter of his enclosed plain some forty or fifty foot. The Country people flock from all sides, many miles off, to hear and see it; for they have therein devices and devils to delight as well the eye as the ear; the players con not their part without book, but are prompted by one called the Ordinary, who followeth at their back with the book in his hand, and telleth them softly what they must pronounce aloud.

Survey of Cornwall (T3 v)

This seems to imply illiterate actors, who were not professionals and did not rehearse enough to get their parts: it implies also a succession of single actors or at least a very few at a time with speaking parts. Carew describes the prank of a gentleman who took a part, and given his cue—'Go forth, man, and shew thyself'—repeated the words aloud; a distressed 'O, you mar all the play' was also proclaimed, and the prompter's 'passion' mimicked in action. As he fell to railing, the gentleman 'with set gesture and countenance still soberly related' all, till the Ordinary in rage gave over the play.

Which trousse, though it brake off the interlude, yet defrauded not the beholders, but dismissed them with a great deal more sport and laughter, than twenty such guaries could have afforded.   (T4 r)

For medieval spectators there must have been little difference between live actors and effigies in a tableau; a mechanical figure, as being rarer and more costly, might have provoked more interest. A common emblematic or heraldic tradition linked these figures to others embroidered on copes, wrought in stained glass, worked into a fresco or the border of a manuscript, moulded in marchpane for the 'sottlety' of a feast. Lydgate designed a Life of St George for the Livery Hall of the Armourers' Company and the famous Danse Macabre for St Paul's Churchyard, painted on the north wall of the cloister; he also wrote 'devices' for the confections (sottleties) at feasts.

In the great open-air theatre there had been so little sense of the co-ordination of parts that it was possible for the Seven Deadly Sins to discuss the seduction of Mankind 'who sits among them beaming on his throne, hearing every word they say, yet missing the drift'

> *Let each of us take at other,*
> *And set Mankind on a stumbling stool.*
> *While he is here on live,*
> *Let us lull him with our lust,*
> *Till he be driven to damning dust.* (3)

The opposite extreme is shown in ready give-and-take

between the world of life and the world of the interlude, as in the induction to *Fulgens and Lucrece*, played perhaps half a century later in the Hall of Cardinal Morton. Two players enter, posing (prophetically!) as servingmen; one says

> *I thought verily by your apparel*
> *You had been a player*

and with a brisk 'I will be doing, I make God avow', thrusts himself into the play; though, when the second half is postponed because the guests have not fully dined, he refuses to come back.

Anyone who can amend this comedy is invited by the prologue to do so. The intervention of spectators in an Offering, since quarrelling is a form of intercourse, might please the players, especially if their lord condescended to interrupt for a jest, even at their expense. It meant the Offering had been accepted; their service was acknowledged. Shakespeare shows young courtiers displaying their wit in the theatre of the Hall at the players' expense, with no sign of disapproval.

The transition from narrative engendered confusion, for the nature of drama was not clear. Irrational fears as well as rational puzzles perplexed both actors and audience. A play that was an Offering, like a Mumming or Carnival, or the rule of a Christmas Lord, was but half emerged from the life of the moment to separate existence. Pure acting seemed to confront Self with Rival Self as in a Comedy of Errors.

The Chief Spectator was often represented within a pageant; Katherine of Aragon and Elizabeth Tudor were both welcomed to London by images representing themselves. By the time of Gosson and Rankins, the actor who personates kings is 'acting a lie', because he is 'claiming' to *be*, and not to *represent*, royalty. But a quarter-century later, Sir Henry Wotton's only observation on the procession of Garter Knights in Shakespeare's *King Henry VIII or All is True*, is that 'this representation makes greatness very familiar if not ridiculous'. He does not doubt its morality, because he knows what drama is.

Offerings intended to scorn the Lord's enemies were played by antics, mute figures wearing animal heads, like those of the Carnival or country Mummers. They were both comic and terrifying; akin to the tales of satiric beast fable, but vaguely 'enchanted'. The strange figures of cardinals, bishops and abbots with the heads of crows, asses and wolves who appeared in Elizabeth's first Christmas revels, were akin to the ape and fox into which in *Mother Hubberd's Tale* Spenser transformed Alençon and Burleigh: to Circe's herd and Comus's rout. . . . The fashion did not remain in favour at Elizabeth's court; a woman ruler did much by her mere presence to curb scurrility, as comparison with the customs of Henri IV of France makes plain. (4)

The degree of confusion between 'show' and 'play', antics and actors, is suggested by a passage from a scurrilous antipapal narrative, *Beware the Cat* (1570), in which Baldwin, author of *The Mirror for Magistrates*, and George Ferrars, King Edward VI's Lord of Misrule, are introduced discussing the King's players' comedy of *Aesop's Crow*: Baldwin objected

It was not comical to make either speechless things to speak, or brutish things to common* reasonably. And although in a tale it be sufferable to imagine and tell of some things by them spoken or reasonably done (which kind Aesop lawfully used) yet it was uncomely . . . and without example of any author, to bring them in lively personages to speak, do, reason, and allege authorities out of authors.   (A4 r and v)

Such rough animal mockery seems especially associated with 'religious' quarrels. (5) It long remained popular on the common stages; in 1615, Thomas Greene, the clown, leader of Queen Anne's Men, appeared in indecent disguise at the Red Bull, as a baboon 'with long tail and long tool'.

* to 'common' is to converse in some set form by way of courtly game. See p. 110.

Meanwhile, in the mid-sixteenth century, two forms flourished which exercised the actor's versatility; the medley and the moral interlude. The medley depended upon spectacle; so however did the moral interlude, and the two are afterwards allied in the plays of Robert Wilson—to be considered in a later chapter.

One difficulty of the moral interlude lay in the constant fear of libel (6) Even the medley seems to have been libellous at times; a few dangerous words would be dropped in a flood of nonsensical patter by way of 'prophecy'. The medleys of the mid-century and of the sixties and seventies accepted 'variety' or rich confusion as first aim. Some might object to an action that rambled, or thrust in clowns by head and shoulders, as Sidney did in his *Apology* (pointing out that this happened because the writers did not know the difference between reporting and representing); but a later critic of the popular stages sees the advantage.

A man is not wearied, be it never so tedious, because they do not only (as I say) feed the ear with sweet words, equally balanced, the eye with variable delight, but also with great alacrity doth swiftly run over in two hours' space, the doings of many years, galloping from one country to another, whereby the mind is drawn into expectation of the sequel, and carried from one thing to another with changeable motions, that although he were unacquainted with the matter before, yet the cunning he seeth in the conveyance maketh him patiently attend the catastrophe; when as at a lecture and holy exercises, all the senses are mortified and possessed with drowsiness. (7)

This account, from the last years of Elizabeth's reign, would apply to the popular medleys of the seventies; it would apply also to the restless confusion and proliferation of entertainment of the Revels. The multiplication of troupes of poor players in the late sixties and early seventies probably meant that new depths of incoherence were plumbed. Tales of wandering knights, in the style of the minstrels' romances, mixed with scurrility and the comic-horrific sports of antics, resulted in such abortions as *Sir Clyomon and Sir Clamydes* and *The Pedlar's Prophecy*. Here, the actors from five or six 'tents' or 'mansions' mingle their 'Five Tales in One' just as if all the Canterbury pilgrims were to begin their Tales together. These plays are the last broken shards of medieval popular Romance, which Chaucer had parodied in *Sir Thopaz*, and the Oxford scholars mocked in *Thersites*; the degenerate relics of a genuine tradition of simultaneous statement, such as the alliterative poets, Chaucer's contemporaries, had once known. Their best effects were spectacular. Ordinary people who did not want to follow a debate would be prepared to gape at a show and wait for the fighting to begin, or for the appearance of the devil with his fireworks.

An example of simple moral spectacle is *The Cradle of Security* as given at Gloucester about 1570. It seems a mixture of show, song and lament. The hero, whom the writer describing him realized to be 'a king or some great prince', was enticed into a huge cradle and rocked asleep by three ladies, but

in the mean time closely conveyed under the clothes wherewith he was covered, a vizard like a swine's snout upon his face, with three wire chains fastened thereunto, the other end whereof being holden severally by the three ladies, who fall to singing again, and then discovered his face, that the spectators might see how they had transformed him. While all this was acting there came forth of another door at the farthest end of the stage two old men, the one in red with a drawn sword in his hand, and leaning with the other hand upon the other's shoulder, and so they two went about in a soft pace round about by the skirt of the stage, till at last they came to the cradle, when all the court was in the greatest jollity, and then the foremost old man with his mace struck a fearful blow upon the cradle, whereat all the courtiers, with the three ladies and the vizard all vanished, and the desolate prince starting up barefaced, and finding himself thus sent for judgment, made a lamentable complaint of his miserable end and so was carried away by wicked spirits. (8)

POET'S ART AND PLAYER'S QUALITY

In his Bartholomew sermon of 1578, Stockwood distinguishes between the allurement of 'lively gesture', and 'voice' in players of interludes; the artisan players of *Histriomastix* doubt if ability to 'sing and say' will qualify them as real actors unless their action 'answer the extempore' of the poet. The Vice praises Sir Thomas More as a 'rare player' when he steps in to improvise the part of Good Counsel (played by one Luggins, who has run to the costumier to borrow a beard).

> *Did ye mark how extemporically he fell to the matter and spake*
> *Lugginses part almost as it is in the very book set down?*
>
> Sir Thomas More (4, 1, 298-301)

To which Wit replies:

> *Peace! do ye know what ye say? my lord a player? let us not*
> *meddle with any such matter; yet I may be a little proud that*
> *my lord hath answered me in my part.*   (4, 1, 302-4)

The chime of voices could have been learnt from songs and madrigals; but the transition from dumb show with recitation to 'deeds and language such as men do use', the full incarnation of the common life, represents a different way of conceiving action.

This integration of drama was fully achieved in Marlowe, assisted by the absolute predominance of Alleyn

> *Whom we may rank with (doing no one wrong)*
> *Proteus for shapes and Roscius for a tongue* (9)

He created the tragic parts of Tamburlaine, Faustus and Barabas; the emergence of integrated drama came with the emergence of tragedy. Tarlton, the first modern actor, created his own rôle as a solo turn. Marlowe, in spite of, or perhaps because of, the towering egoism of his characters, produced first a 'tragical discourse' and then a full tragedy, while Greene and Peele were still fumbling with inductions, where characters glided in and out between the stage and the world amid all the perplexity of unmastered perspective.

Marlowe's sculptured, freestanding characters move almost without comment or intervention (the Chorus in *Faustus*, or Machiavel in *The Jew of Malta* are outside the action). This implies a new kind of attention to *the object*, free from the cauls of 'dream' and 'shadow' in the older story-teller's art, which established his imaginative relation with his audience. The dramatist leaves the establishing of *direct* relationship with the audience to the actors; his art involves a kind of abdication. Conflicts of states-of-being, the interior drama of the morality play, gave way to flesh-and-blood battles; the actors were conceded full objectivity and independence. This incarnation of the story, this putting on of flesh and blood, was an imaginative feat of detachment on the part of the poet, as well as an imaginative feat of integration on the part of the actors. Voice and action, shape and speech, above all one part and another part, were co-ordinated, in the solid world of the theatre. The dim forests and fleeting visions of Spenser represent the old art, delicate modulations within the imaginative realm, the king-dom of fairy; the embodied action of the stage, when it ceased to be an offering, became the Mirror of Nature. The difference made by dramatic objectivity in the poet's art of character drawing is comparable only with the difference that knowledge of anatomy made in painting, as such knowledge was applied by Leonardo da Vinci and Michelangelo.

Marlowe's greatness did not provide a good model; almost all imitations of his style, except Shakespeare's, are appalling huff-snuff. The craftsman Kyd gave later writers their scaffolding.

General development can be traced in the transitional figure of the Vice, through the first great tragic type, Kyd's Revenger, to the oldest 'live' tragic part commonly acted today, that of Shakespeare's Richard III. In all three figures, their relative independence may be gauged by the degree of contradiction that can be included in the one part; this occurs only to figures 'in the round'.

The Seven Deadly Sins, like emperors and angels of the street pageant, existed in display—they were exhibited, rather than employed. The variety shows of the minstrels—their juggling, singing and fantasy—also lacked 'a soul diffused quite through to make them of a piece'. Contentions from the schools and universities were trimly shaped and well planned but they were limited in scope till the Vice, incarnation of wit, mockery and iconoclasm, took the lead. The Vice is not fully dramatic because he is not confined within the framework of the play, but stands with the audience partly outside it; he engineers the action, and also explains it confidentially; so far, he has something in common with the Presenter. But he is always disguising himself and playing a false part; he has this in common with the mime. He feigns joy and grief, piety and remorse, displaying his cheats shamelessly to the audience; he gives the exposition of his own part as well as acting it. Rhetorically his style is vivid and 'low'—a churl's style; it is familiar, jogging the listener, Protean of mood, incessantly waggish.

The Vice embodied the imp of irreverence within the audience; his wit included many Freudian slips of the tongue. (10) Disrespectful, airily familiar, engagingly good humoured, he stood for deflation of the virtuous, he was all that authority feared. The official representative of the audience in a moral play was the victim—Humanum Genus, Lusty Juventus, or Mankind; from the spectator's point of view, what was to be rejected overtly was the enticing of Inclination or Merry Report, the Vice; what was rejected covertly was his dull, simple dupe.

However close the sermons of the Virtues to the sermons of the preacher, mood and occasion determine the meaning of even the most impeccable sentiments; the identical words of the pulpit will sound very different in the atmosphere of a feast. The closer such plays came to religious phrasing, the more likely they were to rouse clerical opposition, (11) and stories were told of summary vengeance from on high.

Yet the preachers adopted their tricks: Stockwood attacked by pretended slips of the tongue: 'The bawdies de Gaul—I would say, the *Amadis de Gaul*'—'toyish, I had almost said Popish', 'latrones' for 'patrones', 'chameleons' for 'comedians'.

In college plays, since some of the audience were themselves likely to be preachers, the old spirit of parody from the Feast of Fools may have helped the Vice, who always betrayed a familiar knowledge of members of the audience. The first Protean figure of the stage, the Vice demanded Protean art. His attack on authority remained witty, comic, youthful; he was a jester, and privileged; yet he was not fully human, for, however convincing himself, he inhabited a world of abstractions.

The tragic rôle of the Revenger, once it had been created by Kyd and Alleyn, remained a model for later writers and actors. Revenge tragedy evolved among common players and their poets, and supplied not only a story, and a group of rôles, but a body of poetic imagery to Shakespeare, Marston, Tourneur and Webster. This 'black tragedy' embodied in figures, drawn from the enemy realms of Spain and papal Italy, the perpetual tragic issues of guilt and sacrifice; it allowed the projection of deep fears, the exorcism of guilt which the actors and audience shared. In the terrifying figure of Hieronimo the Revenger as created by Edward Alleyn, *the punitive and denunciatory aspects of the religious attack upon the stage were unconsciously absorbed and mastered.* Within the tragedies of the public stage may be seen, contained and assimilated, the rage and fear which the actor aroused and the mirror image of that rage and fear evoked in himself. It is no coincidence that the climax of this play is a murder in a masque; this catastrophe remained a favourite one, into the middle of the next century.

Such a reflexion is, of course, indirect and distorted; but it accounts for the extraordinary energy, the sense of depth in the Revenger's part. Kyd's Hieronimo sprang directly from the theatre, the work of a man not otherwise remarkable as a writer. The power of *The Spanish Tragedy* lies in ironic co-ordination; as theatre it is superb. The 'antic' boy who silently points to the empty box which the wretch Pedringano thinks to contain his pardon, and dupes him to the scaffold; the Machiavel Lorenzo; the Ghost of Andrea and the looming figure of Revenge all foreshadow the planned, dominating, inescapable doom which Hieronimo finally accomplishes in his play, where all the deaths are in earnest and not in jest. The rhetoric of this play is rhetoric in action; the cut-and-thrust dialogue, or grand *tirade*, are parts of its structure.

The figure of the human Revenger represents assimilation and mastery of fear evoked by such a work as Dr Thomas Beard's *Theatre of God's Judgments* (1597), where, upon the stage of the whole universe, God is seen as the supreme Revenger. Arden of Feversham, Antony and Cleopatra, Tamburlaine, Richard III and the Duchess of Malfi are among the examples of wickedness justly punished whom Beard cites; and he has no doubts about any of them.

'Negative prohibitions are commoner than affirmative commandments' he observes, and his plan is based on the Decalogue. God appears as a revengeful Father Deity, not scrupling to use evil men as instruments of his wrath and then destroy them (such were Bajazet and Tamburlaine); like a Machiavellian, using His slaves as 'nails to drive out one another' according to the player's maxim. Beard stresses the absolute obedience owed by subjects, servants and children, commending the severity of parents to children. Except for the always useful Richard III, the punishment of wicked rulers occurs only in distant antique examples, such as Ahab's.

Each brief tale is subordinated to its moral; the power and singleness of impression in the *Theatre of God's Judgments* derives from this conviction. Under the all-seeing eye of Beard's God, *Vindicta Mihi* gains new intensity.

> As we see murderers hang upon gibbets to terrify others from committing the like offence, so here are thousands as it were, hung upon gibbets, to terrify us from these sins and bring us to repentence....

Christian stoicism placed the universe under the guidance of Providence, with God in remote control; but for Beard, God was directly active in His universe, so that

> nothing in the world cometh to pass by chance or adventure, but always and only by the prescription of His will; according to the which He ordereth and disposeth by a straight and direct motion . . . and that after a strange and admirable order.   (A5 r)

This direct intervention is shown by the ingenuity and exactness with which punishment fits the crime; miraculous patterns are continually imposed on natural events. If the Wizard Earl of Northumberland dies in prison, it is God's judgment; if three drunkards fall off their horses and are drowned, it is God's judgment; as all men are mortal, such judgment can always be found. Weight of examples is reinforced by most striking coincidences; Dr Whittington condemned a poor woman to be burnt as a heretic at Chipping Sodbury, only to be instantly gored by a mad bull. The death of Christopher Marlowe, with a little manipulation of the facts, provided an example for Beard.

> As he prepared to stab one whom he ought a grudge unto with his dagger, the other party perceiving, so avoided the stroke, that withall catching hold of his wrist, he stabbed his own dagger into his own head, in such sort that, notwithstanding all the means of surgery that could be wrought, he shortly after died thereof; the manner of his death being so terrible (for he even cursed and blasphemed to his last gasp, and together with his breath an oath flew out of his mouth) that it was not only a manifest sign of God's judgment but also an horrible and fearful terror to all that beheld him. But herein did the justice of God most notably appear, in that he compelled his own hand which

had written those blasphemies to be the instrument to punish him, and
that in his brain, which had devised the same. . . .

(K5 v, Ch. xxv)

The tragic part of a Revenger, in a world where God did
not demonstrably intervene to protect the innocent, was to
take God's rôle upon himself. His concealed stratagems, the
neat correspondence of crime and punishment, the sudden
unveiling of purpose behind events, the irony and the patient
biding of time are all copied from the model provided by
Omnipotence. Macbeth foresees, what Beard so often
illustrates, that crows, and maggot-pies, and choughs bring
forth the secret man of blood.

To have reduced this frightful God to dimensions merely
human, and shown him in the end as falling to death's mace
himself, must have given sweet if unrecognized relief to fear.
Confronted with the God which such men as Beard created
in their own image, the magnitude of Faustus, Richard and
Hieronimo in their defiance can be more readily com-
prehended.

Richard III opened Burbage's career as a supreme
tragedian; the story was familiar and stately. The diabolic
Richard—a potent figure in the mythology of the Tudor
State—was perhaps remembered to have had a troupe of
players; for like the Vice, he is given the part of an Actor,
comic as well as tragic. 'I do the wrong and first begin to
brawl' he observes; among the many parts in his wardrobe,
that of the Plain Blunt Man is his favourite. With Clarence
he plays the Honest Soldier, with Anne the Lovesick Hero—
in which part he boasts of the murders he has committed.
He makes melodramatic offer of his throat to be cut; then,
when he has conquered, turns round and mocks at his own
triumph.

> *She finds, although I cannot*
> *Myself to be a marvellous proper man.*

(1, 2, 255-6)

133

Such masterly dialogue demands discipline and fire in the actor—it demands rehearsal and a professional sense of pace and timing. This cut-and-thrust is informed with terrific power; the snap and crackle of the exchange depends on rhetorical figures of speech strung out between headlong fits of passion. A wooing over a coffin, underpinned by a cynical soliloquy, shows Richard's complete detachment from the part he is playing. This scene is still used as a training exercise for young actors, as it was in Shakespeare's own day when Heywood wrote a prologue for 'a young witty lad playing Richard III at the Red Bull, to encourage him'.

Richard enjoys his acting and enjoys explaining it; even the dullest member of the audience would not need four soliloquies to tell him that Richard is a villain. His chameleon variety is something which the audience could enjoy, while at the same time they could also enjoy the fluent curses of his victims. 'I seem a saint when most I play the devil', he exclaims, and the devil's is the rôle for which he is most often cast; in dozens of ways he is called 'minister of hell', 'foul devil', 'diffused infection of a man'. For he is an actor in the 'real' life of his victim: he deals death not in jest but in earnest: his rôles are taken for truth: he is counterfeit one way, deadly earnest another.

The audience's feelings about Richard clash; he is so clearly fated to be condemned in his 'detested life and most deserved death' that his wit, dash and early spectacular success appeal to the sporting instinct: the end is known to the audience from the start. In acting, he creates a highly emotional situation; by turns indignant, sententious ('we are not safe, Clarence, we are not safe!'), soldierly, garrulously simple or heartily bluff.

In Act III he is joined by another Actor, the 'deep revolving witty Buckingham'. They invent a plot against themselves, armed with the 'confession' of a man they have already killed.

RICHARD: *Come, cousin, canst thou quake and change thy colour,*
Murder thy breath in middle of a word,
And then again begin and stop again,
As if thou wert distraught and mad with terror?

(3, 5, 1-4)

To which Buckingham replies that he can play at being an actor.

Tut, I can counterfeit the deep tragedian,
Speak and look back and pry on every side,
Tremble and start at wagging of a straw,
Intending deep suspicion. Ghastly looks
Are at my service, like enforced smiles:
And both are ready in their offices
At any time to grace my stratagems.

(3, 5, 5-11)

With sardonic enjoyment he later describes the farce of his appeal to a hostile audience in the City Guildhall; then he acts as Presenter, to Richard appearing in his rôle of Pious Contemplative, between two bishops. Having gained the crown, Richard no longer needs to be an actor; he wakes to a new sense of himself. Mephistopheles had said 'Myself am hell', and Richard, starting in terror from his haunted sleep cries:

Richard loves Richard; that is, I am I.
Is there a murderer here? No. Yes. I am.

(5, 3, 184-5)

He is left stripped of every rôle, a King and nothing. In the end he is willing to throw away all; Burbage made a byword of the line

A horse, a horse, my kingdom for a horse.

(5, 4, 7)

This brilliant, many-sided study shows the evil image of the Actor-Hypocrite drawn within the imaginative world of the play, given the crown—and conquered.

The audience could identify themselves in a new way with the actor. The old reciprocal exchange had been one either of compliment or detraction, in which neither party surrendered to the play itself. Donne, most dramatic of lyric writers described it to Wotton in his second *Epistle* (as an image of courtly futility).

> *Believe me, sir, in my youth's giddiest days,*
> *When to be like the Court, was a play's praise,*
> *Plays were not so like Courts, as Courts are like plays.*

> *Then let us at these mimic antics jest,*
> *Whose deepest projects and egregious gests*
> *Are but dull morals of a game at Chest.*

Now the audience were completely carried away, and could not separate the actor from the rôle; they too lost themselves in the action, as a number of stories about the effects of Burbage's playing Richard III survive to show.

Shakespeare at last achieved the final objective view, the fully dramatic interplay between actor and actor, actor and audience; he had the great advantage of being a player himself. Marlowe and Alleyn imposed themselves by grand, obliterating majesty; Shakespeare and Burbage were more truly Protean.

Tributes to Burbage as an actor suggest his more flexible style, his greater sense of the ensemble. Flecknoe praises Burbage for 'docility' as well as excellence:

He was a delightful Proteus, so wholly transforming himself into his part and putting off himself with his clothes, as he never (not so much as in the tiring house) assum'd himself till the play was done.

A Short Discourse of the English Stage (1664). (*E.S.* 4, 370)

POET'S ART AND PLAYER'S QUALITY

In the 'Parnassus' play, Burbage looks to the young student for a good 'conceit' of a part; (12) Hamlet mentions the importance of a player's 'conceit' and Heywood in his *Apology for Actors* says it will compensate for lack of natural ability. The player's 'conceit' is his notion of a particular part, his realization of it as a coherent identity. Alleyn remained ever himself, and his career shows that he was as remarkable and forceful off the stage as on it. Burbage subdued himself to his part:

never falling* in his part when he had done speaking; but with his looks and gesture maintaining it still unto the height.

So imagination bodied forth the shapes of men and women, who were not, like Wilson's Three Lords of London, or even Marlowe's Tamburlaine, enlarged images of the Self, playing at Kings and Queens; but part of a complex, organic group, in the two hours' traffic of the stage.

If all the world appeared on the stage of the Globe, there yet remained the older kind of play, where life and art were mingled. This survived in the imaginative game of courtly rivalry for power where sometimes, as Walter Ralegh, one of the most gifted actors observed, men might truly die, in earnest and not jest.

The courtly 'game' was in turn reflected in the revelry of other great households. This imaginative play was akin to that which Chaucer knew. His celebration of the good Queen Alceste in the Prologue to the *Legend of Good Women* is more elegant than his pupil Spenser's spring vision of Elizabeth in the April Eclogue of *The Shepherd's Calendar*; yet it seems likely enough that the very real social power of her projected imaginative 'form', which Elizabeth used with superb adroitness as an instrument of government, was another manifestation of the power to create a fluid, dynamic order within the realm of traditional art.

Elizabeth's dominating position will be seen in the next

* 'Falling' means 'sinking' or 'falling off'.

chapter. Here there will be a return to 1575, the midpoint of her reign, the period of the rise of Leicester's Men; for the general development which has now been outlined will be illustrated by some particular examples, showing in terms of representative actors the rise of the Common Player.

PART TWO

Common Players, 1575-1600

CHAPTER VI

LEICESTER'S MEN AT KENILWORTH

Laneham's Letter

Country sports—included in Kenilworth activities—Laneham's
Letter compared with Whythorn's work—not really by a Mercer
—the author as depicted an imaginary figure, the true writer
probably John Laneham of Leicester's Men—banter of the town
players, who, like the common players, are attacked by the clergy
—the song of the Minstrel a professional burlesque—the social
status of the writer corresponds to that of a player—but includes
in his 'character' traits of a friendly citizen—the author's
justification of his own learning—his defence of writers
—the subsequent career of John Laneham the actor.

MERRYMAKING and ceremonial games provided a
foundation for the Elizabethan theatre. Festive
seasonal sports persisted among countryfolk,
linked with the phases of the agricultural year—Mayday or
Hocktide, Whitsun and Harvest. Even in towns, the
Sheriffs had their summer feast and the Livery their Midsummer Watch, and in London at Bartholomew Tide the
Lord Mayor of London went in procession to the fields and
'the mob began to wrestle before him, two at a time'. (1)
Such wrestling could turn easily into a Robin Hood play.
Jesting and flouting by Summer Lords—who enrolled men
in their livery and gave out badges and cognisances—would
employ mock testaments, mock proclamations, and the like.
The ridicule of unpopular characters in these sports did not
differ very much from the mockery of the clown's jig (2).
Somewhere about 1575, a Scottish account of such sports,
Peblis to the Play, was copied into the Maitland MS.

Triumph as well as detraction was part of the game; the crowning of May Lord and May Lady, with the procession of Maypole and Maygarland, was followed by weddings with rush rings, and lovers going two and two a-Maying. The animal spirits of the merrymakers, whether expended in dancing, feasting, wooing or fighting were a source both of apprehension to their governors and of rebuke from their pastors. The momentary generous oblivion of *meum* and *tuum* in communal feasts, the ready gifts to 'gatherers' in money or kind, were looked on sourly by such characters as Stubbes, for on these occasions other distinctions were also lost.

... then march this heathen company towards the church and church-yard, their pipers piping, their drummers thundring, their stumps dancing, their bells jangling, their handkerchiefs swinging about their heads like madmen, their hobbyhorses and other monsters skirmishing among the throng; and in this sort, they go to the Church (though the minister be at prayer or preaching) dancing and swinging their handkerchiefs over their heads in the church like devils incarnate ... then after this, about the church they go again and again, and so forth into the churchyard, where they have commonly their summer halls, their bowers, arbours and banqueting houses set up, wherein they feast, banquet and dance all that day, and (peradventure) all that night too. And thus these terrestial furies spend the Sabbath day.

Stubbes, *Anatomy of Abuses*, 92-93

In this matter, Puritans and Bishops were for once in full agreement. The chief opponent of the Puritan Martin Marprelate, Thomas Cooper Bishop of Winchester, ordered the suppression of 'Church ales, May Games, Morris Dances and other vain pastimes' in May 1575—at a moment when local sports, professional playing, and courtly allegory were all to be combined; for the Queen was about to set out on a progress which culminated in the most stately of all sylvan games—the Princely Pleasures of Kenil-worth. (3)

LEICESTER'S MEN AT KENILWORTH

The most famous and costly of Elizabeth's country welcomes lasted from 9 to 27 July 1575. The Earl of Leicester's spending was princely; he was reputed to have provided at the rate of £1,000 a day, but to have recovered two hundred thousand crowns in royal grants by way of recompense. The Earl laid on his merriments as lavishly as everything else; to support his display of costumes, jewels, fireworks, music and poetry he dispensed gifts to all the household. With all its hangers-on, its baggage, its open bravery and rapacious competition, state for the few and cramped discomfort for the rest, the Court found at Kenilworth a magnificence equal for once to its Gargantuan appetite.

Two accounts of these Pleasures survive (at least one other appeared in print, though now lost); they show that beneath the festive gaiety sharp cleavages could still be felt, although the delight in ceremony which could devise these welcomes sprang from something better than mere calculation. George Gascoigne's version of plays, both those acted and those rejected, written from the point of view of a gentleman poet, is dealt with below, in Chapter XI. The present chapter is concerned with an anonymously printed letter, dated from the court at Worcester 20 August 1575, 'from a freend officer attendant in the Coourt, unto his freend a Citizen, and Merchaunt of London'. (4) This work, usually known as Laneham's Letter, is written with more attention to country sports which Gascoigne excluded as beneath his notice or that of the 'studious and well disposed young gentlemen' he addressed. Hitherto, though well known and several times reprinted, it has been assumed to be no more than its title states it to be; the 'quaint' spelling and the vivid descriptions have excited a rather amused curiosity. It is my view that this document was written by a member of the Earl of Leicester's Men, John Laneham, and that it represents the common player's point of view; that its merriment is by no means naïve, but conceals a sting and that it is a social document of importance for the historian of the theatre, the sole surviving literary production of the first great Elizabethan acting company. No plays from the repertoire of Leicester's Men have survived, but if my view is correct, this work provides the text of one of their 'merriments' or afterpieces, in the burlesque song of the Minstrel of Islington.

It is fairly certain that the Earl of Leicester's Men were at Kenilworth, for as the letter tells, on Sunday, 17 July

after supper waz thear a play prezented of a very good theam, but so set foorth by the Actoourz wel handling, that pleazure and mirth made it seeme very short, though it lasted too good oourz and more.

(p. 39)

Leicester's Men would have felt very ill used had the Earl invited any players than his own to give this performance.

This specimen of Laneham's spelling is enough to show its likeness to that of Thomas Whythorn, whose *Autobiography*, written in the following year, 1576, has recently come to light, and been edited by James M. Osborne. Whythorn belonged to the highest class of musicians and entertainers; he had been Music Master at Lambeth. His 'Orthography' is based on the system of John Hart, Chester Herald; though Laneham's is not the same it is clearly related, and is no proof of rustic quaintness but rather of elegant sophistication, for Hart's system was evidently fashionable, especially among language teachers.

The letter appears to be a formal, imaginative composition. The character of the writer is vividly drawn; his account of himself has hitherto been taken at its face value. In the course of the letter he calls himself Laneham, others call him Langham (pp. 44, 84), and finally he subscribes:

Yoer contreéman, companion, and freend assuredly; Mercer, Merchantaventurer: and Clark of the Councel Chamber Doore, and also kepar of the same; *El Prencipe negro.* Par me R. L. Gent. Mercer

(p. 87)

A little earlier he observes that he is summoned to his livery 'by the name of Ro. La. of the Coounty of Nosingham Gentlman'.

It seems however improbable that the writer is really Roberte Langham, admitted to the Mercers' Company in 1557, having been apprenticed to William Leonarde; for at the beginning of the letter he describes how he travelled to France 'under my Master Bumsted'. Christopher Bompstead *could* have been Langham's Master, for he himself was admitted to the Mercer's Company in 1541; but in fact he was not. If there is one thing which even the most careless writer would not mistake, it is the name of the master to whom he had served his seven years of apprenticeship, in whose house he had resided—when not engaged upon his travels. (5)

Many readers from the time of Walter Scott onwards have been fascinated by Laneham's character as revealed in the letter, without realizing how different is this impression from the glimpses afforded in real correspondence. He is a bluff, lively citizen with a great taste for company, a great interest in heraldry and display, colour and shows, a good knowledge of music and of languages ancient and modern; but above all a jovial fellow and a friend to pastime. His character is 'touched in' at the beginning and end of the letter; it is not revealed by the writer, but built up artificially and dramatically, for the reader.

To choose a name that was nearly, but not quite, that of a well-known citizen was a familiar clown's jest; to describe himself 'of the Coounty of Nosingham' is to thumb a nose at the reader; similar jests about 'the tribe of Mani-asses' or —more daringly—the 'Just-asses' are known from May Games elsewhere. (6)

The letter is addressed to Humfrey Martin, a young Mercer who was admitted in 1570, the son of Sir Roger Martin of Long Melford, Suffolk, twice Lord Mayor of London; in 1571, as a Bachelor of the Company, he was one of the two who supported the 'Mercer's Maid', the company's pageant, in the City show, where as the senior of the Great Companies, they would lead the way. He was perhaps a friend to players, for his family was of the old faith; and certainly a friend to Leicester, who knighted his father. (7)

A 'countryman' of Martin would then have been a Suffolk man; the Visitation discloses no such name among the gentry. Laneham is however a place-name in Suffolk; Lavenham is pronounced Laneham. It occurs as a surname in eastern England, including Bury St Edmunds; it is also, as has been often observed, the name of one of the leading actors in the Earl of Leicester's Men—John Laneham. And if Laneham had already heard that his fellow James Burbage was thinking of leasing a certain plot of land in Holywell, with the idea of starting something new in the way of a playing place, he might have heard the name of Christopher Bompstead, who at one time had owned the property, and whose name could therefore appear in any document of conveyance. (8)

The writer's description of his office is likewise imaginary —at least it finds no support in the Queen's household accounts. The Four Clerks of the Privy Council were supported by a postmaster and thirty standing posts, who were used to meet out of court in the house of one of their number. The servants of the Queen's privy chamber included groom porters, grooms and yeomen. The Yeomen Warders who kept the door were drawn from the Yeomen of the Guard, and on state occasions the door would be guarded by the Captain of the Guard in person—Hatton or Ralegh. (9)

Laneham describes his duties at length in the letter; they are those of a doorkeeper. 'Clerk' was a senior title and the Clerk of the Council-Table served in the Office of the Lord Privy Seal. To 'act' the porter was a recognized comic rôle; on Elizabeth's entry to the Castle, the part of the porter was played by the Esquire Bedell of the University of Oxford, of which Leicester was Chancellor.

Laneham pictures himself also as waiting on the Earl of Leicester in the mornings with a servant's duty, as well as eating his manchet at the Earl's cupboard, where it was left overnight for his livery:

for I dare be az bolld, I promis yoo, az any of my freends the servants thear: and indeed coold I have fresh if I woold tary.   (p. 82)

In other words he was a serving man. When the Queen's troupe were later formed, in 1583, they were allowed livery as grooms of her chamber extraordinary. When in 1572 they had petitioned to become his household servants, Leicester's Men could have been given this office—and the general conservatism in such matters would suggest that the Queen had simply followed custom. If so, when a miniature of the royal household was set up at Kenilworth, one of Leicester's Grooms of the Chamber extraordinary may well have found himself given the privilege of serving as groom in the Queen's chamber, and this might have included keeping the door. (10)

Familiar Letters were a common device for any controversial or topical pamphlet; the Queen's entertainment at Woodstock, in September of the same year, was described in another Familiar Letter (11)—the scurrilous attack on Leicester himself, afterwards known as *Leicester's Commonwealth*, first appeared as *A Letter from a Master of Arts to his Friend in London*; above all, the popular half-jocular, half-satirical pamphlet such as Chettle's *Kind Hart's Dream*, took this form. Although it is nearly twenty years earlier, this Letter has much in common, both in style and matter, with the pamphlets of the nineties; there is large borrowing from it, for example in Greene's *Farewell to Folly*.

The informality of parts of the Letter is calculated. It has a double aim; a report of the Castle pleasures (this would be the best selling point) and a glorification of the Earl of Leicester. It is possible that it had also a further aim; to celebrate the triumph of the common players—a merry

147

triumph recorded over their sourer opponents, in the year between getting their Patent and opening the Theatre, when triumph must have been sweet indeed.

The work opens with a lengthy history of Kenilworth and Mercia, from Saxon times—a set piece, though graced with touches of verisimilitude as 'Nay, noow I am a little in, Master Martin, Ile tell you all' but ending

Thus proface* ye with the preface. And noow to the matter.

(p. 7)

The matter of the sports, which follows, is highly selective. Pride of place is given to the country shows and indoor merriment which Gascoigne ignored. 'The Merry Marriage' opened with hideous elderly bride (a man in disguise?), clownish groom, and tilting at the Quintain by riders without stirrups and without boots, who were probably antics mounted on one another's shoulders. This was the passage which attracted Robert Greene, who copied it almost word for word in the description of 'a wealthy farmer's son' who was 'going up very mannerly to be leader of a morris dance'.

The bridegroom formost, in his fatherz tawny worsted jacket (for his freends wear fayn that he shoold be a brydegroom before the Queén) a fayr strawn hat with a capitall crooun steépl wyse on his hed; a payr of harvest glovez on his hands, az a sign of good husbandry; a pen and inkhorn at his bak, for he woold be knowen to be bookish, lame of a leg that in his yooth was broken at football; well beloved yet of hiz mother that lent him a nu mufflar for a napkin that was tyed too hiz gyrdl for lozing . . . for though heat and coolnes upon sundry occazions made him sumtime too sweat, and sumtime rumatick: yet durst he bollder too blo hiz noze and wype hiz face with the flapet of his fatherz jacket, then with hiz moothers mufflar. Tiz a goodly matter, when yooth is manerly brought up in fatherly loouve and motherly aw. (p. 27, p. 30)

* 'Welcome to the preface.'

This formal procession is far from the rowdy morris dance denounced by Stubbes, but it is a morris none the less. It anticipates much burlesque pamphlet literature of the next generation; Barnaby Rich's description of the marriage of Ruffling Richard and Mannerly Margery is in this same detailed style, which may be modelled upon the Prologue to the Canterbury Tales, and thought of as a popular English fashion of the old time. (12) It is particularly suited to a player, for his costume often made his part.

Such good-humoured chaff would be very well suited to a professional actor watching the simple countryman's efforts, as well as to a city merchant enjoying the joke with his crony. It gave to country sports the bantering approval which professional actors might have taken from their lord. More heroic burlesque develops in the martial show of the Coventry men, led by Captain Cox, Mason, Master of the town musters, and Aleconner (or president of town feasts).

But aware, keép bak, make room noow, hear they cum. And fyrst Captain Cox, an od man I promiz yoo; by profession a Mason, and that right skilfull, very cunning in fens, and hardy az Gawin, for his ton-sword hangs at hiz tablz end; great oversight hath he in matters of storie . . . Captain Cox cam on marching valiantly before, cleén trust and gartered aboue the knee, all fresh in a velvet cap (master Goldingham lent it him) floorishing with hiz ton-swoord, and another fensmaster with him; thus in the foreward making room for the rest.

(p. 34, p. 36)

The royal visit thus enabled Captain Cox and his men to revive their Hock-Tuesday 'storial show', which the local clergy had put down, notwithstanding it had been recommended to Henry VIII as a model of national sentiment. The Coventry men came out with their show on Sunday, 17 July; but as the Queen was drawn away by dancing in the great chamber they were invited to give it again two days later and rewarded with two fat buck, and five marks in money. At a time when the well-rehearsed plays of the gentlemen were being thrust aside, this must have inspired the revellers with fresh courage in their struggle with local divines, and proved the sympathy of the Queen.

The thing said they iz grounded on story, and for pastime woont too bee playd in oour Citee yeérely . . . tyll noow of late laid dooun, they knu no cauz why onless it wear by the zeal of certain theyr Preacherz: men very commendabl for their behaviour and learning, and sweét in their sermonz, but sumwhat too sour in preaching awey theyr pastime: wisht therefore that, az they shoold continu their good doctrin in pulpet, so, for matters of pollicy and governauntz of the Citie, they woould permit them to the Mair and Magistratez: and seyd by my feyth, Master Martyn, they woold make their humbl petition untoo her highnes, that they might have theyr playz up agayn.   (p. 33)

The show was a mixture of procession, drill display and Hocktide battle between men and women. It commemorated the defeat of the Danes by the English at Coventry on St Brice's Day, 1002. The procession, led by 'Danish lannsknights on horsebak' and then the English 'each with their alder poll martially in their hand' kindled 'from a hot skirmish unto a blazing battail', first with spear and shield, then with sword and target. Two parties of footsoldiers next marched in, and turned from ranks into triangles, and from that into rings and so out again till 'a valiant captain of great prowez, as fiers as a fox assaulting a gooz' gave the first blow; whereupon the fight resumed with the Danes twice getting the advantage 'but at the last conflict, beaten doun, over com, and many led captive for triumph by oour English weémen'.

The martial triumph is of the same sort, though not as grand as that of London against Spain in Wilson's play which is discussed in the next chapter; but it also represented a triumph of players over preachers and would therefore have been particularly acceptable to the Earl of Leicester's Men, less than a year from that glorious moment when by Letters Patent they had secured their own victory over the zealous

preachers of London. It anticipated also what was to prove
the London players' best getpenny—the English history.
Coventry men revived the play next year; and in 1591
returned to their old theme with *The Defeat of the Danes and
the Life of Edward the Confessor*. (13)

Captain Cox's library of romances, ballads and almanacks
as listed by Laneham has always excited great interest; but
as the writer records upwards of sixty titles, it might be
thought, unless the Captain carried round a card catalogue,
that the list is an ideal one, and represents what such a
collector might be thought to possess. It represents also the
kind of source on which all popular plays were based—those
tastes among the common people on which the players
relied, when they produced the 'medleys'. Captain Cox is a
character everyway resembling Laneham himself; a good
fellow yet bookish—drawn rather larger than life. He
remained so famous a figure that Ben Jonson revived him for
a *Masque of Owls* given at Kenilworth as late as 1626.

Even more space is given to the description of another
'ridiculous device' of which Laneham says he saw a rehearsal.
This was a song of King Arthur by a 'Squire Minstrel' of
Islington, evidently presented as a member of the town waits.
His burlesque title might be translatable as 'The Right
Honourable Gentleman, the Village Fiddler'. The minstrel's
costume, down to the very colour of his points and the fresh
blacking on his old pumps is specified; hanging from his
neck by a pewter chain is a scutcheon with mock-arms for
Islington—the crest of a bowl of furmenty stuck with horn
spoons. (14) These arms, proudly blazoned by the minstrel,
are flouted by a member of the audience. The minstrel was
about forty-five; yet like Humfrey Martin 'he was but a
bachelor yet'.

The mockery of Islington's civic pretensions—'well
knooen to be one of the most auncient toounz in England
next London at thiz day' (p. 48)—reflects on the glory of
her great neighbour. The song sung by the minstrel, which

extends only to one 'passus', is based on the *Morte D'Arthur*.
This 'solemn song', like the show of the Coventry men, is
'warrented for story': its burlesque manner is close to the
burlesque story of the show; it recounts the kind of tale that
Captain Cox would have enjoyed. The 'doughty dwarf' who
demands King Arthur's beard in tribute, to line the mantle
of Sir Ryance of North-galles, causes a tremendous uproar in
which princes puffed, barons blustered, pages and yeomen
yelled out in the hall. They were quieted by the entry of Sir
Kay with the courteous command of 'Silence, my sovereigns',
and the dwarf, having been feasted and rewarded, received
his answer from Arthur

> *Say too Sir Ryens thou Dwarf quoth the king,*
> *That for his proud message I him defy,*
> *And shortly with basinz and panz will him ring*
> *Oout of Northgalez whereaz heé and I*
> *With sweards (and no razorz), shall utterly try,*
> *Which of us both iz the better Barber;*
> *And thearewith he shook his sword Excalaber.*

(p. 54)

This provides the climax of Laneham's account of the
festivities. He says that there was more of the song, which
he could not obtain; but a mispagination which occurs at
this point in the printed text, with the elimination of p. 55,
suggests that a cut has been made deliberately. As the
signatures are regular, this must have occurred before
printing began.

The comic double rhymes of the song, like his ridiculous
armorial badge, prove that the 'minstrel' was burlesquing the
old-fashioned tradition he stood for. (14a) The language of
the song is quite a fair imitation of traditional phrases, in the
manner of Chaucer's *Sir Thopaz*, to which kind it seems to
belong. This being so, badinage from the courtly audience
would be expected and played up. Jokes were handed to
them ready-made by the performer. Audiences enjoyed

'dashing' a comedy, and the courtly interruptions were part of the game.

If the letter were what in some ways it resembles, a Bad Quarto, there would be no doubt of the Pirate Actor's part. John Laneham would be recording one of his own merriments, and like Gascoigne, putting in print part, at least, of what he had not been able to present in person.

The writer of the Letter was clearly a skilled musician; on both occasions when he lets slip his own name (as distinct from the clues 'planted' at the end), it is because he is carried away either by the pleasures of song:

for the smal skyl in musik, that God hath sent me (ye kno it is sumwhat) Ile set the more by myself while my name is Laneham and grace a God. A! musik is a nobl Art. (p. 44)

or the intoxication of being asked for an encore by the ladies —'Anoother, good Langham, anoother!' (p. 84). For a skilled musician, parody of a town minstrel would be a tempting part.

But behind the surface jollity and gay burlesque, a more personal and dangerous jest may perhaps be concealed. The matter of this song, especially as transmitted by one London citizen to another, might reflect upon the state and dignity of the London archery band, the Ancient Order, Society and Unity Laudable of Prince Arthur and his Knightly Band of the Round Table, incorporated as such by King Henry VIII, who also bestowed on the leading archer the mock title of The Duke of Shoreditch. The city archers held ceremonial parades and shooting matches, not unlike the parade of the Coventry trainbands; their society was limited to three hundred and was led by fifty-seven 'knights' named from heroes of the Round Table, whose arms were to be solemnly blazoned by their historian. (15) Here the City was aspiring to ancient titles of dignity; this song was intended only for the genuine nobility. The song appears devoid of anything like personal allusions; but much would depend on the manner in which it was given—a scandalous play like *The Isle of Gulls* also reads harmlessly enough. In the version given here, which is apparently not complete, it remained popular, circulating in manuscript for many years, as dangerous burlesques had a habit of doing. (16)

After enumerating in detail, the very ruffles on this non-performer's shirt, Laneham takes leave of him with the casual remark 'Az for the matter, had it come to the sheaw, I think the fello would have handled it well inoogh.'

Such a merriment or afterpiece in private would have not been thought worthy of more than informal production; and it might have been misinterpreted on this occasion, because the Arthurian theme of the whole Kenilworth entertainment was designed for the glory of Leicester. The gigantic Arthurian trumpeters and the Lady of the Lake who came to welcome Elizabeth were meant for pure state and glory.

The 'ridiculous device' ends Laneham's description of the festivities, which cover the first ten days only. He says that he did not keep any further notes—it may have been that the players, having given their Offering, hastened off to reap the extra large rewards that they would have gained by showing at once the play which had been acted before the Queen.

He records with delight the Queen's answer to the Lady of the Lake; her gracious words when the overacting of the amateur George Gascoigne had caused her horse to rear: 'No hurt! no hurt!' which

we wear all glad to heer and took them too be the best part of the play.

(p. 21)

These signs of favour were calculated to catch the professional ear of a player, as the gorgeous devices took his professional eye. He concentrates on the spectacular entry of the Queen (where the heraldic devices particularly interest him), hunting, bear-baiting, the feats of an Italian tumbler and the fireworks. He spends his time as an entertainer, singing and playing to the ladies, teaching courtship in a variety of languages, visiting the great in their chambers, yet he gets a peep into the private garden and the marvellous aviary of tropical birds only by help of a fellow-servant, when the courtiers are out hunting; while he feeds with one 'Master Pinner', who is sometimes put off his food by rebukes administered from above. The self-characterization presents a bluff gay companion, a somewhat Falstaffian friend for young Master Martin, who jokes about his own red nose, but who is knowledgeable in music, heraldry and devices, gifted with a mercer's or a player's eye for fine stuffs.

The figure of the narrator represents that part of the City which was favourable to sports and therefore to the common players' cause. A jovial man, addicted to sack and sugar, his hunting and sporting tastes might have developed in a really wealthy citizen. The 'token' sent to his friend Mr Customer Smythe (the magnificently bearded captain of Prince Arthur's Knights, incidentally) sounds like a proverb which may not have been unknown to merchants: 'Set my horz up to the rak, and then let's have a cup of Sak' (p. 87) 'He wil laugh, I hold ye a grote.' Not all City men were enemies to good cheer; some may have opened their houses to the common players.

The character is built up with a good but not quite sufficient knowledge of the Mercers' Company; the London reader is directed by the Mercer's shop-sign *El Prencipe Negro*, (17) although at the beginning of the letter it is implied that he is no longer trading. To make a merchant adventurer, with such distinguished connexions in London, into a household servant is to create a most improbable social hybrid. Even the powerful Hunnis, Master of the Chapel Royal, only dabbled in trade; and Whythorn, another Musician, temporarily took charge of his affairs for the London merchant Bromfield.

On the stage the Jovial Citizen was to receive his best embodiment in Simon Eyre, hero of Dekker's *Shoemakers'*

Holiday; here, the good cheer of the country is presented dramatically through the eyes of a City good fellow, to enhance the regal magnificence of the Queen's pleasures and the glory of Leicester. The Mercer serves to bring the Londoner into the picture as it were; to relate the City to the Country and the Court; he puts the ideal reader into the story, making him not only Chief Spectator but also one of the actors in the scene.

Laneham excuses his fragmentary account by saying that after the first ten days the court expected to remove and therefore he did not keep any more notes. He adds however:

If I dyd but ruminate the dayz I have spoken of, I shall bring oout yet sumwhat more, meat for yoor appetite (thoogh a deinty tooth have ye) which I beleve yoor tender stomak will brook wel inoogh.

(p. 56)

For another thirty-seven pages, almost half the work, he expatiates, beginning with some mystic numbers, contriving all his praise to the Queen and the Earl of Leicester. The seven gifts of the seven gods which greeted the Queen had shown that by his princely power Leicester commanded Jupiter and all the rest; to his further glory, in his capacity as Master of the Horse he had evidently supplied Laneham with a licence for beans [horsebread] and given his old father the right to purvey for the stable.

Laneham indulges a fancy that the Fates did not spin a single thread of the Queen's life while she stayed (pp. 63-5). He digresses to describe the splendours of the castle, with its curious closed garden, containing a fountain with a hidden spout, that 'with the wreast of a cock' would drench the onlooker 'from top to toe; the hee's to some laughing, but the shee's to more sport'. Returning to his theme, he notes that the hands of the great castle clock were stopped at two o'clock throughout the visit, which he takes as a sign of amity and 'oracle certain'. This moralizing he admits is 'a windlass':

And but mark a lyttl I pray, and seé hoow of all things in the world, oour toongs in tallk do alweyz so redily trip upon tooz payrz and cooplz. . . . (p. 75)

This is his nearest approach to the hope, more openly expressed by others, that at Kenilworth Elizabeth might find 'a world of wedded bliss'; but his loyalty to Leicester is enthusiastic and pervasive. 'God save the Queene and my Lord, I am well, I thank you', he exclaims in joyous climax to his recital of the Earl's bounties. He had been given suits from Leicester's own back—an old-fashioned favour indeed, except for players, who depended on the cast suits of the great for their wardrobe. If it were not for the Earl's protection, this doorkeeper, who ends by sending his affectionate commendations to the great Mr Customer Smythe, to Alderman Pullison (a future Lord Mayor) and 'to my mery cumpanion (a Mercer ye wot az we be) Master Denman, *mio fratello in Christo*' would go in cut canvas instead of satin, and afoot instead of on horseback. He eats with servants, though he mingles with lords and ladies to entertain them; at one moment he boasts of his acquaintance with Sir George Howard and Lady Sidney; the next, he is begging for a peep at the aviary. This ambiguous mixture of familiarity and humble station is characteristic of the common player; it is shared by Laneham with Tarlton, as his heraldic interests and his love of pageantry are shared with Robert Wilson.

Finally, Laneham finds it necessary to account for his Latin quotations. His eulogy of Leicester is well studded with Latin tags and provides a great contrast to the popular style which he uses for describing the country folk; the climax is naturally reserved for Leicester's liberality

So great in liberalitie, az hath no wey to heap up the mass of his trezure, but only by liberal gyving and bounteous bestoing his trezure; folloing (az it seémez) ye saw of Martiall that sayth.

Extra fortunam est quicquid donatur amicis,
Quas dederis, solas semper habebis opes.

157

Oout of all hazered, doest thou set that to thy freends thoou
gyvest:
A surer trezure canst thoou not have every whyle thoou
lyvest. (p. 80)

Earlier in the letter, scraps of French, Italian and German and learned quotations from Conrad Gesnerus and Diodorus Sicurus had shown his skill in the tongues. So the mercer explains that he went to school both at St Antony's in Threadneedle Street, and St Paul's. According to Stow, the 'pigs' of St Antony's and the 'pigeons' of St Paul's spent the midday hour disputing and fighting in St Paul's Churchyard which rang with cries of 'Salve!' 'Salve te autem!' 'Placet tibi mihi disputare?' 'Placet!' St Antony's was famous for rhetoric and Laneham certainly knows both the high and the low style. But the ingenuous observation that his friend may wonder to see him so bookish followed by an over-weighted explanation that no friend should have needed is one of the conventional touches of self-characterization. It helps to join together the superimposed figures of Langham the Merchant and Laneham the Player. The interest in languages is similar again to that shown by Robert Wilson; and the Latin is not beyond a common player's reach. (18) The style of the Letter, ranging from lofty panegyric to familiar banter, implies not only good training but good practice in rhetoric.

Especially significant is the Latin verse which appears on the title page, more particularly its last half-line, which is an adaptation of Vergil, *Eclogues* 7, 26. It shows that the Letter is a defence against envy, detraction of poets, and the accusation of disorder with which players were charged.

De Regina Nostra Illustrissima.
Dum laniata rūat vicina ah regna tumultu
Laeta suos inter genialibus ILLA diebus
(gratia Diis) fruitur; rūpantur et ilia Codro. (19)

Another latin quatrain closes up the Letter with Elizabeth's praises; as three years before the players had closed with a little quatrain their petition to the Earl for admission to his household.

Music and merriments in Tarlton's vein seem to have been the speciality of Laneham the Player. He remained with Leicester's Men till the Queen's Men were formed and was then chosen for the royal troupe. He played a spirited part in the attack on Martin Marprelate. Martin appeared on the stage as an Ape, where he was wormed and lanced; and one of the anti-Martinists suggests that this is the only level on which he should be answered.

> *Ye grave men that answer Martin's mowes,*
> *He mocks the more, and you in vain lose times:*
> *Leave apes to dogs to bait, their skins to crowes,*
> *And let old Lanam lash him with his rimes.* (20)

In another anti-Martin pamphlet, *Martin's Month's Mind,* the Puritan mocker is shown on his death's bed declaring, 'All my folly I bequeath to my good friend Lanam and his consort [his troupe] from whom I had it.'

In the Familiar Letter, the country players are bantered kindly—for they were ready to welcome the City Actor, no doubt; while the 'poor fellowship of the minstrels' are rather more pointedly shown as old fashioned curiosities, and made to carry some 'squandering glances' at the City dignitaries, who prefer them to players. Playing is supported against the zeal of sour divines, and the triumph of actors is celebrated. The one performance of the Earl of Leicester's Men at the Castle is recorded with proper reserve; for on this occasion they were no longer common players, but acting as their lord's household servants in the entertainment of their sovereign lady. A fine social sense of different levels in entertainment—not to mention a professional superiority— is already seen.

If they encountered it, the document must have given pain to the godly. To question the Queen's right to her Princely pleasures would be disloyal, yet how could a painful preacher thunder against sinful sports and pastimes, while the Deborah of the Reformation was setting such a bad example?

The Letter shows the early troupes' interest in display and music, heraldry, colour and shows rather than drama in the strict sense. It fits in well with such a work as Wilson's *Pleasant and Stately Moral*; but comes before it by thirteen years. It appeals in the same way as Wilson does to the more generous and convivial members of the City, and dramatically assumes such a rôle, for the author.

Whatever the story behind this Letter, and whether or not it is actually from the pen of John Laneham, it was surely an unsophisticated reading which transcribed from the Letter as literal fact every detail in the life of that Nottinghamshire worthy, Robert Laneham, for the Dictionary of National Biography. He never existed; he is a 'ghost'. Such a confounding of art with nature yet might have pleased a player. For in the Letter, all the world is seen as a stage, with dramatic possibilities in everyday things, a 'conceit' to be sought for in all common events. The Queen herself created drama by her presence, and life then took on the dimension of art.

This apparently harmless little production was issued without printer's name or provenance, which means presumably that it was not licensed. Yet a loyal tribute of this sort would not in the ordinary way have offered difficulty. If, however, the appropriation of the names of worthy citizens had been known to the Wardens of the Stationers' Company, they would have made some difficulties; and if the device of the Squire Minstrel, with its flouting of civic glory and bearding of Prince Arthur's Knights had been presented, the difficulties might have grown insurmountable. It is the joining of genuine celebration with flouts and jests, the royal triumph and the covert glee of the common stages that give the Letter its depth; like dignified plot and farcical subplot in a comedy, they intertwine to make a complex web of merriment and scorn.

LEICESTER'S MEN AT KENILWORTH

Yet in this work the professional players are still close enough to the rural games of Coventry and the songs of the minstrel for a later generation to be unable to distinguish between them. This same misunderstanding was to occur over the merriments of Laneham's contemporary, the first great English actor, Richard Tarlton the clown.

Afterword 1978

In *English Literary Renaissance* VII, 3 (Autumn 1977), pp. 297–306, David Scott convincingly proves *Laneham's Letter* to be the comic but unsuccessful jest of a minor author, William Patten (*fl.* 1540–89), writer of the Latin verses set above the gateway at Kenilworth to welcome the Queen. Dramatically fathered on at least one real person, Robert Langham, who provided the Council Chamber with tongs and fireshovels, herbs and flowers, and was termed its Keeper, the work offended as being 'disrespectful' of the honourable entertainment; Langham himself complained. The author, who had printed and distributed one or two gift copies only, excused himself in a letter (now at Hatfield) to his patron Lord Burghley, dated from London 10 September 1575—just twenty-one days after the subscription 'from Worcester 20 August' to the pamphlet itself.

Patten, a Teller of the Exchequer and Customer of London Outward, had served under the Earl of Warwick in 1548 against the Scots. He writes in the peculiar spelling of the *Letter* (his annotations can be found in the Huntington Library copy). The prudently ambiguous *persona* of the 'author' suggests both Langham the Keeper and Langham the Mercer, but possibly also Laneham the player, with whom Patten would probably have worked in devising the sports. Though the detail is careful, the device misfired, and the work was evidently ordered to be suppressed only a few days after its appearance. Patten obeyed. Such are the hazards of the jester.

CHAPTER VII

THE QUEEN'S LIVERY

Richard Tarlton

Tarlton's career outlined—the nature of his acting—its subsequent misrepresentation—his extempore verses—his ballads—
his lost play—some posthumous descriptions—the paradox
of his career—his *Tragical Treatise.*

H IS contemporaries knew that Tarlton the clown was
no fool; they did not confuse the parts he played with
the man himself. They knew that he wrote plays as
well as acting; his *Play of the Seven Deadly Sins* was very
popular, though nothing of it now survives but the prompter's
'plot', preserved with Alleyn's papers at Dulwich.

By the seventies, Tarlton was a national figure, the first
actor to achieve stardom; perhaps the first man to be known
all over England simply in terms of his personality. His
individual achievement was as revolutionary as that of the
Great Companies themselves; to create an entirely new kind
of relationship between one man and the rest of the community is to justify Nashe's playful description of him as the
King of his epoch.

Wilson, his fellow-actor, said Tarlton was apprenticed to a
water carrier in the City of London—as who should say,
articled to an ice-cream vendor. As he is generally asserted to
have kept a tavern, this joke may imply that Tarlton watered
his liquor. If he had been a freeman, Tarlton would have
been a Vintner. Tradition asserts that his father lived at
Ilford—and Tarlton is described as of Ilford in his will. He
is thought to have kept the Tarlton Inn at Colchester, the
Saba tavern in Gracechurch Street, and an ordinary in
Paternoster Row. He acted at the Bull, the Bell Inn in

Gracechurch Street and the Belsavage by Ludgate, and may
well have graduated to the stage from comic turns at his own
inn; for since the days of Chaucer's Harry Bailly, innkeepers
had been traditionally jovial and witty. (1)

A dull but godly ballad on recent floods in Bedfordshire,
published in 1570, is the first relic of him to survive; he
joined the Lord Chamberlain's (Earl of Sussex) players, who
often came to Court between 1577 and 1583; in the latter
year, when the Queen's troupe was formed, he became one of
the twelve. He was already famous for his 'wonderful plentiful pleasant extemporal wit'. Five years later he died, on
3 September 1588, in the house of 'one Em Ball in Shoreditch, she being a woman of very bad reputation'. A squabble
broke out between his old mother, his brothers-in-law (one
was a butcher) and his lawyer over his will and the custody of
his small son, Philip, whose godfather had been no less a
person than Philip Sidney. Tarlton's dying appeal to Sir
Francis Walsingham, to protect the child, shows the player
already enjoying that familiarity with greatness and with
squalor, with social extremes, which is the price and reward
of a career outside normal social limitations. (2)

Ballad singers went to work and produced songs of
repentance and farewell, now lost; while Robert Wilson
wrote a scene showing London's grief for the death of
Tarlton, putting the praise of the dead clown into the new
clown's part. (3)

Stories of his favour with the Queen, and his frankness,
are likely to have been improved in the telling. He had a
drunken act—a stock item with all clowns—which he played
before her; and a contemporary note describes

how Tarlton played the God Luz with a flitch of bacon at his back,
and how the Queen bad them take away the knave for making her
laugh so excessively as he fought against her little dog Perrico de Faldas,
with his sword and longstaff, and bade the Queen take off her mastie;
and what my lord Sussex and Tarlton said to one another. (4)

Such mock combats were an old sport; Shakespeare gave his first great clown a man-and-dog act in *Two Gentlemen of Verona*. Skill, precision and polish are needed for this kind of clowning to succeed; Tarlton was a master of 'activities'. He was also, as it happened, a Master of fencing, gaining this coveted title by challenging seven other Masters in 1587; his pupils fought for their own titles before him as judge. He dealt summarily but not bloodily with a bully set on him by a drab—getting within his guard, picking him up and throwing him down bodily into the tiltyard. At Norwich, when in June 1583 the Queen's Men were involved in a fight, he tried to restrain the ardour and the sword of his fellow-actor Bentley.

Ben Jonson describes a two-man act with John Adams—also a member of Sussex's Men; Peacham remembered seeing Tarlton come in himself as 'a rogue, in a foul shirt without a band, and in a blue coat with one sleeve, his hair full of straw and feathers' as the third son of a miserly old father, who said he had nothing to bequeath such a knave in his will but the gallows and rope.

Tarlton, weeping and sobbing upon his knees (as his brethren) said O father, I do not desire it, I trust in God you shall live to enjoy it yourself. (5)

The apocryphal *Jests* describe him as doubling Clown and Lord Chief Justice to Knell's Henry V—a situation which, though it is impossible in the *Famous Victories of Henry V* as it has come down, may have left traces on that play; but his most celebrated acts were his afterpieces, jigs and extempore merriments, which often were solo turns. Tarlton's art represented the first stage of separating clowning from the traditional folk sports which in style and subject it still recalled. He raised the jig, originally a country song-and-dance, to a professional 'number' which kept the stage long after his death, and developed into the German *singspiele*. Jigs sprang from the same boisterous farcical

tradition as Dunbar's 'Ballad of Kind Kittok', Skelton's verse
and the later collections of *fabliaux* in which Tarlton appears
in person. The favourite topics were wooing and coneycatching; but like Dunbar and Skelton, actors transmuted
this popular material into a more sophisticated form. In
Tarlton's case, the transmutation lay in the quality of his
acting; he was a Common Player of uncommon brilliance.
Sounding the pipe and tabor of the morris dancer he entered,
drumming furiously but dancing lightly, clad in the baggy
breeches and enormous shoes of an Elizabethan Charlie
Chaplin, or the country clown's dress of russet, 'with a
buttoned cap on his head, a great bag by his side, a strong
bat in his hand'. He was 'artificially attired for a clown' however, a cockney who assumed the rôle of a countryman, whose
quickness of wit and movement were set off by his mock
rusticity. A quarter of a century after his death he was falsely
idealized as the embodiment of simple country merriment;
art was confounded with nature.

> *Let us talk of Robin Hood,*
> *And little John in merry Sherwood,*
> *Of poet Skelton with his pen,*
> *And many other worthy men,*
> *Of May game Lords, and summer Queens,*
> *And milkmaids dancing on the greens,*
> *Of merry Tarlton in our time,*
> *Whose conceit was very fine,*
> *Whom death had pierced with his dart,*
> *Who loved a Maypole with his heart.* (6)

Nothing could have been more metropolitan than Tarlton's
country mirths; Nashe tells how somewhere in Norfolk 'the
people began exceedingly to laugh when Tarlton first peeped
forth his head' and a foolish Justice went round belabouring
them for their lack of respect for the Queen's livery, in
daring to laugh at the royal players. The tale shows the gap
between genuine rustics and those 'fine conceits' that every-

one praised. Tarlton's was an art of paradox. His companion Robert Wilson exclaimed

> *O, it was a fine fellow as ever was born. . . .*
> *The fineness was within, for without he was plain.*

His shock of curly hair, squint eyes, squashed nose and stocky figure were among his chief assets. Being asked in extempore rhyme how he came by his flat nose, he replied with an intricate stanza that he had got it when separating fighting dogs from bears, but that it would still serve to smell out an honest man from a knave.

The extempore verses which he composed upon themes provided by his audience were among his most popular acts; his successors did not often follow him in this. (7) Probably they depended on adapting something from his repertoire to fit the event; but speed, point and quickness on the comeback were essential. In his give-and-take with the audience, they might find themselves under attack or might be invited to share the discomfiture of a common enemy. One of the *Jests* describes how Tarlton was hit by an apple from the crowd and replied with a verse; but when the same assailant followed up the pippin with a crab, Tarlton replied with a sour jest involving the virtue of his opponent's wife.

A pretty new Ballad entitled The Crow sits upon the wall, signed R. T. might have been sung as a jig; the different lines could have been fixed on to suitable members of the audience by gesture.

> *Please one and please all,*
> *Be they great, be they small*
> *So pipeth the crow*
> *Sitting on the wall,*
> *Please one and please all.*
>
> *Be they white, be they black,*
> *Have they a smock on their back,*

Or a kercher on their head,
Whether they spin silk or thread,
Whatsoever they them call,

Please one and please all.
Be they sluttish, be they gay,
Love they work, or love they play,
Whatsoever be their cheer,
Drink they ale or drink they beer,
Whether it be strong or small,
Please one and please all,
Please one and please all . . .

What it was that really would please one and please all can scarcely have been left in doubt. Chaucer described how the crow betrayed adultery, in the Manciple's Tale; and it is the impropriety of this 'very true ballad' on the lips of Malvolio which makes it so preposterous. He must be presumed to quote it in all innocence.

Mar-Martin, in his accusation of scurrility

These tinker's terms and barber's jests, first Tarlton on the
stage,
Then Martin in his book of lies hath put on every page

is probably well founded but somewhat ungrateful, since Tarlton hit out at both Papists and Puritans with more force than decency. John Laneham developed the attacks on Martin Marprelate after Tarlton's death; they were probably given as jigs or shows. But the *Jig of a Horse Load of Fools*, against Gosson, must have been fathered on Tarlton by J. P. Collier; it contains modern turns of phrase like 'He makes dying quite a pleasure'.

Tarlton's play of *The Seven Deadly Sins* treated of such classic stories as Sardanapalus and Tereus. The proud author invited Gabriel Harvey to see it, and Harvey described how afterwards he condescended to ask Tarlton which of the seven deadly sins he himself affected. 'By God, the sin of other gentlemen, lechery', was the vigorous reply; but when Harvey pursued his smooth banter 'O, but that, Master Tarlton, is not your part upon the stage; you are to blame that dissemble with the world . . .', Tarlton returned the 'countercheck quarrelsome'.

Nashe declared that Tarlton put Gabriel's brother Dick Harvey in a play; and after his death he was certainly associated with Robert Greene in the popular mind—Greene, the quick-silver spirit, Harvey's chief mocker, as speedy in his writing as Tarlton in his quips. Energy, zest and astringent wit had made him a fighting clown, with 'a quart for his friends and a sword for his foes' as he boasted; though Sir Roger Williams observed 'our pleasant Tarlton would counterfeit many acts; but he was nobody out of his mirths'. (8) Harvey pityingly speaks of Greene's 'piperly extemporizing and tarltonizing'. Both led reckless lives and after their deaths provided material for godly moralizers. Both were invoked as patrons of the literature of roguery. Both appeared in popular pamphlets, presented by Robin Goodfellow, whom they were held to resemble 'and such like sprites as they term of the buttery, famoused in every old wives' chronicle for their mad merry pranks'. From these works, more may be gathered of Tarlton's merriments.

Tarlton's News out of Purgatory (1590), subtitled 'Only such a jest as his Jig' and supposedly published by 'Robin Goodfellow', opens with an apology for Tarlton's lack of learning; 'he was only superficially seen in learning, having no more but a bare insight into the Latin tongue'. (9) In his dream-vision near the Theatre, the narrator is visited by Tarlton's ghost, which he attempts to conjure, in the voice of a Puritan

Ab infernis nulla est redemptio. Upon these conducive premises, depart from me, Satan, the resemblance of whomsoever thou dost carry.'

At this, pitching his staff down on the end, and crossing one leg over the other, he answered thus: 'Why, you whoreson dunce, think you to set Dick Tarlton non plus with your aphorisms?. . . . Oh, there is a Calvinist; what, do you make Heaven and Hell contraria immediata? . . . yes, yes, my good brother, there is quoddam tertium.'

(Ed. Halliwell, pp. 55-6)

Tarlton proceeds to dispute in favour of Purgatory, urging that men of old would never have paid so much in diriges and trentals for nothing, and taking a high hand with authority from Scriptures:

If any upstart Protestant deny, if thou hast no place of scripture ready to confirm it, say as Pythagoras' scholars did, ipse dixit, and to all boon companions it shall stand for a principle. (p. 57)

Eight scurrilous tales, anti-papal and distinctly bawdy, supply the 'news', describing the earthly discomfiture and purgatorial pains of popes, friars, millers and other unpopular characters. *The Cobbler of Canterbury*, an 'invective' against this pamphlet, meant to start a merry war, describes it as 'somewhat too low for jests, somewhat too high for style' to be Tarlton's own; 'Tis not merry enough for Tarlton's vein, nor stuffed with his fine conceits and therefore let it pass for a book and no more.' (10)

Tarlton's boon companion is shown visiting other eternal regions in *Greene's News from Heaven and Hell* (1593), where the poet's ghost returns to say he is shut out of heaven for writing against lesser coneycatchers only, and shut out of hell for writing against any of them, so that he ends as 'the maddest goblin that ever used to walk in the moonshine'. When in the course of this third collection of *fabliaux*, the author Barnaby Rich comes to make a hit against his personal enemy, Adam Loftus, Archbishop of Dublin, he underscores the point by introducing Tarlton, singing a scrap of Elderton's famous ballad, *The Pangs of Love*. The prelate was said to be 'fit for the devil's chapel' and this brought Barnaby Rich before the Privy Council. Tarlton's extempore jests, whether against Puritans or Archbishops, might be launched at the Bull or Belsavage, but print was a different matter. These grotesque, scurrilous, hobgoblin tales are as close as anything that has survived, it may be presumed, to Tarlton's lost works.

Tarlton's ghost appears to speak the prologue in William Percy's *Cuckolds and Cuckqueans errant* (*c.* 1600). Here he mimics the accents of the Puritan.

I need not superstitiously recapitulate into your ears now either my name or my person, for without all paravauntour (that by your licence I may use mine own phrase and mine own dialect unto you) most infallible demonstrations and arguments will prompt the same unto you—my drum, my cap, my slop, my shoes, yea, even that same merry old master Tarlton. . . .

Then noticing his picture outside as the sign of the Tarlton Inn

At a wine tavern too! O, my heavenly Maker! . . . shall I invest on me the bull case of such a Monstrum Horrendum? God forbid, says the Apostle Paul. Yet a little compliment, and yet a little compliment, I beseech you, as whylom I intimated oft the same unto you, sweet Gentlemen.

The most revealing portrait of Tarlton is Henry Chettle's. *Kind Hart's Dream* (1592) provides the first printed vindication of popular pastime. It combines dream vision and packet of news, and among the letter writers, Greene and Tarlton appear; Tarlton is given the main defence. 'To all maligners of honest mirth, Tarlton wisheth continual melancholy.' He starts off briskly with the clown's familiar 'Here we are again', but appearing to detect some Puritans, falls into their style, and begins a mock denunciation of players.

Now, masters, what say ye to a merry knave that for this two year day hath not been talked of? will ye give him leave, if he can, to make you laugh? What, all amort? No merry countenance? Nay, then, I see hypocrisy hath the upper hand and her spirit reigns in this profitable generation. . . . Fie upon following plays, the expence is monstrous; upon players speeches, their words are full of wiles; upon their gestures, that are altogether wanton. . . . (p. 39)

Zealously he advocates the players' expulsion from the City;

expelled, quoth you? that hath been prettily performed to the no small profit of the bowling alleys in Bedlam and other places, that were wont in the afternoons to be left empty.

The godly earnestness of 'this profitable generation' is shrewdly exposed; retailers at the far end of the town have lost custom; whores lost trade; alehouses are desperate. The landlords not only impose high rents but heavy key-money and force tenants to buy in the landlord's shop; every ale-house needs a supplementary source of income, and further competition is quite intolerable, especially as players betray the cheating tricks of the tradesmen—'they make it common, singing jigs and making jests of us, that every boy can point out our houses as they pass by'. This no doubt was Tarlton's own speciality.

Speaking 'sadly' and in his own person, Tarlton hopes 'a time may come when honest recreation may have his former liberty'. He pleads with the audience not to start up their 'shameful disorders and routs' (11) and boldly attacks the opponents of plays—'some of them do more hurt in a day than all the players (by exercising their profession) in an age'. He admits the players have faults, but they are in every man's eye 'and see not how they are seen into, especially for their contempt, which makes them among men most contemptible'.

The letter has turned into a dialogue:

Quaintly concluded, quoth Peter Pandar; somewhat ye must be and a bawd ye will be. Ay, by my troth sir, why not I as well as my neighbours since there's no remedy. And you, sir, find fault with plays. Out upon them, they spoil our trade, as you yourself have proved.

(p. 42)

Tarlton ends with a fling at the Puritans; 'With you I would end in a song; yea, an extemporal song on this theme.' But in Kind Hart's postscript there is a final hint on Tarlton which I suspect refers to Em Ball, or another of her kind. (12)

Tarlton had made his will, died and was buried on the same day. The lawyer who drew the will may have been a shark, as suggested in Tarlton's dying petition to Walsingham (printed by Halliwell) against the 'sly fellow Adams, being fuller of law than virtue . . . to teach such unconscionable men how they seek the utter undoing by fraudulent means of a silly old widow of fourscore years of age and a poor infant of the age of six years'. Adams was quick to retaliate against the Tarlton family with countercharges that they were unruly, turbulent, troublesome and of no credit, and claimed that being childless, he was prepared to treat the child as his own. The fate of this small son is unknown; but in addition to his mother and his lawyer, Tarlton had appointed as trustee William Johnson, a fellow-player, who was afterwards to act as trustee for Shakespeare. Perhaps Johnson, who took no part in the general brawl, was the most trustworthy of the three.

Paradoxes of fame and squalor, brilliance and coarseness, wit and roughness fascinated Tarlton's contemporaries.

I was not taught and yet I did excel . . .
I was extold for that which all despise.
T. B., *Chrestoleus* (1598), p. 155

His memory was cherished by the common people; he was given the popular canonization of the alehouse sign. His picture hung outside inns as a token of good fellowship; it was hawked in the streets of London; it was also used as a sign to indicate the doors of jakes. A ballad sung to the tune of *Tarlton's Carol*, though signed with his name, seems to be a lament for him, and its conclusion would have fitted his sardonic humour. It may adapt some wooing ballad which he sung to the same tune:

THE QUEEN'S LIVERY

Time caused my Willy to come to the court,
  And in favour to be with the Queen:
Where oft he made her Grace for to smile,
  When she full sad was seen.

A groom of her chamber my Willy was made
  To wait upon her grace
And well he behaved himself therein
  When he had obtained the place.

Regarded he was of gentlemen all
  That in the court did remain
And ladies desired his company oft
  Because of his pleasant vein.

Like Argus my Willie had eyes for to see
  Least any he might offend
And though that he jested, his jests they were such
  As unto reason did tend.

           L'envoy.

Thus Peggy bewailed the loss of her friend
  Whom fates had taken away
And wished her body entombed with his
  In grave whereas he lay.

But seeing thy Willie is gone
  What needs thee to wail and moan?
Be merry, I say, let sorrow alone,
  Some other will love thee as he hath done. (13)

One of his works of a serious kind has survived; the
fragment of *Tarlton's Tragical Treatises*, of which a copy is
preserved in the Folger Shakespeare Library, (14) was published in 1578, at the beginning of the City attack, and

consists of a passionate and simple defence, not of the stage
but of poetry in general—'the author's judgment of such
rash verdicts as are given in dispraise of poets'. Tarlton's
wonder at the strange variety of creation bears an innocent
childlike conviction. Poets create a second nature; their
'learned heads'

> *cunningly disclose*
> *The strange variety of things,*
> *The choice of men's delights,*
> *The heavens, the earth, the seas, the shores,*
> *The gods and ghostly sprites.*

All creatures from the creation of the world, Christ's life and
death, princes and degrees, the invention of ships, the art of
astronomy, all learning and all history are so reflected that
they

> *serve us as a christal glass*
> *To gaze upon our folly,*
> *Wherein our faults are portrayed out,*
> *Though shews do make us holy.*

Tarlton rejects both those who rely on Nature alone, so that
'Art can stand them small in stead' and the pedants of Art
who argue according to prefixed notions, who

> *in finding fault with other's works*
> *Have Argus' hundred eyes:*
> *They rifle volumes leaf by leaf*
> *Verbatim to survey*
> *The substance or the circumstance,*
> *And then in scorn they say:*
> *This problem here is ill applied,*
> *That term is much abused,*
> *Here is a lame discourse indeed,*
> *There Priscian's head is bruised.*

Admitting that he himself has no learning to boast of,

> *Yet am I as a subject true*
> *To reverence their deeds.*

Poetry is a *deed*; Tarlton's deeds consist in action, and in action he will pay his tribute. If God and Fortune had allowed him to claim but the lowest room among the learned, he would have inscribed in gold letters the fame of Apollo

> *But wishes nought prevail,*
> *I yield to loss of time.*
> *Sith verse and I so different are,*
> *I'll press in ragged rhyme*
> *To manifest the mere goodwill*
> *That I to learning owe,*
> *No painted words but perfect deeds*
> *Shall my invention shew.*

He does not write for grace, but if he wins grace

> *Then have I scaled the doubtful fort*
> *The victory is mine. . . .*

With these words, not inappropriately, the fragment breaks off.

In its naïvety it may be thought to confirm Sir Roger Williams' view that Tarlton was 'nobody out of his mirths'. The commendatory sonnets, stressing his lack of learning and gifts of nature, urge further publication of his Themes upon him. The earnest simplicity of his tribute to learning is touching and, in its plain enthusiasm, far superior to the flowery grandeur of his dedication to Frances, wife of Sir Thomas Mildmay of Chelmsford, and daughter to the Earl of Sussex:

I might have taken sufficient occasion in these superfluous pamphlets to have entered into a necessary Enchomiasticon of your honour's sundry good virtues and noble qualities, if without the help of my barren blazoning they were not already so notified to all the world, that your ladyships just praises are in every man's mouth.

He asks her only to accept these treatises as

a perfect testimony of the good heart and dutiful zeal of your honour's most humble at commandment, Richard Tarlton, servant to the Right Honourable, the Lord Chamberlain, Earl of Sussex.

With a flourish the clown lays his tribute to Apollo at the feet of his 'Minerva'.

The last picture of him should be Chettle's, as he stands between the two ragged figures of the ballad singer and the piper, faltering pleaders for the old kind of pastime which was so rapidly passing away. Between these two 'old fellows' there dances forth one who

by his suit of russet, his buttoned cap, his tabor, his standing on the toe and other tricks, I knew to be . . . Tarlton, who living for his pleasant conceits was of all men liked, and dying, for mirth left not his like.

Kind Hart's Dream, p. 12

In the affair at Norwich, since he wore the Queen's livery, Tarlton is described with his fellow-actors as 'generosi'; but in spite of his flourishes and bravery, he made no real claims to this status. He was a servant of his lord; he might have licensed freedom to jest, though it seems incredible that as a late report declares he once said of Ralegh in the Queen's presence, 'See the Knave commands the Queen', and when she frowned, went on to jest about Leicester. (15) These stories represent the legend of his freedom, as they grew up in a later and more organized age. Tarlton had no ambitions for the solid benefits of gentility such as Alleyn and Shakespeare achieved, it would appear; still less for the modest citizenship of Heywood. He belonged to the violent, fluid life of the early stages; his noisy and familiar admirers were still an assembly rather than an audience; they provided his chorus. Kempe, his successor, though he was called 'Jest-

monger and Vice-Gerant General to the Ghost of Dick
Tarlton', was more strictly a member of a company; he is
shown in a Cambridge play giving auditions to hopeful
graduates along with Richard Burbage.

In Shakespeare's household fools, with their bitterness,
their scraps of song, their readiness to take to the wandering
life, however different the atmosphere surrounding them,
Tarlton's position in society perhaps finds some reflection.
He was a household jester who also took the whole City for
his home. Nashe put him with Knell, Bentley and those who
advanced the dignity of the stage, but this was the consequence of his excellence in his quality. His place was
never filled; he remained in the popular memory for nearly a
century, when his contemporaries had been long forgotten.

CHAPTER VIII

THE QUEEN'S LIVERY

Robert Wilson

Wilson often coupled with Tarlton—member of Leicester's Men
—his *Three Ladies of London* adapted from academic play—the
Clown's part played by Tarlton—his *Pleasant and Stately Moral*
a triumph over the Spanish foe, the enemies of the stage, and
a lament for Tarlton—his *Cobbler's*
Prophecy satiric in intention.

ROBERT WILSON'S name is several times coupled
with Tarlton's, for both excelled in extempore acting.
No legend grew about him; yet his achievement
supplemented that of the great clown, for he was the *literary*
creator of the Clown's part. His plays range from moral to
triumph and to satiric medley; and in them the Clown becomes a central figure, the Wise Fool, instinctively on the
side of the angels, invulnerable though always cheated,
triumphantly irrepressible like the players themselves.

Wilson was the first Common Player to gain wide
reputation as an author. Nothing is known of his origins; of
all the men named Robert Wilson who appear in Oxford
and Cambridge registers, the only one whose dates might
fit the dramatist's career matriculated as sizar of King's
College at Michaelmas 1548, and apparently took no
degree. (1) This would suit Wilson, putting him in the same
class of poor scholar as Gosson, for he was certainly, in distinction from Tarlton, credited with learning. By 1572 he
was evidently established as a member of Leicester's Men,
for he signed the letter asking for enrolment among the
Earl's household servants. He is named in the Patent of

1574, and appears also in later lists of the company. He was coupled with Tarlton as one of the two extempore actors chosen on the formation of the Queen's Men; but while Tarlton's wit was 'plentiful' and 'pleasant' Wilson's was quick, delicate, refined'. Four years earlier, in a burst of mock indignation against Spenser, Gabriel Harvey had likewise joined the two:

How peremptorily ye have prejudiced my good name for ever in thrusting me thus on the stage to make trial of my extemporal faculty and to play Wilson's or Tarlton's part!

Letter Book (Camden Society 1884), p. 67

In November 1585 Wilson went to the Netherlands with Leicester's Men and stayed two months. (2) He may have left the Theatre after the great plague of 1592-4, since neither Nashe, nor Thomas Heywood who joined the stage about that time, appear to have known him; yet in 1598, ten years after the death of Tarlton, Meres, in *Palladis Tamia*, to his praise of the dead clown, adds:

So now is our witty Wilson, who for learning and extemporal wit . . . without compere or compare, as to his great and eternal commendation he manifested at his challenge at the Swan on the Bankside.

(E.S. II, 349)

This was presumably a general challenge to a match of witticism or perhaps of invective. In November 1599, £8 was paid for his *Henry Richard*, which was more than the usual price of a play (3); finally, Robert Wilson, yeoman, a player, was buried in St Giles, Cripplegate, on 20 November 1600. (4)

Wilson started before Alleyn, and outlived Tarlton; his career offered a model to Shakespeare. Meres described him as 'the best for comedy amongst us', but the most revealing praise comes in a Latin letter written by the player Thomas Bayleye on 25 April 1581, from Sheffield, the Earl of

179

Shrewsbury's seat, where a St George's Day play had just been given. Bayleye writes to Thomas Bawdewyne, with an order for new plays of the popular kind called medleys or gallimaufreys:

librum aliquem brevem, novum, iucundum, venustum, lepidum, hilarum, scurrosum, nebulosum, rabulosum et omnimodis carnificiis, latroceniis et lenoceniis refertum.

This tall order Bayleye hopes can be met by Wilson of Leicester's Men who 'is willing and able to do much'. (5) In his day he was as much of a Johannes Fac Totum as Shakespeare, in the same tradition of 'easiness' and 'facility'.

Three of Wilson's plays survive; lost plays recorded by Henslowe show that he collaborated with Chettle, Mundy, Dekker and Drayton. In *Three Ladies of London* (c. 1581; printed 1584, 1592) he adapted the traditional Moral to new uses; in *The Pleasant and Stately Moral of Three Lords and Three Ladies of London* (1588; printed 1590) he completely transformed it to a secular Triumph. In *The Cobbler's Prophecy* (1594), the only play to appear under his full name, he used the medley for a satiric purpose, which, like all his plays, reflects upon the fortunes of the Common Player.

Three Ladies of London, though entitled a Comedy, is also described as 'a perfect pattern for all Estates to look into', and the theme is the seduction of all estates of the realm by the power of Lady Lucre, working through her four wicked followers and servants, the 'four knaves of the pack'. These knaves are the chief reason for setting the play in London, their tricks being of the kind known in the London underworld. They prey upon society, robbing and corrupting scholars, divines, lawyers and artificers, but they are themselves half-way between social types and allegorical figures— Dissimulation the farmer with 'his poll and beard painted motley'; Fraud the ruffian; Simony the churchman; and

Usury. At a higher level than these are the Three Ladies, Lucre, Love and Conscience, who make the first entry with Fame sounding a golden trumpet before them; but Love and Conscience sink to the level of waiting maid and bawd to Lucre; Love is married to Dissimulation, and in the final judgment scene Lucre and Love are condemned to Hell and Conscience sent to durance till 'the Day of general Session'.

But the moral aspect is only lightly pressed home to a London audience; the play was probably adapted from an academic Moral, perhaps from Oxford. (6) In this graver part of the play, gorgeous costumes and spectacular transformations would be the chief attraction. When married to Dissimulation, Love grows into a monster with two faces— a familiar figure for Fortune in other plays—and Conscience, reduced by the extortions of Lady Lucre, becomes a broom wench crying her wares; when she accepts a bribe from Lucre she is spotted over her face with ink from 'the box of all abomination'. These picturesque pageants are characteristic of the Tudor interlude—other plays show Money in a dress sewn all over with dancing coins, Vanity in a garb of feathers, and Rumour, like the Prologue in Shakespeare's *King Henry IV*, 'painted full of tongues'. The purpose of this part of the play is declamation and display; in the subplot, the coneycatchers and the Clown provide action. The 'London' part—as distinct from the academic part—centres upon Mercadorus, the cheating Italian trader, and on Simplicity the Clown.

Tarlton took the part of Simplicity, for his phrase 'Faith, I'll go seek peradventures and be a serving creature' uses one of Tarlton's catchwords. He enters first as a miller, all mealy, that the traditional white of innocence, even if comically assumed, may contrast with the motley evil of Dissimulation. Millers, however, were traditionally cheats and Simplicity has not prospered as a miller; so he takes service with Love, but is turned away when she marries Dissimulation, and falls to filching in company with two beggars. He soon leaves them, only to suffer the strolling players' own indignity of a whipping—

Enter Servicable Diligence the Constable, and Simplicity with an officer to whip him, or two if you can. (F1 v)

Like Lancelot Gobbo, Simplicity is a great feeder, and susceptible to the charms of his mistress Love; like Gobbo, he abounds in 'mistaking words'—comportance, bonfacious, bequest (for request), resist (for assist), markle, conspatch, competually, reparliament, semblative (for dissembling) and miserable (for merciful). He sings, riddles, takes his final punishment with a wry jest:

> *I pray you, be miserable to me and let me go,*
> *For I labour to get my living with begging, you know*

and asks to be whipped 'in the skin' to save his clothes.

But as the son of Plain Dealing and the cousin of Sincerity, a poor scholar, he can always detect the four knaves. He tells their past history, especially the career of Fraud as an ostler, for whom, with a surprising display of heraldry, he devises mock bearings: yet in spite of his truth-telling he is always cheated by

> *Fraud the clubbish knave, and Usury the hard-hearted*
> * knave,*
> *And Simony the diamond-dainty knave,*
> *And Dissimulation the spiteful knave of spade.*

Unheeding and invulnerable, he asserts the rights of the common man at his most childlike to gaiety and a place in the scheme of things. It is the crime of Fraud, by now a respectable burgess, for which poor Simplicity suffers his whipping. The coneycatching knaves escape from final judgment; Mercadorus, the Italian cheat who has tried to cozen his Jewish creditor by turning Turk, is finally robbed by English Fraud on the orders of Lady Lucre; the good old man Hospitality, protector of Love and Conscience, is murdered by Usury; when the Judge asks

> *What is become of Usury?*
> DILIGENCE: *He was seen at the Exchange very lately.*
> JUDGE: *Tell me, when heard you of Simony?*
> DILIGENCE: *He was seen this day walking in Paul's having conference and very great familiarity with some of the clergy.* (F2 v)

There is no easy commonplace about virtue triumphant. When Simplicity tries to escape his whipping by accusing the real culprit, he is smoothly ordered a double whipping by the criminal himself, who in his rôle of worthy burgess observes 'It stands not with my credit to brawl.' This passage must have given satisfaction to the players, smarting under the injustice of their own condemnation.

> *Simplicity sings it, and 'sperience doth prove,*
> *No dwelling in London for Conscience and Love.*

That the connexion was seen, Stephen Gosson testifies; for in *Plays Confuted* he says that 'towards the catastrophe' Wilson inserted a passage in defence of plays. Love and Conscience hold debate about them, Love condemning plays because they expose her tricks to the world, but Conscience approving. Gosson triumphantly points out that by this stage of the play, Love and Conscience are both defiled and their approval would itself be a condemnation. There is no trace of this passage in the printed text.

A 'moral' could vary from the elegant offering of Westcote, *Liberality and Prodigality*, designed to compliment the Queen, to the sardonic intensity of *Enough is as Good as a Feast*; the 'colouring' of these plays by serious or festive intent might shift from one performance to another; but Wilson's play shows a straightforward Moral turned to the same kind of mocking jest as those in *Tarlton's News out of Purgatory*.

It is a protest masked protectively by fooling, and supported by allegory; a Comedy neither purely academic nor merely popular. The irony is given a further twist in the sequel, where Servicable Diligence himself is cozened by Fraud with a purse containing counters; Fraud and Dissimulation a second time succeed in evading justice. This happens in *The Pleasant and Stately Moral* which, in the months of triumph following the defeat of the Armada, celebrated London's victory over Spain and the players' victory over Puritans. Wilson dexterously seized the national rejoicings as a moment to justify his own cause. (7) In the winter of 1588, Londoners would loudly applaud, when in place of the familiar figure of Respublica or Widow England they saw

Enter for the Preface a Lady very richly attired, representing London, having two angels before her, and two after her, with bright Rapiers in their hands.

London speaketh.

> *Lo, Gentles, thus the Lord doth London guard,*
> *Not for my sake, but for his own delight . . .*
> *By a power and providence unseen,*
> *Even for the love wherewith God loves our Queen . . .*
> *And that hath bred our plenty and our peace,*
> *And they do breed the sports you come to see. . . .*

London is surrogate for the noblest Lady of all, the miraculously preserved Elizabeth. The London Lords who are the heroes of the play embody the unity of London actors and London audience. The Preface echoes the humble prayer that ended the gorgeous triumphal procession of Sunday, 24 November when the Queen in a chariot-throne was borne through the cheering throngs of citizens to thanksgiving at St Paul's, while on London Bridge the captured flags of the Spanish navy fluttered from the spikes reserved for traitors' heads.

This pious preface introduces a most gorgeous show, in which the magnificent costumes of the London Lords and their Spanish foes, the blazoning of their armour, the full wedding procession of the Lords and Ladies must have cost the players a pretty penny; it was justified as a celebration of triumph and noble fellowship. For in the usual Moral, London's Lords would have been of the Devil's party—in fact, Policy, Pomp and Pleasure, might well have appeared as the Infernal Trinity of the World, the Flesh and the Devil.

Here, the triple wedding of Policy to Love, Pomp to Lucre and Pleasure to Conscience humanizes Policy, justifies Pomp and safeguards Pleasure. Applied to the players' own case, it constitutes a reply to the new attack.

The year before, William Rankins had used revelry to attack revels and elaborated the infernal nuptials of Pride and Lust in the Chapel of Adultery in Holywell (i.e. the Theatre) —a marriage graced with a masque sent from Satan. (8) Gosson's *School of Abuse* had also been republished in a second edition. *The Pleasant and Stately Moral* issued a triumphant Vaunt, Counterblast or Challenge, in which proclamation replaced argument. Pleasure most directly represents the players' cause, and as he hangs up his shield at the opening in general challenge to all comers, his words to his page, Will, include a veiled threat of staging his enemies (particularly strangers born, like Gosson) to their public ridicule.

> *I bid thee mark him well, whate'er he be,*
> *That London's pleasure doth in malice scorn,*
> *For he's a rascal or a stranger born.*
> *Good boy, mark well his gesture and his look,*
> *His eye, his gait, his weapons and attire,*
> *And dog him to his lodging or his den,*
> *For I will make him scum and scorn of men.* (B2 r)

At the beginning Pomp is carefully characterized by his page Wealth as 'rather Magnificence than Pomp in bad sense, and rather Pomp than Pride in best sense'—Pride, in fact, is a Lord of Spain whom Pomp singles out as his special enemy. Policy fights Ambition and Pleasure, Tyranny. These Spanish Lords, in the characteristic way of Vices, have taken the name of virtues; Pride disguises as Majesty, Ambition as Honour and Tyranny as Government. The triple challenge by three heralds, insignias and titles fully set forth, is a stately image of a tourney, and far removed from any popular sword-and-dagger act; the dignity and symmetry of these triumphant shows recall great courtly and civic events, which they are clearly meant to do; for Policy, in issuing his orders against the Spanish invaders, commands Pomp and Pleasure to such acts, to assist morale. Pomp is to arrange for grand display, and Pleasure for humbler pastimes.

> *My lords, I would I might advise ye now*
> *To carry as it were a careless regard*
> *To these Castilians and their accustomed bravado;*
> *Lord Pomp, let nothing that's magnifical,*
> *Or that may tend to London's graceful state*
> *Be unperform'd. As shews and solemn feasts,*
> *Watches in armour, triumphs, cresset lights,*
> *Bonfires, bells and peals of ordinance.*
> *And Pleasure, see that plays be published,*
> *Maygames and masks, with mirth and minstrelsy,*
> *Pageants and school feasts, bears and puppet plays.*
> *Myself will muster upon Mile End Green*
> *As though we saw and fear'd not to be seen.*

The last phrase was one of the taunts regularly hurled at the audience by Puritans—as adapted for martial display, it links together the pomp of patriotism and the pomp of plays, which was to be so thoroughly exploited in the English Histories of Wilson's successors. The heroes of *The Pleasant and Stately Moral* are the citizens of London collectively seen; the Spanish Lords are given a few tags of Spanish, calculated to call forth the patriotic hiss. 'Fuoro Viliagos, fuoro Lutheranos Angleses, fuoro, sa, sa, sa!' The herald of the Spaniards is given an Irish name, Shealty, since the Spaniards supported Irish rebellion.

By the time this play was put on, the Queen's Men must have already presented *The Famous Victories of Henry V*: Wilson himself wrote a lost play upon Cœur de Lion, and he had a share in the popular *Sir John Oldcastle*, as well as writing essays in local patriotism such as *Black Bateman of the North* and *Pierce of Winchester*.

The friendly rivalry of all three London Lords, who all at first wish to marry Lucre, does not prevent their issuing a joint challenge to any foreigners who presume to dispute their right. (9) After the defeat of the Spanish Lords, three Lords of Lincoln appear, but they are sent away bearing only the stones of repentance on which the ladies sat.

London's fellowship includes heroes and clowns; Simplicity is now a freeman and very proud of his title. Clad 'in bare black like a poor citizen', his mourning attire, as he sets up his ballad stall, bears witness to the fellowship of the stage. For Tarlton had died in the September of Armada year, and Simplicity, singing his ballads and setting out his picture, mentions the dead clown's claim to be part of London too:

WILL: *What was that Tarlton? I never knew him.*
SIMPLICITY: *What was he? a prentice in his youth of this honourable city, God be with him; when he was young, he was leaning to the trade that my wife useth now and I have used, vide lice shirt, waterbearing; I wiss he hath tossed a tankard in Cornhill ere now. If thou knewest him not, I will not call thee ingram, but if thou knewest him not, thou knewest nobody. . . .*

    O, it was a fine fellow as ever was born,
    There will never come his like while the earth can corn;
    O passing fine Tarlton, I would thou hadst lived yet . . .

WEALTH: *He might have some, but thou shewest small wit.*
There is no such fineness in the picture that I see.
SIMPLICITY: *And thou art no Cinque Port man, thou art not*
wit free.
The fineness was within, for without he was plain,
But it was the merriest fellow and had such jests in store,
That if thou hadst seen him, thou wouldst have laughed thy
heart sore. (C1 v)

Like the London Lords, players were members of more than one estate: 'citizens born, and courtiers brought up, for they that be born in London are half courtiers before they see the court', as the Pages explain to Simplicity. Although the Four Knaves of the Pack return, supported by new companions in mischief, they are taken in the end. Their judgment provides a wedding day merriment for the Lords, and Simplicity suddenly shows himself as a watchdog of the commonwealth. In a parody of the City's objection to upstart players, he comes in to denounce novelty:

I would have no new orders, nor new sciences set up in the City, whereof I am a freeman and please ye, as ye may read in my bill there, Simplicity freeman. (H3 v)

Detecting great risk to the commonwealth in the three dangerous trades of those who cry 'Old Iron', those who seek to buy up gold and silver and those who chop wood, (10) he next spies Fraud concealed in a serving man's coat among the wedding attendants. Fraud is bound to one of the stage posts, and Simplicity set to run at him blindfold with a wedding torch in his hand to burn out Fraud's tongue. He charges against the contrary post 'and all to burns it', while Dissimulation unbinds Fraud and both slip away. Simplicity thinks he has been more than successful:

Well, all London, nay all England is beholding to me, for putting Fraud out of this world, I have consumed him and brought him to nothing, and I'll tread his ashes under my feet, that no more fraud shall

ever spring of them. But let me see, I shall have much anger, for the
Tanners will miss him in their leather, the Tailors in cutting out of
garments, the Shoemaker in closing, the Tapster in filling pots, and
the very oystermen to mingle their oysters at Billingsgate.

(13 v, 14 r)

The play closes with a prayer for Queen, Council and Commons, 'chiefly in London'.

In the very year after this triumph, the players found
themselves under inhibition for their too-vehement attack in
the Marprelate controversy. Wilson's latest play, *The
Cobbler's Prophecy*, is a medley—the kind of play Bayleye
expected of him, and which evidently he practised, (11)
further. Roman Gods, allegorical figures, Estates of the
Realm, and the clownish hero Ralph jostle together. After
the clear and definite lines of his previous work, this hotch-
potch looks like a sad falling off. But the 'variety' might in
itself be put forward as an aim, especially when the variety
consisted of elements in themselves familiar; as another playwright, Thomas Lupton, put it in the preface to his *Thousand
Notable Things of Sundrey Sorts*.

Perhaps you will marvel that I have not placed them in better order,
and that things of like matter are not joined together. Truly, there are
many of such divers and sundry effects, that it could not be altogether
observed. And in my judgment, through the strangeness and variety
of matter it will be more desirously and delightfully read; knowing
that we are made of such a mould, that delicate daintiness delights us
much; but we loathe to be fed too long with one food; and that long
wandering in strange, pleasant and contrary places, will less weary us,
than short travel in often trodden ground.

Five 'houses' are shown upon the stage in this medley, and
at the end one of them is burnt down. (12) It is the Cabin of
Contempt, the villain of the piece—Contempt, the players'
besetting sin. Contempt who calls himself a 'little God' and
is called by Ralph the Cobbler 'a little, little *seeing* God' is

the opposite of Eros; he miscalls himself Content, and in a most fantastic scene, after Venus has lulled Mars asleep with a song 'Sweet are the thoughts that harbour full Content' he comes in and kisses her, they dance and leap over Mars as he lies asleep with his head in Folly's lap, 'making horns at every turn'.

The play opens with an assembly of the gods; they are introduced by Mercury, as they pass in dumb show, while he conjures attentiveness from his audience;

> *I see a sort of wondering gazing eyes,*
> *That do await the end of this conceit,*
> *Whom Mercury with waving of his rod,*
> *And holy spells enjoins to sit and see*
> *The effectual working of a prophecy,*

while his companion Ceres does her best to produce content in the audience by throwing sweets.

> *Ceres sheds her sweetest sweets in plenty*
> *That while ye stay, their pleasure may content*
> *ye.*

Then there is a second induction in which Thalia attempts to write a play but finds her pen is broken; she is penning the pageant which is to pass by, in which Sorrow masks in Pleasure's weeds; neither Tragedy nor History can find matter worthy for their pen. The action takes place on two planes; the sphere of the Gods in which Venus (alias Lust) and Contempt (alias Content) are finally punished while Mars and Mercury finally preside; the earthly plane, in which the kingdom of Boeotia is threatened with invasion and Ruin by the treachery of a courtier. Ralph the Cobbler is given the gift of prophecy by Mercury, and his mad wife Zelota kills the traitor. On the celestial plane Ruin is born of Contempt and Lust. Roughly the first half of the play belongs to the Gods and the second to Boeotia, with Ralph the Cobbler moving freely in both worlds.

An entirely unrelated satiric episode brings on Charon, ferryman of Hell, in dialogue with Codrus, enemy and detractor of poets, a human embodiment of Contempt. The medley ends with a flock of jailbirds being released to help repel the invasion of Boeotia—the sharpest sardonic contrast to the heroic defence of London in *The Pleasant and Stately Moral*. Though it has no unity of theme or characters, *The Cobbler's Prophecy* has a unity of tone. Underlying all is the bitterness of the Clown, with his prophecy. The strange, half-nonsensical, half-threatening rhymes and riddles of such characters as Peter of Pomfret, (13) Thomas of Erceldoune, or of John Ball constitute the tradition for his speech of warning to the worldly court of Boeotia: it is threatened with the fire of Judgment Day.

The high hill and the deep ditch
Which ye digged to make you rich,
The chimneys so many and alms not any,
The widows' woeful cries,
And babes in street that lies,
The bitter sweat and pain
That tenants poor sustain,
Will turn to your bane, I tell you plain,
When burning fire shall rain
And fill with blotch and blain
The sinew and each vein.
Therefore the poor that cry
Being lifted up on high
When you are all forlorn
Shall laugh you loud to scorn.
Then where will be the scholars' allegories,
Where the lawyer with his dilatories,
Where the courtier with his bravery,
And the moneymaking knave with all his knavery,
Bethink me I can nowhere else,
But in Hell where Dives dwells.   (B3 v, 4 r)

He warns the scholar:

> *The time shall come, not long before the doom*
> *That in despite of Rome,*
> *Latin shall lack,*
> *And Greek shall beg, with a wallet at his back,*
> *For all are not sober that goes in black.*
> *Go to, scholar, there's a learning for your lack.*

In the end, the scholar repents of his contempt for the humble cobbler's wisdom:

> *The gods, when we refuse the common means*
> *Sent by their oracles and learned priests,*
> *Raise up some man contemptible and vile,*
> *In whom they breathe the pureness of their spirits,*
> *And make him bold to speak and prophesy.*   (F3 r)

The broken bitterness of this play is eloquent of defeat. And though its inconsequence makes it now extremely difficult to read, most of the figures were traditional and familiar; its mingling of natural and supernatural is in the tradition of popular romance. Both in his triumphs and in his defeats, Wilson reflects the difficulties of his generation— one half-way between traditional pastime and full drama. Courage and sardonic energy are the marks of his work, as they are of what we know of his fellow-players of the 1580s.

His plays embody the older traditions of spectacular display, familiar morality turned to new use, and clowning (14); they have no independent poetic life, for at this stage the verbal aspect of playing had not yet asserted itself as the dominant one upon the common stage. The generation of Marlowe, Greene and Shakespeare, in a few years reformed and unified the theatre, and plays such as Wilson's remained only in the repertories of the lesser companies or of country players. There are in fact better Morals than Wilson's; it is as player-poet and for the light that he throws on the players' struggles that he deserves his place in the story of the

Elizabethan stage. And it should not be forgotten that Wilson's tradition of spectacle remains as part of Shakespearean drama—transmuted into such scenes as the cauldron scene in *Macbeth*.

Wilson was given the Queen's livery, but his career suggests that he remained attached to his old associates, Leicester's Men, and that the absence of any regular form of incorporation for the royal players is no accident. The Queen's Men of the eighties were the élite of the London players, but perhaps they never formed a fellowship, or company of sharers; membership may have been coveted by the actors as modern actors covet a knighthood. The City Fathers who had hoped to find the numbers of troupes reduced, found only that the privileges of the Queen's Men were extended to all the leading companies by exemplification. The provincial strollers of the nineties who were known as Queen's Men have nothing but the name in common with the early players.

Among members of this later generation, Shakespeare alone successfully combined the poet's and the actor's art. Professionalism meant that different functions were developed by different people; the greater actors of Shakespeare's days were not writers. The greatest of all, born two years junior to Shakespeare, was Edward Alleyn, whose career was recognized in his own lifetime as a great vindication of the actor's art.

CHAPTER IX

MASTER OF THE ROYAL GAME

Edward Alleyn

Alleyn's early career—alliance and association with Henslowe—
domestic life—various enterprises including bear-baiting and
building of the Fortune Theatre—retirement from the stage and
later career—his building of his College—second marriage—Alleyn's general abilities and his ideals.

THE first of Elizabethan tragedians ended his days
Lord of the Manor of Dulwich, son-in-law of the
Dean of St Paul's, and founder of the College of
God's Gift. For nearly thirty years he had been retired from
the stage, having, as the City Fathers might approvingly
have said, other trades to live by (1); as an actor, Edward
Alleyn belonged to the sixteenth century.

He was born 1 September 1566, the son of a Bishopsgate
innholder, who died four years later. Alleyn's mother re-
married with John Browne, a haberdasher, who does not
seem to have taken up a father's duties, for at the age of
sixteen Alleyn appeared at Leicester as a leading member of
Worcester's Men; they had their Lord's licence but had
lost Tilney's, which had been picked up by ragamuffin
players; they defied the Mayor's ban on playing with 'evil
and contemptuous words'. This is the one time Alleyn is ever
recorded as involved in the troubles and uncertainties of the
stroller's life; the players stopped to apologize and beg that
their lord should not be informed; the Mayor allowed them
to play after all. The ruffled youth rose quickly to the level of
a City player. By the end of the eighties he had joined the
Lord Admiral's Men; he created the leading rôles in
Marlowe's plays—Tamburlaine, Faustus, Barabas—as well

as playing Hieronimo and Orlando. Strikingly tall, with a splendid voice and presence, he excelled in majestic parts.

Among his papers at Dulwich is a finely executed invitation, with his name written in gold, where he is called upon to meet a challenge for the 'English Crown' by playing before chosen judges any of the great parts made famous by the best tragic actors of Tarlton's day: the wagerer

hath now given you liberty to make choice of any play, that either Bentley or Knell played. . . . I see not how you can any way hurt your credit by this action; for if you excel them, you will then be famous; if equal them, you win both the wager and the credit; if short of them, we must and will say Ned Allen still. Your friend to his power, W. P.

> *Deny me not, sweet Ned, the wager's down,*
> *and twice as much, command of me or mine:*
> *and if you win, I swear the half is thine,*
> *and for an overplus, an English Crown.*
> *Appoint the time, and stint it as you please,*
> *Your labour's gain; and that will prove it ease.* (2)
> (*Henslowe Papers*, ed. Greg. pp. 32-3)

The very name of Ned Allen on the stage was able to make an ill matter good, as Nashe, one of his staunchest admirers, declared; but the foundations of his fortune as distinct from his fame were laid when on 22 October 1592 he married Joan Woodward, stepdaughter of Philip Henslowe, the wealthy owner of the Rose Theatre. Henslowe himself had started life as a servant in the Woodward household, and had acquired wealth by marrying his widowed mistress; he adopted Alleyn as a son into his highly respectable Southwark home, while Alleyn, having found the father he had lacked, seems to have played the part with genuine feeling. This was a season of plague; and, driven off to Chelmsford, Bristol, Chester and York, Alleyn sent home instructions to his young wife for the disinfecting of the house, while Henslowe replied for her with affirmations of the superior efficacy of prayer. One letter ends with a player's flourish—

'Thine, and nobody else's, by God of Heaven but otherwise his endearments forecast those of the worthy Citizen
from *The Knight of the Burning Pestle*: 'Jug', 'sweetheart',
and—matching her vocal powers against his—'farewell,
mecho moussin and mouse'. Joan signed as 'your poor mouse
for ever' and once 'your assured self till death', Alleyn's letters
often being addressed to the household under his own name,
whose fame would assure their more easy delivery. Domesti-
cities about his white waistcoat and orange tawny stockings
are piously headed 'Jesus' or 'Emmanuel', while on the
boards Alleyn was audaciously playing Faustus in a surplice
with a cross upon his breast (3)—perhaps as protection
against the personal appearance of the devil, 'credibly
reported' to have materialized in this play both at London
and Exeter.

With his own hand Alleyn wrote for his prentice John Pyk
a jesting letter whose climax is a mocking pun upon his own
powers to play the Christian King's part.

Mistress, your honest ancient and loving servant Pige hath his humble
commendations to you and to my good master Hinsley and mistress,
and to my mistress' sister Bess for all her hard dealing with me I send
her hearty commendation hoping to be beholding to her again for the
opening of the cupboard; and to my neighbour Doll for calling me up
in a morning and to my wife Sara for making clean my shoes and that
old gentleman mounsir Pearl that even fought with me for the block
in the chimney corner and though you all look for the ready return of
my proper person yet

> *I swear to you by the faith of a fustian king*
> *Never to return till fortune me bring*
> *With a joyful meeting to lovely London.*

I cease.

Your petty pretty prattling parlying pig. By me, John Pyk.

Mistress I pray you keep this letter that my master may see it for I
got one to write it (Mr Downton) and my master knows not of it.

(*Henslowe Papers*, p. 41)

The cosy family group of husband, wife and prentice, with father, mother and sister—'Bess Dodipoll'—in the background is supported by all the civic virtues. Joan wrote on a later occasion to ask the amount of rent due from Alleyn's tenants, and paid what was due from her husband before witnesses:

the quittance cost me a groat; they said it was the bailiff's fee. You know best whether you were wont to pay it; if not they made a simple woman of me.   (*Henslowe Papers*, p. 60)

She added that when a plausible young trickster came to borrow money, though he was well dressed and had contrived to steal a horse, 'he gulled not us'. By the early nineties it is clear that Alleyn was a man of property, one of those wealthy players whom Greene detested for their loftiness towards the poets. It does not seem, however, that Alleyn demanded parts to suit himself from the hack writers of Henslowe's service though he witnessed and drafted the bonds which bound them to it; and in December 1594, when plague had abated and the playhouses reopened, he turned to another form of pastime and became lessee of the bear-baiting at Paris Garden, as deputy to the Master of the Royal Game of Bears, Bulls and Mastiff Dogs.

Players and bear-wards were associated in the public mind, as well as in various statutes; they used the same playing places, and in the eighties had presented mixed entertainments. The most popular of all Elizabethan plays, *Mucedorus*, features a live bear; in his account of the Princely Pleasures at Kenilworth, Laneham includes the story of a great bear-baiting, with thirteen bears worried at once for the delectation of the Queen. He thought it 'very pleasant' to 'see the bear with his pink nyez leering after his enemies' approach, the nimbleness and wait of the dog to take his advantage'. Bets on the bear were probably more profitable than playing a challenge for an actors' crown, and in turning to this form of entertainment Alleyn could rely upon his father Henslowe, whose own father had been Master of the Game in Brill Park and Ashdown Forest. It was not a pretty sport, as an advertisement among the Alleyn Papers at Dulwich makes plain; a chief attraction, as with cockfights, was betting:

Tomorrow being Thursday shall be seen at the Bear Garden on the Bankside a great match played by the gamesters of Essex, who have challenged all comers whatsoever to play five dogs at the single bear for five pounds and also to worry a bull dead at the stake and for your better content shall have pleasant sport with the horse and ape and whipping of the blind bear. Vivat rex.

(*Henslowe Papers*, p. 106)

The most sympathetic passage of Stubbes's *Anatomy of Abuses* is his plea against it:

What Christian heart can take pleasure to see one poor beast to rent, tear and kill another, and all for his foolish pleasure? And although they be bloody beasts to mankind, and seek his destruction, yet are we not to abuse them, for his sake who made them and whose creatures they are.

(Q2 r)

Most Elizabethans would think the cruelty of the Bear Garden less dangerous than the irreverence of the players, and the filth of the Ring less noisome than a 'filthy' word.

Alleyn, like other gifted players, moved freely from company to company: the plague conditions of 1592-4 made all groupings insecure. Such was Alleyn's fame that in 1594 a play was described as given, not by the servants of the Lord Admiral, but by 'Ed. Allen and his Company'. In 1597, Alleyn sold his stock in the Admiral's Men, while retaining a specially privileged share, without liabilities. He was now beginning to purchase country properties; one of his gentlemen tenants helped in the difficult court-play to secure the Mastership of the Game, when the holder should die. The Lord Admiral was approached; and the Master of Requests;

Lady Edmonds even spoke to the Queen for Alleyn and Henslowe, and a patent was drafted. Too late; the place was promised to a gentleman pensioner, and so in 1598, at an annual fee of £40, Henslowe and Alleyn had to continue as deputies.

Next year, however, Alleyn launched upon the great venture of building the Fortune Playhouse, which called for delicate negotiation as well as a large capital outlay. (4) In later years he calculated the cost at £1,320 in all, ejaculating as he noted the figures down, 'Blessed be the Lord God Everlasting!' His accounts, like Henslowe's, were kept minutely and often adorned with pious expressions.

At royal behest, Alleyn would still appear upon the stage; at the City's invitation, he played a leading part in the pageant welcoming James I to London, where he appeared as the Genius of the City, with 'excellent action' and 'well-tuned and audible voice'. He was enrolled among Prince Henry's Men and when, a little earlier in the year, an outbreak of the plague had sent him touring as a player once more, Joan wrote in the old strain:

Though you have worn your apparel to rags, the best is you know where to have better, and as welcome to me shall you be with your rags as if you were in cloth of gold or velvet, try and see.

(*Henslowe Papers*, p. 60)

In the summer of 1604 the Master of the Royal Game died, and was succeeded by one of James's hungry Scots who refused either to licence Henslowe and Alleyn or to take over the sport himself, but forced them to buy the patent. They purchased it jointly from him at what they considered the exorbitant rate of £450, promptly petitioning the king to have the Master's fee from the Crown raised from sixteen pence to two shillings and fourpence a day. A long lugubrious recital of all charges and hindrances attached to the Mastership ends by invoking the Act for the Restraining of Vagabonds—for Alleyn was now in a position to be able to complain of strollers, and played the part as if he had been born to it:

. . . whereas there are divers vagrants, and persons of loose and idle life, that usually wandreth through the countreys with bulls and bears without any licence, and for ought we know serving no man, spoiling and killing dogs . . . for the restraining of such, your Majesty would be pleased . . . to grant us and our deputies power and authority to apprehend such vagrants and to convent them before the next Justice of Peace there to be bound with sureties to forfeit his said bears and bulls to your Majesties use, if he shall be taken to go about with any such game. . . .

W. Young, *History of Dulwich College* (1889), ii, 22-3

The chief advantage of the Mastership was the right to take up bulls and bears and dogs for the royal use—which meant, of course, for exhibition at Paris Garden. Deputies were sent out to recruit dogs, much as they were sent out to recruit choir boys; but Justices of the Peace were not always co-operative, especially in Cheshire and Lancashire, where the best dogs were to be found. The Masters hoped that some towns would covenant to send a mastiff up yearly to the Bear Garden and so save themselves from visitation; among other places, Manchester compounded to do so.

No doubt by using these powers Alleyn and Henslowe raised the standard of the City game till it surpassed the countryside, as the City players did the country strollers. Prince Henry improved the sport by setting prize dogs to bait the lions in the Tower; but he could not have improved the breed, for most of the dogs were killed in the process.

Moving steadily forward on his planned ascent, Alleyn bought the first pieces of land in Dulwich the year after he gained the Mastership, though he still resided in the neighbourhood of the Clink at Southwark, where he could supervise his deputies of the Bear Garden, the unsavoury grounds of his wealth. Where there's muck, there's money; the parishioners of St Saviour's were so far from sharing the opinion of Stubbes that 'the Devil is Master of the Game, bear-ward and all' that in 1610, in succession to Father Henslowe, Alleyn became churchwarden. This gave him several new rôles to play, for within the liberty of the Clink churchwardens performed many of the duties of a magistrate.

Establishing his College of God's Gift drew out Alleyn's skill as a planner, his patience in negotiation, his firm desire to leave a monument to posterity and in the absence of an heir to perpetuate his name. Fourteen years were needed to accomplish his design, though probably his purpose was known by 1612 when Heywood praised the bountiful public spirit of great actors. (5) Alleyn's grandeur must have seemed to merit the comparison with Roscius that so often was made.

The Dulwich estate was acquired gradually, the title secured by a Chancery suit, and in 1613, a building plan was drawn up for the chapel, almshouses and school of the College. (Upon this great foundation Alleyn was to expend in all ten thousand pounds.) The group of buildings, which are still standing, were set in the traditional place for almshouses, at the gates of the great park, and on Alleyn's fiftieth birthday, 1 September 1616, the chapel was consecrated by the Archbishop of Canterbury in the presence of a concourse of gentry. One who in youth might have heard himself denounced from Paul's Cross was now described as 'the honourable gentleman, Edward Alleyn, moved by pious and religious devotion'

So Adam had his oratory in Paradise; and Jacob his praying place in the fields; Moses his holy ground in the wilderness and the Israelites their tabernacle for Thy worship in the land of promise; till it pleased thee at the last to put it into the heart of king Solomon to build a temple to Thine honour in Jerusalem.   (Young, I, 26)

The flowing periods of the Archbishop were echoed by the plaintive voice of one of Alleyn's old associates Dekker, who wrote from King's Bench prison, where he lay for debt:

... it best becomes me to sing anything in praise of charity, because albeit, I have felt few hands warm through that complexion, yet imprisonment may make me long for them. If anything in my Eulogium or praise of you and your noble act be offensive, let it be excused, because I live amongst the Goths and Vandals, where barbarousness is predominant. Accept my will, however, and me ready to do you any service. Thomas Dekker.

(*Henslowe Papers*, p. 92)

Again the old poet wrote, asking Alleyn to accept as servant a young man 'son to a worthy yeoman of Kent here prisoner'. He was a namesake of Alleyn and so 'you shall do me much honour if you think him fit to serve you as a servant'.

Dekker evidently knew Alleyn's weakness, which was shown in his taking another 'poor fatherless boy' and giving the child his own name; in stipulating that the future Masters of his foundation should be called Alleyn; in the hopes that inspired his second marriage. This founding of a charity was part pious restitution of God's gifts to Alleyn, part compensation for the absence of an heir; as such, it was attended with fresh difficulties. After drawing up his statutes, for which he consulted the noble foundations of Eton and Winchester, Alleyn required letters patent to establish a perpetual charity. Once more the wearisome business of following the court, pleading, judiciously disbursing, began. Francis Bacon wrote sardonically to Buckingham of 'a patent I stayed at the great seal':

It is of licence to give in mortmain, though it be of tenure in chief, £800 land, to Allen that was the player, for an hospital. I like well that Allen playeth the last act of his life so well; but if his Majesty give way thus to amortize his tenures, the Court of Wards will decay...

(Young, I, 37-8)

Other foundations of more use had been denied 'whereas hospitals abound, and beggars abound never a whit the less'. It was not till 16 July 1619 that the patent passed under the Great Seal.

A traditional foundation of the kind that royalty, gentry and good citizens had established for centuries, the College of God's Gift with its Master, Warden, four fellows, six poor brethren, six poor sisters, and twelve poor scholars was designed to rescue from vagrancy and beggary the aged poor and the orphan children of St Botolph's parish where Alleyn had been born; St Saviour's, Southwark, where he had lived; St Giles, Cripplegate, where his playhouse the Fortune stood; and Camberwell, where his foundation lay. During his own lifetime, Alleyn did not put his draft Statutes into operation but supervised the charity himself, buying clothes and shoes for his orphans, turning away unsatisfactory pensioners (sometimes the brethren got drunk, at other times they married the poor sisters). He kept his accounts, feasted his neighbours, more especially on his wedding anniversary, and patronized decayed gentry; to Sir James Blogg, a 'poor knight' who dined with him one night, he recorded the gift of half a crown.

The career of an Industrious Apprentice could not be better illustrated; only by missing the knighthood he sought did Alleyn fall far short of Dick Whittington. His fortune was about six times greater than those of Burbage or Shakespeare. Yet, though Henslowe and Alleyn were both charitable, they were not easy men; along with the begging letters of Dekker and Nat Field there are 'articles of Grievance and Oppression against Philip Henslowe' drawn up in 1615, alleging among many other charges that 'within three years he hath broken and dismembered three companies'. Though he did not take an active part in his father-in-law's ventures of this kind, Alleyn had never adhered to the world of the playhouse as did the Burbages, who spoke of the Blackfriars as 'our inheritance', and gave as their arms the sign of revelry, the Boar's Head. Alleyn noted laconically the burning of his playhouse (which he had sublet first to his father-in-law and afterwards to a shareholders' group), and at once set about having it rebuilt at the cost of a new set of shareholders, who all contributed.

The Fortune was burnt down on 9 December 1621 and rebuilt next year; in the following year Alleyn suffered a much heavier loss. The death of Joan Alleyn on 29 June 1623 provided him, however, with an opportunity he did not neglect to ally himself with the church and the gentry, and less than six months later, on 3 December, he married a girl of twenty. There was much comment and some amusement; one courtier writing to another observed:

The strangest match in my opinion is that Allen the old player hath lately married a young daughter of the Dean of Paul's, which I doubt will diminish his charity and devotion towards his two hospitals.

(Young, II. 35)

John Donne had prudently and hard-headedly married his Constance to a man nearly three times her own age and five years older than himself for a settlement of £1,500; having but newly arrived at the affluence of the Deanery, the Dean struck a bargain with the doyen of a profession that forty years before his predecessors had stigmatized with infamy. Young Jack Donne, 'a great frequenter of plays', must many times have sat with the gentlemen of his acquaintance to watch Ned Alleyn playing Tamburlaine, with 'Bajazet encag'd, the shepherd's scoff' (*The Calme*, l. 33).

Alleyn's relations with his second father-in-law by no means equalled in cordiality those with his first. He had hoped that a common interest in livings might have developed; instead he found his wife's dowry withheld, himself refused a loan, denied the courtesy of the Dean's household in his visits to London and saddled with a sister-in-law whom he was expected to support. All sorts of trifles—a ring, a favourite horse, her mother's child-bed linen—were kept back from Constance, and the situation after a year is shown by a fiery letter from Alleyn.

My language you took so harsh was this; that I now perceived you esteemed £500 before your honesty, your own reputation or your daughter's good; you presently being inflamed twice sung it was false and a lie, words in my mind more fitting you thirty years ago when you might be questioned for them, than now under so reverend a calling as you are, but as false as you suppose them. . . .

Before this violence brake forth you called me a plain man. I desire always to be so for I thank God I could never disguise in my life and I am too old now to learn rhetoric of the curiousest school in Christendom. . . .

For a conclusion let me entreat you, as I find you no way willing to my furtherance, so be not any way a means of my hindrance; and as your daughter Luce is good company for my wife, so your ability is better able to bear her charge than mine. And thus being a plain man, I hope you will pardon me delivering my mind in plain terms.

(Young, II, 36-8)

If the Lord of Dulwich Manor had to live down the memory of Ned Alleyn, the Dean of St Paul's had to live down that of Jack Donne; and if in such moments of disagreement the 'old player' was expected to give all, and get nothing but the honour of alliance, he well knew how to retaliate. In hopes of an heir, Alleyn tried to recover some of the land granted to his foundation; not till the last month of his life did he sign the statutes, even then retaining a life interest. He died 25 November 1626, and was buried in the choir of the college chapel, where he lies under a plain black slab bearing a plain English inscription. His portrait, with its old-fashioned spade-beard, joins to an expression of sage simplicity the hale complexion and strong blunt features of the country squire.

Alleyn's rise to fame and munificence, springing from solid commercial foundations, shows how the adaptable intelligence which made him a Proteus of the stage could be turned to advantage in other ways, as he seized his chances with Marlovian audacity. He combined the actor's charm and versatility with an unusual shrewdness; with his energy and natural authority, he joined perseverance and the capacity to plan ahead. In an age of patents, monopolies and farming of office, he skilfully united practical supervision with the knowledge of when to delegate, and when to manage directly; the landlord of the Fortune, the owner of estates from Sussex to Yorkshire, he knew also how to distribute his investments. Yet the safest foundation for capital enterprise was still the family unit; the Henslowe-Alleyn combine was based on the strongest social bonds. Henslowe trained Alleyn in matters of finance; but in his later years Alleyn ventured upon investments in land; Henslowe never ventured on this. As a travelling player Alleyn probably came to know the districts and the people as far north as Yorkshire where he made his purchase of estates.

Within the theatrical profession itself, Alleyn's social position resembles more closely that of the Masters of the Choristers in an earlier generation than that of the common player; his many activities make one think of William Hunnis rather than William Shakespeare; although Shakespeare too ended as a country gentleman—of a minor kind—whilst Hunnis died, like most courtiers, more in need of charity than able to bestow it.

In the form of Alleyn's foundation there may be traced his own sense of good fortune's instability. He decreed that all elections were to be made by lot between two nominated candidates; the winning lot to carry the inscription 'God's Gift'. It was an old objection to gaming that lots were a serious matter involving God's providence, and to use the lot lightly, as in games of chance, was to blaspheme Providence. (6) If Alleyn interspersed his accounts with such phrases as 'Blessed be the Lord God, the Giver of All'; if he stoically noted his greatest financial loss in half a dozen words; he had learnt this lesson in the hazards of meeting a challenge on the stage, and at 'the Bears' College'.

Moreover, at the very end of his life, he tried, though unsuccessfully, to enlarge his college for the benefit of such poor handicraftsmen and musicians as he had known in his earlier days. He wanted six chanters or minor fellows to be added to the foundation—singing men who might bring to his chapel something of the art which had been his own in youth. Two were to be organists and masters of music to the orphan scholars; the other four were to be tradesmen, tailors or shoemakers who would clothe the children and teach their trades. Here are shadowy figures typifying his own orphan childhood, lack of apprenticeship, fellowship with the artisan players, transformed after forty years into a pattern which he piously hoped would endure for ever. (7)

Alleyn founded a College; James Burbage founded the Theatre, which he left to his sons Cuthbert and Richard. Richard also inherited some of Alleyn's rôles, and equalled his fame; he is perhaps the 'one man' with whom country players are invited to 'play Hamlet for a wager' in 1605, when Alleyn had already 'grown weary of playing' and bought 'some place or lordship in the country' as a player

'whom Fortune hath so well favoured that [he] expected to be knighted or at least conjoint in authority and to sit with men of great worship on the bench'. *Ratseis Ghost* (see Chambers, *E.S.* I, 350)

The next chapter will follow the story of the choristers' theatre; this is not a story of success but of failure. Here children, who might have expected to receive a good education, were exploited by a succession of masters, some of whom possessed talent as well as audacity; none commanded any capital. To trace the history of this attempt to put 'closed' entertainment in its closed Hall, upon a commercial basis, it is necessary to return once again to the crucial period of the mid-1570s.

PART THREE

Household Players, 1574-1606

CHAPTER X

THE LIVERY AND THE SURPLICE

The Rise and Fall of the Choristers' Theatres in London, 1574-1606

The choristers of St Paul's and of the Chapel Royal—their traditions—performances of the Children of Paul's under Westcote—and of the Chapel Royal under Farrant at Blackfriars—organization of the Chapel Royal—activities of Hunnis and Lyly—an outline of Lyly's career as dramatist—the second period of activity at Paul's—and at Blackfriars—kidnapping of Thomas Clifton—nature of the plays at Blackfriars—James I prohibits acting by choristers—decline of the boy's companies.

W H O maintains 'em? how are they escoted?' Hamlet's questions about the little 'yasses' cut deep. Twenty years earlier, as little Clergeons, the singing children of St Paul's and of the Chapel Royal had represented the true succession of household players; they were genuinely part of great households—the only kind of households which could have maintained them. Their skill, displayed by their Master, who trained them, composed for them and pocketed all the profits, lay in the arts of music and rhetoric, for which they had been picked out from the whole land.

Though the Master was himself a servant, a lay clerk without resources to launch an expensive venture, the children needed no payment; few assistants were required; St Paul's must have supplied a stock of vestments, and the Revels Office a wardrobe which could be cheaply borrowed, cut down or made up for the little players. Expensive effects would be beyond their means, unless an Oxford, a Derby or a Percy were willing to spend money upon an Offering at Court. In contrast with the common players, the choristers' theatres of the seventies must have sounded as though a string quartet were competing with a Works' Brass Band; but their sophistication, polish and discipline taught their elders; Shakespeare's debt to Lyly is as large as his debt to Marlowe.

The chapels had behind them a magnificent tradition, and in musical achievement their performances must have been unmatchable in the country. The musical centre of a great household was expected to sing at feasts, or to provide other kind of entertainments, to maintain the splendour of its lord in the worship of God. The great chapels of the Renaissance were the most sumptuous ornaments of princely courts. Elizabeth's chapel inherited the tradition of Tallis, and its members included William Byrd, John Bull and Thomas Morley. Henry VIII, himself a composer of skill, had enlarged the establishment; the boys were increased by him from eight to twelve; and these Elizabeth inherited, together with the establishment of the Chapel of St George at Windsor, the singing boys and lutanists of her chamber and other musicians of her household. Wolsey's great chapel at Whitehall, which had rivalled Henry's, no longer existed as a body of musicians, and the building itself had come to the Crown; but several of Elizabeth's greatest nobles, Norfolk, Oxford, Derby, maintained notable chapels.

In providing music and shows for a small public the chapel children were carrying on a familiar and noble festive tradition. The fact that there was an admission charge, and that the Master was making profits, might have seemed at first a minor matter. The group, the nature of the performance, the livery were splendid; they acted in household premises. Under cover of this quite acceptable practice, however, something new was developing, something not so very different from the activities of the common players. But there was continuity of tradition.

THE LIVERY AND THE SURPLICE

The choristers' theatres started in the seventies, and continued into the eighties—with some intermissions, and increasing difficulties, till the end of the eighties. But in the crucial decade of the nineties they were shut. The children of Paul's did not play in London for a decade, the Queen's children did not play for sixteen years. When they reopened, in 1600, the common players were fully established, the Admiral's and the Chamberlain's Men settled in their houses, and favoured at Court. All forms of entertainment were becoming public affairs, no longer a matter of the great household. In drama, Marlowe and Shakespeare had utterly transformed the art, as the acting of Alleyn and Burbage had given new depth and passion to the painted scene.

Household players and craft players disappeared before this formidable development. When the children were revived, they became a species of common players put on by a group of citizens, actors and playwrights who had no interest in their education or their future. The royal choristers became completely detached from the chapel, and lost their old security, which had ensured them a career at the University as choral scholars and possibly a return to the chapel as Gentlemen. As Hamlet observed, and as truth bore him out, they were being trained for the common stages. In a society where youthful training was as significant as it was to the Elizabethans, such misdirection of talents would have appeared a grave matter.

By 1600, these boys could not have constituted a threat to the powerful companies of the Lord Chamberlain and the Lord Admiral; or Burbage, who owned the Blackfriars, would never have given their Masters the lease. But the malicious wit of their playwrights could bring about a general inhibition of plays. Having tamed their audience, the common players now found themselves exposed to a new threat by these puny competitors, whose chief asset and weapon was a saucy frankness. Shakespeare gave their efforts the throw-away treatment, conceding them a mock victory and putting his real case in the form of rhetorical questions: Who is behind them? Who pays the rent? . . . and what are these children but common players who one day will come to recognize their proper station? (He refrained however from giving them the publicity of print; the passage was not allowed to appear in the Quarto of *Hamlet*.)

Two men's companies had emerged to lead the London theatres; but from the first, two companies of boys had given a long lead to all competitors. The second half of Elizabeth's reign, which saw the rise of the Great Companies, saw also the rise and fall of the choristers. Their household bases gave them special rights, which disappeared as their playing grew openly professional. At first, since they had fixed habitations, were directed by gentlemen, and did not collect large assemblies of the vulgar, they created no problems for the magistrates. Of these two troupes, one sheltered by the protection of the cathedral church had been able to establish a playing place in the heart of the city before Burbage built his Theatre; the singing school of St Paul's had its eyrie in the precincts. The Master of the Children of the Chapel Royal and of Windsor set up within the Liberty of Black-friars which still kept its old clerical privileges, where the Lord Mayor could not intrude; in the great hall of the Priory, scene of the divorce proceedings between Henry VIII and Katherine of Aragon, the children played between August 1576 and Easter 1584.

Based on privilege, the choristers' theatres flourished on social equivocations even more ambiguous than that of the men. Plays were a regular school exercise, by which Udall of Westminster and Mulcaster of Merchant Taylors' taught 'good behaviour and audacity'; their children were regularly summoned to Court; Westminster, St Paul's, St Antony's and Merchant Taylors' as regularly provided child speakers for City pageants. (1)

Different children's troupes rise or decay and dissolve with the appearance or disappearance of some talented, energetic or greedy promoter. Their history is the history of the men who trained the children. When, some time before 1551, Sebastian Westcote transferred from being Yeoman of the King's Chamber to Master of the Children of Paul's their future as the leading boys' troupe was assured. They were the earliest child performers in London; they were also the best.

A somewhat doubtful record of performance of Old Testament plays at St Paul's in 1378 is followed by much clearer traditions about the mumming of Boy Bishops; and by the mid-sixteenth century the singing boys were appearing at the feasts of city companies. By 1574, the choristers of Paul's had been giving public performances for some time, (2) and must have enjoyed the first regular playing place in the City; Richard Farrant brought the royal livery to Blackfriars in 1576, only three months after Burbage signed the lease for the Theatre. The late seventies saw the heyday of both boys' companies. Farrant died in November 1580, Westcote in April 1582, at the height of the first City campaign against plays. There was some attempt to join the two companies; acting ceased in 1584, though Paul's Boys reopened in 1587 for another three years. The most successful years for the boys coincided with the rise of Leicester's Men—their best plays belong to the era of the Queen's Men.

As they grew in popularity in London, the choristers lost the lead at Court. Elizabeth's interest in child actors, strong up to 1567, declined, at first slowly, but after 1576, when the public theatres were opened, very sharply. She no longer invited Westminster or Merchant Taylors' to Court; at the point where the public fortune of the singing boys began to waver, the Queen's Men were established, and her chapel ceased to perform. It may be no coincidence that the Queen's delight in child players fell off at a time when she might be supposed past the age to hope for children of her own.

'Sebastian's Boys', as the Children of Paul's were known, led because Westcote was a personal favourite of Elizabeth. He had played before her when she was a Princess at Hatfield; royal favour alone explains how he contrived to keep his position as almoner, organist, vicar choral and subdean of St Paul's, in spite of his being, like Byrd, a Recusant. In 1563, Leicester, although the Protestant champion, appealed vainly on his behalf to another Protestant champion—Grindal, Bishop of London, who, not unmoved by what he suspected were 'crocodile tears', excommunicated Westcote in the Consistory Court. Westcote gave his bond to conform or resign; yet a decade later the City Remembrancer came to protest to the Dean about 'one Sebastian that will not communicate with the Church of England', who kept plays 'to great gain, and peril of the corrupting of the children with papistry'. From December 1577 to March 1578 Westcote was committed to the Marshalsea 'for Papistry'. Yet, with more than the common player's audacity and defiance, he kept his position in St Paul's precincts till his death in April 1582, when he left handsome remembrances to many of the clergy and was buried in the choir. Some of his furnishing (not the best) he bequeathed to the Almonry where his boys were lodged; he remembered old pupils, the gatekeeper and 'Shepard that keepeth the door at plays'. (3)

Both the Master and his boys, being part of the cathedral establishment, were nominally under control of the Dean; Alexander Nowell, who held that office through most of Elizabeth's reign, was a more powerful character than many of his Bishops; moreover, he had a Puritan distrust of singing. None the less, in the very precincts where so many godly preachers, including Grindal, thundered against plays to an approving audience of City Fathers, a Papist could lead the singing boys to chirp up with their comedies.

They were never more than part-time players, however. Their living was secured by endowment, as was their Master's; the profits which they made must have constituted almost pure gain. Unlike the men, they had 'other arts to live by'—arts which directly contributed to the charm of their performance, accompanied as it was by a concert of music. Trained and disciplined by Westcote, and with further instruction from the Grammar School, the ten singing boys—probably supported by a number of beginners—led a happier existence than those who wore the Queen's livery: and they were such Court favourites that when in December 1575 one of Sebastian's boys, a principal player, was stolen from him, it became a matter for the Privy Council.

In King Henry's time, Thomas Tusser, who was impressed to sing in the royal choir, knew both troupes:

> *Sundry men, had placards then*
> *Such child to take.*
> *The better brest, the lesser rest,*
> *To serve the choir, now here, now there,*
> *For time so spent, I may repent*
> *And sorrow make,*
> *But mark the chance, myself to 'vance,*
> *By friendship's lot, to Paul's I got,*
> *So found I grace, a certain space*
> *Still to remain.*

He found himself under the kindly author of *Wit and Science* (4)

> *With Redford there, the like nowhere*
> *For cunning such and virtue much*

and perhaps the boys were already performing their Master's plays, either in the Almonry, in the hall of the College of Minor Canons, or in the parish church of St Gregory, built up against the south-west wall of St Paul's and home of the song school since the twelfth century. In any case the little players were most strategically placed. St Paul's retained after the Reformation that multiplicity of function which most churches lost; it was not only a house of worship but a centre of social life. Within the precincts were two parish churches and many houses; a baker built his shop against the cathedral wall, the oven hollowed out of a buttress; chantries were used for storage, and for a glazier's shop. An ordinance of 1554 forbade citizens to carry loads of ale, bread, beer or fish or to lead horses through the church; but Bankes's performing horse climbed the steeple, and a lottery was held at the West door in 1569 and 1586. The great central aisle was a fashionable promenade; here servants were hired, the needy soldier hawked his sword and the hungry 'dined with Duke Humphrey'. (5)

The boys' plays must have been given after evensong, which ended by four o'clock, and before six, when the great gate to the precinct was shut and the daily bustle ended. They acquired a most distinguished repertory. John Heywood composed for them: Redford's *Wit and Science*, and Westcote's *Liberality and Prodigality*, originally theirs, were rewritten for the common stages.

Westcote's successor called in the most successful young courtly writer of the day to collaborate with him in running the playhouse. Lyly wrote first for Paul's then for joint performances of Paul's and the Chapel; *Endimion, Midas, Campaspe* and *Sapho and Phao* were all played before the Queen. They are nearer to the sub-dramatic forms of welcome and revel than to full drama; they were primarily Offerings. For the select few permitted to attend these 'rehearsals' for Court, an air of intimacy would be kept. Although presumably open to anyone who could pay, the performances were in private quarters; the audience must have felt rather like those who today pay to be 'guests' of a peer. To join the Children of the Chapel in their larger Hall, the Paul's Boys would have had only to cross Carter Lane and enter by a little turngate into Blackfriars precinct. They were as close as the Theatre and the Curtain; conveniently placed both for the young lawyers lodged at the Inns of

Court and for the inhabitants of the great houses in the Strand. (6)

At first entirely decorous, the boys picked up some of that tradition of malice which belonged to the privileged theatre of the Inns and the great Halls. *Mother Bombie* was a harmless merriment, though too broad for Court, it would seem; but Lyly joined the Marprelate controversy, which grew in savagery. He classed the efforts of the common stages with those of Martin Marprelate himself (7); none the less, for fourpence, Londoners could hear the boys' voices raised in shrill defence of episcopacy and shrill abuse of Puritans. A general inhibition of plays for meddling in matters of State was issued by the Privy Council in November 1589. The three-year venture of 1587-90 ended when a commission, which included the Archbishop of Canterbury, was appointed to censor plays. Where neither Dean nor Bishop had succeeded, the Primate prevailed, for in a note to *Endimion*, published in 1591, the printer declared that plays at Paul's have been 'dissolved'.

In hope to atone, in the plague-stricken winter of 1592, the Paul's boys presented his Grace of Canterbury with the charming show of *Summer's Last Will and Testament*, given in his palace at Croydon. In place of the 'May Game of Martinism', this 'bringing in of autumn' assumes a pose of deceptive innocence (it was written by the free-tongued Nashe). The Prologue contains some reference to the little players' 'misfortune', the epilogue offers the players 'wholly to [Your Grace's] service' and appeals to the other onlookers as 'Gods of art and guides unto heaven'. (8)

The much more melancholy history of the Royal troupes of children is one of growing exploitation and gradual divorce from their duties as singing boys. They were a larger group than Paul's, but they were less subject to clerical supervision. Early Masters of the Chapel produced only for the Court, and only one play, *Damon and Pythias*, percolated to the press. William Cornish appeared as Calchas when his boys gave *Troilus and Criseyde*; later, Richard Edwards produced a famous *Palamon and Arcite* at Oxford. Sometimes he took his boys out of Court to his society of Lincoln's Inn and no doubt he would have been ready to appear at the feast of a nobleman, but after his death in 1567 the Chapel Royal yielded pride of place to the boys of Windsor Chapel. It was when their master, Richard Farrant, contrived also to win effective control of the Chapel Royal children, by getting himself installed as deputy to Hunnis, the new Master there, that regular dramatic activity in London began. Fired by the success of Westcote at St Paul's, in the summer of 1576 Farrant boldly opened his new playhouse at Blackfriars. No doubt he had heard, as the City had heard, that the business was highly profitable.

Two things made the venture possible; whenever the Queen's troupes played successfully, one man was in control of the children of both her choirs; and at these times, as throughout her reign, the Chapels Royal had no effective head to see that the children were kept to their pricksong. Perhaps because she did not want her private devotions too strictly regulated, the Head of the Church appointed no Deans to her Chapel Royal. Nominally under the lay control of the Lord Chamberlain, the Gentlemen of the Chapel elected a subdean, and the Master of the Children was supposed to be subject to his authority. But mortality among subdeans was high—there were three between 1567 and 1569; choristers were treated almost as chattels of their Master, having none of the safeguards of prentices, though their education was entirely vocational. A boy was unwillingly surrendered from Wolsey's chapel to Henry VIII, with the proviso that Cornish should treat him 'honestly' which meant 'otherwise than he doth his own'. Farrant's indentures for the Mastership of Windsor stipulated that he should leave the boys as well clothed as he found them; but rich vestments in the choir and rags in their schoolroom were probably the choristers' lot.

These very formal indentures are not in the spirit of a collegiate foundation, but may represent an effort to secure special talent to train the Windsor boys. Farrant, a Gentleman of the Chapel Royal, and married to a daughter of its former Master, did not carry out routine duties at Windsor, though he acquired a house. In 1570, he was also resworn to the Chapel Royal. (9)

The three choirs of Paul's, Windsor and the Chapel Royal kept a close connexion—exchanging and sharing members. Paul's had been the model for Windsor, which was very snug, with free lodging for the boys, masters to teach them and a 'grandsire' from the Vicars Choral to instruct them in scripture. The Chapel Royal, though more loosely organized, also kept some features of a family group, as all departments of the Royal Household must have done; but it was more independent than most, and does not always appear in Household lists. In the time of Edward IV, choristers had lodged in the household; their bread, meat, ale and candles had been assigned them, with one servant to truss and bear their livery, and when the Court moved, fourpence a day for horse hire. But by 1510 they were being boarded out with the Gentlemen or the Master; and in the Statutes of Eltham (1526), to save charges and expense, it was provided that if the King were not resident in one of his great houses, and specially in riding journeys and progresses, the Master of the Children and six Gentlemen only should attend him—less than a quarter of the choir. The children still dined and supped when the king 'kept his Hall' in these great houses; but they did not receive lodging and breakfast (known as bouge or bouche of court). Very liberal 'times of liberty and playing weeks' meant that the chapel did not perform at all, and they were then quite free from the duty of waiting upon the Court. (10)

There was therefore a tradition of dividing the choir, whose headquarters, as it would appear from offices held by the members, tended to be at East Greenwich. Farrant appears to me to have established part of the boys at Black-friars; with ten lawful offspring of his own to house, he could also have spared voices and room at Windsor.

C. W. Wallace, the first historian of the Chapel Children, maintained this view; other writers have not agreed, although it is clear to all that the children were lodged at Blackfriars between 1600 and 1606. It seems likely for a variety of reasons that they were taken there under Farrant.

There were a number of rooms under the Hall where the boys could have lived; to reside on the premises where they played—as tradesmen lived over their shops—was the guarantee that this was an exercise of a private kind, a rehearsal for Court. Blackfriars would in fact furnish convenient lodging when the Court was at Whitehall; the journey from Greenwich took several hours if wind and tide were contrary and included the dangerous passage of London Bridge, a feat to be attempted only at low water. These journeys, performed weekly, would have imposed too much strain on the toughest of children; if Farrant did not think of their comfort, he had to think of their voices, and of the cost of a weekly journey in winter.

If, moreover, the playing troupe was made up by picked boys from Windsor as well as the Chapel Royal, a half-way lodging would be the obvious solution. Farrant had ten children at Windsor and twelve at the Chapel; he could have taken four from each and maintained reasonably full choirs. 'The children of the Chapel and of Windsor' appeared at Court in Christmas revels; in London their season ran from Michaelmas to Easter only, when, by later accounts, they played on Saturdays at three o'clock. They would need to rehearse with their properties; and some plays had fairly elaborate effects. The possibilities of a clash between rehearsals for the theatre and rehearsals with the Gentlemen for Chapel performances would have added to the confusion, had the choristers not divided into selected players resident in Blackfriars and 'daily waiters' upon the Court.

Some difficulties may be imagined from the details in the Revels Accounts of how nine Merchant Taylors' boys went in 1574 to play a Shrovetide masque at Hampton Court. After lodging at the Revels Office to rehearse, they were ferried from Paul's wharf in two tilt wherries, attended by their tutor and their dresser, with their properties following in a barge. For one night they lay in Court and for another at 'Mother Sparo's' in Kingston, with the wherries waiting night and day to take them whenever it should please the Queen to ask for their show. They returned to London on Ash Wednesday, many of them 'cold and sick and hungry', and were landed at the Blackfriars to be warmed and fed, perhaps in the future Chapel quarters. Each child received a shilling; Newdigate who trained them, had forty shillings and the Revels Office paid for transportation and lodging.

Theoretically, there was no reason why the whole Chapel Royal should not have developed into the Queen's household players; its performances had been famous under Henry VIII, when the great pageants had wheeled into the Hall, with children singing sweetly from the height of some huge dolphin's back or mounted on a gryphon. Socially, however, the Gentlemen were far above interlude players, who like Court minstrels were but grooms of the chamber; the Gentlemen had their own servants, sergeants and grooms of the vestry, their yearly feasts, their place assigned—if the lowest place—among the courtiers in Hall. In his study of *Music and Poetry in the Early Tudor Court*, John Stevens said:

They were, just, gentlemen. As such they doubtless cut a considerable figure *outside* the court circle. *In* it they were honourable servants—no more. Among the king's Esquires of the Body and other attendants of noble birth, a singing man would not count for much. (p. 320)

Prince Hal, it will be remembered, broke Falstaff's head for likening his father to a singing man of Windsor. The social position of the Gentlemen was rather like that *claimed* by Laneham; because of their incorporation and traditional rights, it was better than that of Thomas Whythorn, the Archbishop of Canterbury's Music Master, who was sometimes intrusted with important affairs but at other times in his life became an ordinary serving man. In the lists of the Chapel, the same names recur—Mundy, Eveseed, Woodson—implying hereditary succession. They were quarrelsome and disorderly—the yeomen drank, the gentlemen kept their boots in the vestry—and, as it would appear from the system of fines imposed, were given to very lax attendance at service. Yet they would feel far above the level of the common stages. The children, however, were exploitable; and the gentlemanly laxity of the Chapel organization would make this easier.

For this purpose, the Liberty of Blackfriars, being outside the Lord Mayor's jurisdiction, offered advantages almost equal to St Paul's; the Paul's Boys always enjoyed a more settled domicile in the City, while the Chapel enjoyed greater freedom from clerical interference. They also enjoyed better, larger premises; the great Frater of Blackfriars had been used for rehearsals in the time of Elizabeth's predecessors, for the Revels Office had been situated there. It would seem merely a return to tradition when Farrant leased it from Sir William More, executor of Cawarden, late Master of the Revels; though soon it was plain, as More objected, that he kept 'a continual house of plays'.

The definition of that slippery term, 'a private playhouse' —which, however, did not come into use till 1604—might be given as:

A hall within a dwelling, where players, whose chief end of incorporation is not playing, but some more dignified purpose, give performances about once a week, at which a small number of spectators attend; the hall not being let to other performers but in permanent use by the residents only.

Behind its four gated walls, Blackfriars contained noble lodgings, with its own constable and porter to enforce order.

The quarter had royal associations, the children wore the royal livery. It would have been very difficult to protest even when, in the shifting social distinctions of the day, it was realized that Farrant was imitating his friend Westcote across the road. His prices, as befitted his status, were higher than Paul's—sixpence against fourpence. Perhaps Hunnis took some share of his deputy's profits, to add to his fee as Master of the Gardens at Greenwich, his trading interests, and the price of his pious little books of verses. To farm an office was customary.

Farrant successfully maintained his theatre for four years; he died on 30 November 1580, when Hunnis resumed control of the Chapel children. The fiction of rehearsals was coolly kept up; on 19 September, Leicester told More that Hunnis meant only

to practise the Queen's Children of the Chapel, being now in his charge, in like sort as his predecessor did, for the better training them to do her Majesty service.

(Hillebrand, p. 91; from Loseley MSS.)

Hunnis's career had been an exciting one. He had joined the Chapel in Edward VI's time; been imprisoned under Mary for a share in the Throgmorton Plot; kept a mistress and planned a robbery; dabbled in alchemy; acquired money and membership of the Grocers' Company by judicious marriage. He developed some interests in trade, but he was no impresario, and soon ran into difficulties at Blackfriars. In the Christmas season of 1582/3, after Westcote had died, the two boys' companies amalgamated at Blackfriars; this would have compensated the Chapel for the loss of recruits from Windsor, now under separate rule. A certain scrivener named Henry Evans, overseer of Westcote's will, took charge till the Earl of Oxford became interested and encouraged John Lyly to put a finger in the pie. The lease of the theatre was 'tossed to and fro' between them till Easter 1584, when More recovered it and shut down the playhouse.

He let some rooms to the Lord Chamberlain, who complained that the boys had cut up the lead roof with penknives and bored it with bodkins till it leaked.

By November 1583 Hunnis, an astute man, recognized failure. He had always been careful about his rights; his original patent allowed him to commandeer lodgings and fix transport charges; some time after 1578, he exchanged the children's dining rights and their penny a day in breakfast allowance, for a full dietary allowance of sixpence a day. He now put in a long legal plea of his expenses, asking that the children should be allowed to eat with the Court 'during the time of their attendance', for he could keep them no longer. Complaints about other expenses appear to be based on contrast with the better-provided post at Windsor, as defined in Farrant's indentures. Hunnis complains that his predecessors, including Farrant, have died in debt—the common fate of every courtier—but no mention, naturally, is made of the sums that the children had been earning for their Master at Blackfriars. While they lived there, the dietary allowance had been useful; Hunnis now appeared to be seeking full household incorporation, with everything found. In objecting that his fees had been cut, Hunnis never mentions how his allowance for expenses had been increased; it is tempting to say that as an old hand at Court, he saw how to play off one department against another. (11)

Hunnis survived till 1597, when his office fell to Nathaniel Giles, who had already been Master of the Windsor Children for twelve years. (12) The two royal choirs were again under control of one man, and in a few years made a new appearance in London.

One or two classical plays for the Chapel Children survive from the late eighties and early nineties, written presumably for special occasions; Marlowe's *Tragedy of Dido* is the best. When the Court was in Progress in the summer, the children sometimes went on a little progress of their own with their plays; but they must have appeared to be fading out, as the grammar schools had done; they returned to Blackfriars, for the second time, only after Paul's led the way.

During the campaign of 1579-82, the privileged status of the children's companies seems to have preserved them from attack. The Privy Council, in its instructions to the City of December 1578, mentions the two boys' companies as rehearsing for the Court, although both were outside the Lord Mayor's jurisdiction. Under pretence of toleration, Northbrooke contrives to lay down such conditions for child actors as would effectually have cut them out. He will allow comedies in the universities and in other good schools on six conditions; that they contain no ribaldry; that they are mostly in Latin; that they are given rarely; that the apparel is not sumptuous; 'that it be not made a common exercise publicly and for profit and for gain of money, but for learning and exercise sake'; and that the plays contain no love interest.

This passage may be held to describe with fair accuracy the sins of the Children, although they are not mentioned by name. In his first 'pleasant invective' Gosson makes no mention of the boys; in *Plays Confuted* he merely says:

But in plays either those things are feigned, that never were, as Cupid and Psyche given at Paul's; and a great many comedies more at the Blackfriars and in every playhouse in London. (D3 v)

Neither cleric was sufficiently senior to be able to attack Court favourites. Yet this is a mild reference to what must have seemed the abomination of desolation set up in the house of the Lord. As a schoolmaster, Gosson might have been expected also to have disapproved of this interruption of the children's studies. There is no evidence that these earlier theatres were much given to ribaldry, and certainly the boys could not have rivalled Tarlton's robust give-and-take. The audience, removed both from the excitement of the Court and the excitement of the open theatres, must have attended from the first in the mood of connoisseurs. Declamation piped, while passion slept.

Yet by an ancient tradition, children, like Fools, were licensed to play the part of Tom Tell-troth. Shakespeare made subtle dramatic use of the frankness of 'little prating York' in *Richard III*, as later, of little Macduff and Mamilius; the young Coriolanus, doubling his baby fists at his father, has one telling line. Such a privilege, when exploited for the discussion of public affairs, 'freely, carelessly, capriciously', would make them 'sparkle like salt in fire' (*Cynthia's Revels*, I2.).

The risks and limitations, as well the achievements of the choristers' theatre are epitomized in the story of their most distinguished promoter and playwright, John Lyly, successor to Farrant and Westcote in talent but not in authority. Whatever good they had to give is best seen in Lyly's plays. The cause for their decline is discernible in Lyly's career.

Lyly inherited a name famous in scholarship, and a family connexion with St Paul's. His grandfather, the grammarian and friend of Erasmus and More, had been High Master of Colet's school; his uncle had been a prebendary. By birth and connexions Lyly was a gentleman; at Oxford he made his reputation as 'a dapper and deft companion, a pert and conceited youth' and at the age of twenty, with the engaging impudence of one of his own pages, he sought the influence of his patron, Burleigh, to gain a Fellowship at Magdalen. He early became and remained all his life a courtier by profession; at the age of twenty-five, in 1579, he was swept into fame by *Euphues*:

All our Ladies were then his scholars; and that Beauty in court, which could not parley Euphuism was . . . little regarded.

(Blount, preface to Lyly's *Six Court Comedies*, 1628)

Established as the bright young man of the hour he became the 'minion secretary' of Burleigh's son-in-law, the play-writing Earl of Oxford, who in 1580 received the dedication of the sequel to *Euphues*. Lyly tried to curry favour by denouncing his friend Gabriel Harvey for lampooning the Earl; later Harvey bitterly exclaimed:

In my poor fancy it were not greatly amiss, even for the pertest and gayest companions (notwithstanding whatsoever court holy water, or plausible hopes of preferment) to deign their familiars in continuance of their former courtesies . . . Euphues, it is good to be merry: and Lyly, it is good to be wise: and Pap Hatchet, it is better to lose a new jest than an old friend.   (*Works*, ed. Grosart, 1884-5: 2, 125)

The Earl of Oxford kept a chapel; it was natural that his secretary should be led into theatrical enterprise, at that favourable moment when the City was making strenuous efforts against the common stages, and when both the boys' companies were left without dramatic direction through the deaths of Westcote and Farrant. Lyly was actually lodging in the Blackfriars when, during the spring of 1583, Oxford took up the lease of the Hall and transferred it to him.

In the following Christmas season, 'the Earl of Oxford his servants' appeared twice at Court; in the spring of 1584 two plays, *Campaspe* and *Sapho and Phao*, appeared as having being played before her Majesty 'by her Majesty's children and the children of Paul's'. It is probable that at Court the children took their title from their leader, whose lord owned their playhouse and presumably financed their play. When a lord made a personal offering to the Queen, the performers became for the nonce his servants, whatever their permanent connexions might be. It may be that Lyly was trying to amalgamate the children's troupes under Oxford's patronage, as in the previous year the most distinguished men had been joined together under the Queen's protection; and that like the Queen's Men, 'Oxford's boys' represented a temporary amalgamation of all available talents.

However, by the time Lyly's plays appeared in print, Sir William More had regained possession of the Hall; within a twelvemonth of Lyly getting it, Blackfriars closed. By June 1584, Lyly, who had married on his hopes, was flung into the Queen's Bench for debt. He was freed by October, and left Blackfriars for the precincts of St Bartholomew's. He did not recover his Court payment till November 1584, and at Christmas for the last time Evans presented 'the children of the Earl of Oxford' at court, in a play that was none of Lyly's.

Having burnt his fingers, the playwright contented himself with writing for Paul's, who after a discreet interval had regained their footing in the Cathedral precincts; according to his own statement he was given royal encouragement to 'aim all at the Revels'; with a half-promise that the Mastership should be his in reversion. This post had just gone to the energetic Tilney, a follower of the Howards, who stood in no need of a deputy at this time.

Tilney outlived Lyly and blasted his hopes; he raised the Mastership into an important public office, but he did so by supervision of the growing common stages, not by development of the limited Household troupes. He ceased to be a working deviser of shows and became a bureaucrat. His licensing functions were developing most satisfactorily for himself at the time when Lyly's venture at Blackfriars failed; when Worcester's Men found themselves in trouble at Leicester in 1584, they were the poorer for losing an expensive licence which Tilney had issued. Henslowe's diary also shows how regular was his tribute to the Revels Office.

In comparison with such profits, the takings at Blackfriars must have been a very small matter. Lyly could find no position of security. As playwright to Paul's he wrote so well that between 1587 and 1590 the choristers made nine appearances at Court; in 1588, he was created an Esquire of the Body to Elizabeth, a position of honour fitting a possible future Master of the Revels, and many degrees superior to that of Grooms of the Chamber, held by the players. It was, however, equally unremunerative; and it was the only Court advancement Lyly was ever to enjoy.

After 1588, the Earl of Oxford retired to the country, and Lyly probably left his service. In February 1589 he was elected to Parliament, in Lord Burleigh's interest. He sat in three succeeding parliaments, each time for a fresh constituency, as his masters arranged it for him; he had no roots in the country. In this same year he engaged himself in the Marprelate controversy, as a result of which he lost his last theatrical connexion. Occasionally he might be employed by some country lord to write an entertainment for the Queen in progress, (13) but his career was effectually over. After a brilliant start he found himself outdistanced by younger men. The very strength of his original work fettered him, for as a writer he developed little: before the mid-eighties, Philip Sidney was mocking at Euphuism.

In spite of their influence on the common stages, Lyly's plays were not suited for performance there. Their delicate artifice and highly wrought rhetoric belonged to the Hall, to the realm of spangles and candlelight. Donne told Wotton in his second Epistle, that in his youth 'to be like the Court, was a play's praise'. These sub-dramatic Offerings, aimed at the Queen, sometimes took the malicious form of an attack on her rivals, as in *Endimion*, or her enemy, as in *Midas*. The art of detraction had been long practised in court plays, and more often suspected: Lyly's attacks were glancing, interlaced with other matter; the delicate transparency 'like roses overlaid with lawn' loses its subtlety if erected into a heavily allegorical system.

In the Blackfriars or Paul's, boy actors could provide a school of compliment, a gossip shop, an opportunity for the audience to display fine clothes, nice judgment, lofty pretensions.

'I could interpret between you and your love if I could see the puppets dallying', Hamlet told Ophelia at a court play; Lyly's singing children acted out their 'dalliance'—courtship according to the rules of the game of love—on behalf of the audience. They claimed to be no more than 'shadows' of the Queen and her circle, who, watching the play, might imagine themselves to be in a dream-world. The actors are but instruments or toys by which the audience conduct their own 'dalliance' and children were better suited for this game than men actors, although the men, too, at times, must have found their function was to 'become the cause of wit in other men' flattering the complacency of their patrons. At Black-friars or Paul's, court players invited spectators to air their superior insight, and inside information, as well as their critical judgment; the satiric smartness and malicious wit, which Shakespeare shows a courtly audience indulging at the expense of rustic players, were taught to those who aspired to courtly manners. Jonson often satirized this kind of audience, but Lyly was satirical only at the expense of outsiders, or of personal enemies of his patron—such as Ann Vavasour, whom I would take to be the original of *The Woman in the Moon*.

Lyly's ironic treatment of Oxford's enemies, his plentiful use of 'court holy water', brought him no increase. The sprightly 'Cockalilly' of the Presence Chambe rused literature as a means of advancement; he was not, like Spenser, a poet first and foremost. He could not make poetry out of his defeat, or advance with new poets to another style. Nothing in his novels or plays has the passionate depth of his increasingly despairing petitions (which sound more passionate in comparison with the formal, legal, wily plea of Hunnis). In a plaint to Cecil in 1594, he accused Envy of his fall; in one of 1597 he exclaimed:

I hope I shall not be used worse than an old horse, who after service done hath his shoes pulled off, and turned to grass, not suffered to starve in the stable. . . . I find it folly that one foot being in the grave, I should have the other on the stage . . . I only being he to whom her Majesty hath promised much and done nothing.

(A. G. Feuillerat, *John Lyly*, Cambridge 1910, pp. 554-5)

To the Queen herself he first apologized for old fashioned 'tediousness' and reminded her of how he was taken into her service, where 'this ten years I have attended with an unwearied patience'. He begged means to retire from the Court to the country where he might write, instead of plays, prayers for her life 'and a repentance, that I have played the fool so long and yet live'.

Three years later, still unrewarded, in hopes of plucking something from the many fortunes that fell with Essex, his appeals sharpened:

. . . seeing nothing will come to me by revels, I may prey upon the rebels. Thirteen years your highness' servant; but yet nothing. Twenty friends, that though they say they will be sure, I find sure to be slow. A thousand hopes, but all nothing, a hundred promises, but yet nothing. Thus, casting up the inventory of my friends, hopes, promises and time; the summa totalis amounteth in all to just nothing.

My last will is shorter than my inventory; but three legacies, patience to my creditors, melancholy without measure to my friends and beggary not without shame to my posterity. . . . The last and the least, that if I be born to have nothing, I may have a protection to pay nothing; which suit is like his, that following the court for recompence of his service, committed a robbery and took it out in a pardon.

(Feuillerat, pp. 561-2)

Marlowe, Greene and Nashe, his juniors, had run their successful careers in the new style, while Lyly had lingered on to see the plays at Paul's and Blackfriars revived and his Euphuistic court drama mocked by the pert and dapper pages of a younger generation, in the biting satire of a young playwright, Ben Jonson. *Cynthia's Revels* must have stung Lyly, if he heard it; yet its satire of the Court could have been endorsed by no one more passionately than by himself, as he crouched among the brawling washerwomen and plague-stricken inmates of St Bartholomew's.

Lyly's talents show the hopelessness of any attempt to build a theatre upon the uncertainty of Court patronage. The

H*

chief achievement of the boys was the indirect contribution they made to the men's stages. The little fairies whose masque concludes *The Merry Wives of Windsor* (with Evans, their absurd Welsh 'escoter') may represent what Shakespeare took to be the measure of their brief achievement. When the play was given at Court, he might even have borrowed some of those little singing boys fortunate enough to be restored to the Chapel Royal of St George.

In the early part of Elizabeth's reign, men and boys' troupes had sometimes acted together for a Court perform-ance, for at this time, the men had few apprentices. (In the Shakespearean *Sir Thomas More*, one boy has to play three parts in an interlude.) As they established themselves, and acquired their boy-actors, the need for this collaboration vanished; nevertheless they must have kept a not unfriendly memory of the children's troupes, and Kempe reserved it as his highest praise for the Waits of Norwich, when they came out to meet him at the end of his Dance, that they were equal to a Chapel.

The boys' companies had succeeded as one-man enter-prises; Farrant and Westcote combined full authority over the children with creative talent, business acumen and Court privilege. Co-operation did not succeed; perhaps there was never enough profit for more than one man.

But in 1599 a new Privy Council ordinance, limiting the public playhouses to two, tempted promoters to exploit the children once more. Paul's reopened early in the year 1600, in a house near the church (14); here they ran a brilliant repertory for six years, playing Marston, Middleton, and the first play of Beaumont. Yet quite early in the revival the Lord Mayor was ordered by the Privy Council to suppress all plays during Lent 1601, especially at Blackfriars and St Paul's. By now plays were plays, wherever performed, and the notion of 'private' performance had worn too thin for use, (15) although without Privy Council authority, the City officers could still be ejected from Blackfriars. The Earl of Derby had been 'at great pains and charge' to revive the plays at Paul's; both he and William Percy wrote plays for the boys. Edward Peers had relinquished his membership of the Chapel Royal for the richer post of the Mastership of Paul's, and acquired as business associate Thomas Woodford, a nephew of the poet Lodge. Should a particularly libellous play like *The Old Joiner of Aldgate* bring trouble, Peers could blandly disown all responsibility, protesting that he was interested only in the children's education—he added rather inconsistently that he had submitted the play to one of the clergy to read. (16) The mere fact that they acted in the precincts must have meant that some check could have been kept on Paul's Boys by the Dean and Chapter.

Nevertheless, the old tradition of courtly invective, which Lyly had started, was applied during the second phase of the choristers' theatres to general satire of Court and City. Witty young gentlemen from the Inns, like John Marston, wrote in a malicious and highly personal style. Middleton reached new depths of cynicism in depicting the vices of the Londoners. The malice of a 'little theatre' group or of an intimate revue is familiar to modern playgoers but to the Elizabethans it was a scandal. The language was sharper and the taunts much more telling and more wounding than Lyly's glancing mockery had been.

Peers acquired, quarrelled with, assaulted and discarded a variety of business associates. It seems likely that his theatre was closed by order of the Dean and Chapter in November 1606, when the Chapel was prohibited from acting by order of the King; if the clerics of Paul's were not ordered to do so, they would yet have followed the royal example with alacrity. Flecknoe wrote in 1664:

people growing more precise, and plays more licentious, the Theatre at Paul's was quite suppressed and that of the Children of the Chapel converted to the use of the Children of the Revels.

(*E.S.* 4, pp. 369-70)

235

Peers sold off his playbooks; but such had been the reputation of his theatre that two years later, Woodford's rival company paid him twenty pounds a year to keep it shut.

The Paul's boys began the attack on the men's companies, which is known as the Poetomachia or War of the Theatres, with the production of John Marston's *Histriomastix*. Yet they did not get into trouble with the authorities quite as often as the Chapel; they never travelled the country. (17) Their last recorded appearance was before King James and King Christian of Denmark in July 1606, so that they ended in a manner befitting their tradition.

Stimulated by the reopening of Paul's boys, the scrivener Evans took out a lease of the newly enlarged fencing theatre at Blackfriars, which had been acquired by James Burbage in 1596, and fitted up at considerable expense. Burbage could not have regarded the competition as dangerous; nor could the Lord Chamberlain have expected the crowds to disturb his peace and quiet or he would again have intervened, as he did to prevent Burbage's own use of the place. Marston and Middleton, who began by writing for Paul's, were won over to the Chapel; Chapman, Jonson, Daniel, Beaumont and Fletcher were also among the playwrights. They produced at least four plays of a highly inflammatory kind; Daniel's *Philotas*, Chapman's *Byron*, Day's *Isle of Gulls* and *Eastward Ho!* were all thought to reflect on great persons. Jonson's *Poetaster*, the last and fiercest of his contributions to the War of the Theatres, was a Chapel play.

Nathaniel Giles, who after 1597 combined the Masterships of the Chapel Royal and of Windsor, seems to have acted as sleeping partner; the children were collected by his power of impressment and he may have set a song for *Cynthia's Revels*. In organization, the new Blackfriars had little but its name in common with the first —and the presence of Henry Evans. The company was set up by sharers exactly like a common playhouse. Evans's lease ran from Michaelmas 1600; by 13 December the kidnapping of a gentleman's son proved the undoing of the scrivener. Thomas Clifton, a schoolboy of thirteen, was seized as he was coming from Christ Church to his home in St Bartholomew's parish and borne off 'to exercise the base trade of a mercenary interlude player'. When his father found him, he was held by a group of men, including Evans, who brought out the lad, put a playscroll in his hand and bade him learn his part under threat of a whipping. A warrant secured his release from this mockery of impressment; but the men had taken seven other children in the same way 'no way fit or able for singing, nor by any of the said confederates endeavoured to be taught to sing'—these included Nathan Field, the future playwright, and Jonson's small friend Salmon Pavey, who not being the sons of gentlemen, were not released.

Evans appeared in the Star Chamber (after a year's delay) to answer this offence; and the 'confederates' regrouped themselves. Another partner, a Yeoman of the Revels, took over the dieting and ordering of the boys from Evans. Acting a mixture of worn-out old plays and brand new ones, the troupe persisted. A visiting German obtained the impression that the Blackfriars was maintained by the Queen, and that she controlled the building; it says much for their power of self-advertisement and of the splendour they wished to convey. Costumes were gorgeous, and the music was varied; plays were given by candlelight; the cast was twice the size of Paul's. (18) Prices had also doubled and admission now cost a shilling, or for nobility, half a crown.

With the accession of James, matters changed. The Chapel Royal acquired a Dean and the children's Master, a master. The British Solomon recognized facts, severing choristers and players. The nominal connexion between child players and the chapels vanished, and a patent issued on 4 February 1604 to Evans's nominee and three others excluded Giles and permitted the Children of the Queen's Revels 'within Blackfriars in our City of London' to practise and exercise plays and shows. Music was not mentioned. The company became quite openly a special type of common players, in which the actors had no wages, no rights, and no powers to secede.

Later in 1604, a patent confirming Giles in his office as Master of the Chapel, provided that when the boys' voices broke their further education was to be arranged with the Dean at one of the royal foundations in the Universities. On 8 April 1605 a deputy to Giles was appointed at Windsor; the situation was being cleaned up. Two years later, Giles's patent was reissued, the Vice-Chamberlain and Lord Chamberlain joined to the Dean, and Giles excluded from plans for the boys' further education. There was the express proviso that

We do straitly charge and command . . . that none of the said Choristers or Children of the Chapel to be so taken . . . shall be used or employed as Comedians or stage players or to exercise or act any stage plays interludes comedies or tragedies, for that it is not fit or decent that such as sing the praises of God Almighty should be trained up or employed in such lascivious and vain exercises.

This very exceptional patent, issued 7 November 1606, meant that Nathaniel Giles, if he wished to remain in office, must bring up his charges to sing; it implies that he had not done so, or such explicit restraint would not have occurred. Giles, a man reputedly of holy conversation and an excellent musician, bowed to his betters and lived to rule the Chapel Children for many years.[19]

The language was not immoderate, for the choristers' theatres had revived that element of 'courtly' scurrility which was now characteristic only of the clowns' jig. The freedom of attack which Lyly had used against Marprelate was quite out of date. The boys not only mocked at their landlord's (Burbage's) company, but even at the King himself, and they fell into such disfavour that James threatened they should be made to beg their bread. Ben Jonson's masques, not the choristers' satire, supplied the private drama of the Court. In his *Apology for Actors*, Heywood noted:

some abuse lately crept into the Quality, as an inveighing against the State, the court, the law, the city and their governments, with the particularising of private men's humour . . . committing their bitterness and liberal invective against all estates to the mouths of children, supposing their juniority to be a privilege for railing, be it never so violent. . . .

Heywood is not altogether fair in this; for many of the writers hoped to be printed. The repertory of the Chapel though sometimes scurrilous is brilliant, but with the brilliance of bookish rhetoric. Chapman wrote dramatic poetry, not dramas; in the dedication to *Caesar and Pompey*, he made it a boast that this play 'never touched at the stage'. Jonson's early debating plays are made for declamation; there is no depth of character or of plot. A rhetorical type of acting would have suited the boys. The mixture of bold comment on affairs of state (as in the *Byron* play) scandal, invective, and musical interludes must have given the audience such sophisticated pleasure as audiences of today can find in intimate revue.

They enjoyed also satiric inductions, in which the action was criticized; 'Faith, we can say our parts; but we are ignorant in what mould we must cast our actors' as the boy playing the villain declares at the start of *Antonio and Mellida*, a Paul's play; then, finding he is Duke of Venice, he reflects: 'Who cannot be proud, stroke up the hair and strut?'

The malice and bickering of the promoters was much cruder than that of the plays. In 1600, they had defied Thomas Clifton's father, after kidnapping the boy, with ruffling insolence such as the men's companies had outgrown—'If the Queen would not bear them forth in that action, she should get another to exercise her commission'.

Haberdashers, goldsmiths, merchants come and go in brief and violently disrupted partnerships; Woodford, Evans, Kirkham the Yeoman of the Revels reappear from time to time; sometimes a poet, sometimes an old player would join, and start training the boys. In 1606 one Alice Cook bound her son prentice at the Blackfriars for three years 'to practise and exercise the quality of playing', so that the tradesman's model had completely replaced all notion of royal service. In 1608 Martin Slater, a former fellow-player with Alleyn, took boys as prentices at Whitefriars Theatre, again for a period of three years.

The boys had lost that independence of playhouse fortune which had protected them from the worst kind of exploitation; in February 1606 some of them were put in Bridewell for acting *The Isle of Gulls*. Soon they became 'masters themselves', taking the financial risks and paying rent for use of the Hall. Then 'the more to strengthen the service, the boys daily wearing out, it was considered the house would be as fit for ourselves', as Burbage observed; and with a little garnish—one share to Evans—he regained the lease in August 1608. Some of the boys joined the King's Men, while others moved off under the old name to Whitefriars, where Slater's company of boys had just ended a short and stormy career. These later bands seem to have been little better than a City version of Barnses' Boys. Even their audience grew more ill-mannered (20); finally, about the time of Shakespeare's death, after many reshufflings and changes of title, they sank to the level of provincial strollers. 'Silk, satin, kersey, rags'—the children's counting chant gives their history.

Burbage had waited twelve years for Blackfriars; the City Fathers over half a century. In September 1608 a Jacobean charter finally incorporated various Liberties within the City, including Blackfriars and Whitefriars. King's Men and City constables marched in almost abreast for the restoration of good order.

PART FOUR

All the World's a Stage

CHAPTER XI

DRAMA AS OFFERING

The Queen's Summer Welcomes
and Christmas Revels

Elizabeth as actress—her Coronation Entry to London—her
Summer Welcomes—Kenilworth—Woodstock—the growth of
her Legend—the *Misfortunes of Arthur*—difference between
Elizabeth's festivities and those of Henry VIII—decline of
traditional forms—new glorification of secular government in
Gesta Grayorum—revival of Summer Welcomes
in Elizabeth's later years.

ONE actress of consummate skill appeared in Elizabethan England; the Queen herself. 'I thank my
God', she once exclaimed, 'I am endowed with such
qualities that if I were turned out of the realm in my petti-
coat I were able to live in any place in Christendom.' (1)

In her relations with her people, by responsive quickness
she created a part for both to play. The legend of the Queen,
built up throughout her reign, could not have been sustained
had she not herself enjoyed a keen sense of dramatic
possibilities in her rôle. Because of her imprisonment under
Mary, Foxe all but put her among his Martyrs; and the
'troubles' of her early years formed the subject of a popular
play by Thomas Heywood, produced within two years of her
death. Her deliverance was generally accounted miraculous.
Courtiers and poets celebrated her as the chaste and sacred
beauty—if not a Beatrice, at least a Laura, as Gascoigne and
Ralegh both proclaimed. To her people at large she became a
goddess who scattered blessing, wealth and happiness—a
preserver of peace—a 'dearest dread'—a heavenly virgin

exempt from the touch of time. She spoke of her coronation ring as her wedding ring and to her Parliament (while berating them severely) termed herself the nursing mother of her people.

'A foolish song' gave some offence when the common people ventured to make these sentiments their own, adapting a popular tune:

> *Come over the bourn, Bessy,*
> *Come over the bourn, Bessy,*
> *Sweet Bessy, come over to me;*
> *And I will thee take,*
> *And my dear lady make,*
> *Before all other that ever I see.*

It appeared in the burst of high spirits that greeted her accession in the cold winter months of 1558. Nowhere was relief greater than in London, stronghold of Protestant sentiments. To silence the mistimed thunders of John Knox against the 'monstrous regiment of women', at her entry she was presented with a tableau of Deborah sitting in judgment under a palm tree; a scriptural warrant of her right to rule.

The interaction of Chief Actor and spectators was at its height in this New Year's coronation procession. (2) Greeted by 'prayers, wishes, welcomings, cries, tender words' she replied 'by holding up her hands, and merry countenance to such as stood afar off, and most tender and gentle language to those that stood nigh to her grace'; so she 'did declare herself no less thankfully to receive her people's good will, than they lovingly offered it unto her'.

To all that wished her Grace well, she gave hearty thanks, and to such as bad God save her Grace, she said again God save them all, and thanked them with all her heart: so that on either side there was nothing but gladness, nothing but prayer, nothing but comfort.

(Nichols, I, 1-2)

If 'baser persons' offered her flowers she stopped and heard their requests. She drew near to hear the first pageant, at Fenchurch, the welcoming speech of a child

> Here was noted in the Queen's majesty's countenance, during the time that the child spake, besides a perpetual attentiveness in her face, a marvellous change in look, as the child's words touched either her person, or the people's tongues or hearts.　　　(Nichols, I, 3)

The people gave 'a great shout' as the child ended with a prayer.

She sent ahead to order silence at the next pageant 'for her Majesty was disposed to hear all that should be said unto her'.

The Bible in English was presented by 'Truth, the daughter of Time'—' "Time?" quoth she, "and Time hath brought me hither".' She took the Bible with both hands, kissed it and laid it on her breast; and said, 'She would often read over that book.'

When the Recorder presented the gift of the City desiring her to continue their good Queen she replied 'marvellous pithily':

> I thank my lord mayor, his brethren and you all. And whereas your request is, that I should continue your good lady and queen, be ye ensured, that I will be as good unto you as ever Queen was to her people. No will in me can lack, neither do I trust shall there lack any power. And persuade yourselves that for the safety and quietness of you all, I will not spare, if need be, to spend my blood. God thank you all.　　　(Nichols, I, 15)

This produced a 'marvellous shout and rejoicing' 'since both the heartiness was so wonderful and the words so jointly knit'. Later it is said 'the hearers . . . with melting hearts heard the same; so may the reader conceive what kind of stomach and courage pronounced the same'.

Finally, being accosted by poor charity children outside St Dunstan's, she 'stayed her chariot, and did cast her eyes to heaven, as who should say here "I see this merciful work towards the poor, whom I must in the midst of my royalty needs remember." '

If simple people require an image as focus of their loyalty, even the most complex mind has its own level of imaginative needs. Elizabeth's power to satisfy this imaginative hunger made her indeed the nourishing source of poetry, in a much deeper sense than as dispenser of rewards; she could rise to the rôle the poets created for her. On both sides the relationship was shot through with passion and artifice.

She was mistress of the unexpected—of the informal as well as the royal and imperious approach to her subjects. When she rose and trounced the Polish ambassador in excellent extempore Latin, 'I looked for an oration and you have given me a challenge; I expected a legate and I find a herald', telling him his master was too young to know royal manners, she ended 'Farewell and be silent'. The King of Denmark's ambassador was also told his master was too young to know her quarrel with Spain. But when next day he approached her again, begging as it was her birthday she would grant his suit, she said that it was impossible a child born at four in the morning should be able to give answer to so great and learned a man by three in the afternoon.

Her motto was Semper Eadem, but she was like the moon, constant only in change. Unlike the tales of the old gods, or the saints of the old faith, her story was unfolding from day to day; the Legend of Elizabeth was not a static but a dynamic one. A dynamic relation is the basis of drama; instead of the established rapport between minstrel and audience the player has to build up a changing rapport between himself and his audience. So the Queen, mistress of popular arts, would clasp to her breast the Bible presented on her coronation procession; would shake her head and interrupt academic praises with 'Non est verum; sed utinam . . .'; would interrupt a sermon with 'Praising of virginity? Blessing of thy heart, there continue!' The first

courtly drama of the age, that of John Lyly, reflected the
wooing-play of her courtiers—the excitement of a relation
at once formal and mutable, established and risky; as
Spenser was to show it, a perpetual Quest.

Country progresses and Christmas revels divided Elizabeth's year. In the country, her humbler subjects could join
in tribute more directly; little communities dramatized their
own story by way of welcome. Today the descendant of such
great occasions is the pageant or village fête, opened by the
local celebrity, with which every village entertains itself at
some point in a damp English summer. Very often the
Elizabethan speaker was dashed with a shower, while the
Queen obligingly stayed her horse under a tree to hear him
out.

The Summer Welcomes, developing in the seventies,
culminated at Kenilworth, when country folk, gentry and
common players united. During the eighties there were
fewer such entertainments; the course of poetry was diverted
to the great pastoral flowering of Spenser, Ralegh and Peele,
linked to the daily ceremonial life of the Court. The plays of
Lyly provided an Offering to mirror Court life, in a form
half-way between fantasy and compliment. It was essential
in such plays, as at the Welcomes, that at the end the fantasy
should dissolve, that the Queen should be recognized as the
only presiding goddess of the scene, that Virtue should kneel
to her with a prayer:

> *Virtue alone still lives and lives in you,*
> *I am a counterfeit, you are the true,*
> *I am a shadow, at your feet I fall,*
> *Begging for these—for these—myself, and all.*
>   (Dekker, *Old Fortunatus*, 5, 2, 333-6)

In George Gascoigne's account of the Princely Pleasures
of Kenilworth, (3) he presents his Offering quite openly as
part of his suit for Court favour. Gascoigne, gentleman, poet,
experimentor-general, may have begun to practise verse out

of vanity 'To hear it said, There goes the man that writes so well', but he also hoped to repair the fortune that he had wasted. He took part both in Leicester's entertainment and in its sequel at Woodstock, and for a New Year gift presented Elizabeth with a translation of one speech, the Tale of Hemetes the Hermit, which he rendered into French, Latin and Italian. Gascoigne was prepared to serve either as a soldier or as a diplomat; he had already reissued his lyrics (thought too flippant) with a preface where he yielded

> *His pen, his sword, himself and all his might*
> *To Pallas' school, and Mars in Princes' right,*

but his New Year's gift made his object quite plain:

> *Then, peerless Prince, employ this willing man,*
> *In your affairs to do the best he can.*

When the Queen arrived at Kenilworth she was first greeted by a prophesying Sybil, who appeared from an arbour a bow-shot from the entrance; then by a comic porter, in the garb of Hercules—a part written and played by the Esquire Bedell of Oxford University.

Beginning with surliness, he recognized deity in his presence, fell on his knees and offered the keys of the castle. Gigantic wicker trumpeters eight feet high thereupon stepped forward on the battlements, and real trumpeters concealed within sounded a fanfare. These giants, relics of the time of King Arthur, were reinforced by the Lady of the Lake, who floated along to offer her domain. A characteristic retort, mingling the gracious and the regal, came from Gloriana:

> *We thought indeed this Lake had been ours, and do you call it*
> *yours now? Well, we will herein common more with you*
> *hereafter.* (Nichols, I, 7)

The sovereign Lady was wont to date her orders from 'our castle of Kenilworth', 'our manor of Cheneys' or wherever she happened to rest; for all estates lay in her gift.

Here, on the approach over a dry moat, the grand Offering on behalf of the Earl was made. The pillars of the bridge were decorated with seven gifts from seven gods—Sylvanus, Pomona, Ceres, Bacchus, Neptune, Mars and Apollo; they included baskets of live fowl, bowls of fish, and trophies of arms; all with their Master himself, rendered in service. Finally, a tremendous peal of ordinance, which might be heard twenty miles away, greeted the royal entry.

The verses of offering were written by Mulcaster, Hunnis, (4) Paten and Ferrars, Edward VI's Lord of Misrule, who doubtless also designed the gigantic trumpeters, for they resemble his instructions for an earlier masque. The main contribution, at least in Gascoigne's eyes, was however that of Gascoigne himself. It was an opportunity to catch the royal eye which he exploited to the full.

The Queen hunted all Monday; returning by torchlight she met a Savage Man—Gascoigne—who wondered at the extraordinary transformation of his woods and learnt in a song with Echo of the Queen's arrival. This enabled a recapitulation of the previous welcome to be combined with some forecast of the next play, which Gascoigne himself hoped to present. Unfortunately, in breaking his sapling club by way of homage, the Savage Man hurled the top from him with such force that it almost lit upon the royal horse's head. The Queen kept her seat; the grooms rushed forward: 'No hurt, no hurt', quoth her Highness graciously, adding whether in exasperation or excuse, 'The actor was blind'.

Far from being daunted, Gascoigne seized on the accident, and wrote an interlude for his play, in which Audax, Son of the Savage Man, was to appear and to tell the Queen his father had indeed been stricken blind by the power of her word. But in spite of every actor being ready in his garment for two or three days together, 'for lack of opportunity and seasonable weather' the play was not given.

Gascoigne's second opportunity came when he was ordered to compose a farewell. As Sylvanus, God of the Woods, a nobler Savage than before, he appeared when the Queen was out hunting, recalled the offerings of the seven gods and promised many more if she would but remain, to restore the country which pined at her departure. The Queen stayed her horse, fearing he would be out of breath, but with perhaps more zeal than tact he assured her that he could follow for twenty miles afoot, if it would not offend her; and so, running by her stirrup, produced a long tale of the cruelties of a certain nymph Zabeta, who had turned her lovers into trees; one of whom, Deep Desire, pleaded in song from the depths of a shaking holly bush for the Knight of the Castle, Leicester himself.

After seventeen years of courtly wooing, Leicester's attachment must have been habitual rather than ardent; but his followers (happily unaware of his secret marriage with Lady Douglas Sheffield) were ready to press his suit; in this, Gascoigne's cancelled play went beyond the bounds of prudence. Diana, searching for her beloved nymph Zabeta, was enlightened by Mercury who descended to explain that Juno had given her imperial rule, but could not persuade her to matrimony. The goddess was to be presented to the Queen, and the play to end with a speech from Juno's messenger Iris, which Leicester may have thought too pointed for performance.

> *I am but messenger,*
> *But sure she bad me say*
> *That where you now in princely port*
> *Have passed one pleasant day*
> *A world of wealth at will*
> *You henceforth shall enjoy*
> *In wedded state and therewithal*
> *Hold up from great annoy*
> *The staff of your estate,*

DRAMA AS OFFERING

O queen, O worthy queen,
Yet never wight felt perfect bliss
But such as wedded been.   (Nichols, I, 80)

Such prophecy, even from the Queen of Heaven, might have strained the royal temper. Ten years before, in 1565, when a play had been given before the Queen in which the rival claims of virginity and marriage were debated by Diana and Juno, Jupiter decided for matrimony; Elizabeth, turning to the Spanish Ambassador, had said 'This is all against me'.

Gascoigne's was not the only show to be cut—a night skirmish, a masque and a minstrel's merriment were eliminated; the Lady of the Lake came once more to tell how she was freed from captivity by the presence of Elizabeth. She was heralded by Triton and Arion; the latter, being hoarse, boldly tore off his headpiece and declared himself to be 'no Arion, but honest Harry Goldingham, come to bid her Majesty welcome to Kenilworth'. Such boldness pleased the Queen, 'better than if it had gone through the right way'.

Improvising was essential; a kind of serial was evolved in which courtiers cast themselves in whatever rôle suited the moment and their plea. A few weeks later, at the house of Leicester's follower Sir Henry Lee, Gascoigne thriftily picked up some of the material from his unacted play.

At the end of August, Elizabeth arrived at Woodstock, where she was greeted first by another Sybil, then by a combat between two knights, one being Lee himself. A famous tilter, and the Queen's Champion, Lee was a great deviser of mottoes, *impresas* and ceremonies.

The combat was stayed by Hemetes the Hermit—who was blind; who recovered his sight in the presence of the Queen; whose speech, translated by Gascoigne into sundry languages, was to form his New Year's gift. The writer of the Familiar Letter from Woodstock in which all is reported observed:

> In which tale, if you mark the words with this present world, or were acquainted with the state of the devices, you should find no less hidden than uttered, and no less uttered than should deserve a double reading over, even of those (with whom I find you a companion) that have disposed their hours to the study of great matters.
>
> (Ed. J. W. Cunliffe, *P.M.L.A.* XXVI, p. 93)

This story pleased so much that some characters were revived for a little play. But meanwhile the Hermit led her to a splendid bower hung with allegorical devices, too deep for common understanding, relating to her courtiers. Here she was feasted and visited by the Fairy Queen, wearing the personal livery of Elizabeth—black and white colours—who presented her with 'a gown of rainbows'; then she was led home through a grove, where this time a song sounded from an oak tree. It was composed by Dyer, Leicester's Secretary, at this time particularly in need of royal favour.

The play of Contarenus and Caudina recounts further adventures of a knight and his lady, who after many trials part 'for country's good'—since she is of royal blood, and he, though virtuous, but a knight. The debate, which begins with arguments for true love and runs through all the commonplaces to end with a lament, obviously touches on tender possibilities. At the same time, the Fairy Queen, acting as official deputy for the Queen in the play, remains above the strife.

> *Immortal states, as you know mine to be,*
> *From passion's blind affects are quit and free.*
>
> ll. 598-9 (ed. *cit.* p. 117)

None the less, the play was observed to move great passion in the Queen and her ladies, who requested a copy of it, which they studied. Read in cold blood, complex arguments of love and reason, love of desire and love of kind that fill this little drama may appear pedantic; yet from time to time its laments reach a transparent simplicity. The self-banished lover cries:

> *You must regard the commonweal's good plight,*
> *And seek the whole, not only one, to save.*
> *If you do well, I cannot do amiss,*
> *Though losing you, I lose mine only bliss . . .*
> *Good hap light on the land where I was born,*
> *Though I do live in wretched state forlorn.*
>
> ll. 762-5, 794-5 (ed. *cit.*, pp. 121-2)

His Princess remains constant, though aloof.

> *And absent, if your love continue still,*
> *The gain is great who still this ground have laid,*
> *That honest love might think it no disgrace,*
> *Though they that love do hap to sunder place.*
>
> ll. 852-5 (ed. *cit.*, p. 124)

So fortified, he takes his leave.

> *Yet this I am assured, her princely heart,*
> *Where she hath loved, will never quite forget.*
> *I know in her I shall have still a part,*
> *In honest sort, I know she loves me yet.*
>
> ll. 974-7 (ed. *cit.*, p. 127)

In such entertainments, the play was intended for one performance only and for one Spectator only. Like Ralegh's cloak thrown underfoot, the costly gift was to be squandered on royal service. The more closely a secret meaning was shared with the Queen alone, the more exquisite the fancy; while her ladies were given mottoes that matched with those of the lords, her own was extremely subtle, and for more distinction, in Italian.

Norwich would still turn out gigantic shows of wicker work, a flying coach with Mercury attendant, an involved allegory of Cupid and the Philosopher to welcome her;

Cambridge University would attend at Saffron Walden with lengthy disputations by way of entertainment, from which she gracefully retired, leaving Burleigh to preside. A certain shape and coherence appeared in private offerings; the wicker giants, schoolboy nymphs and platitudinous moral virtues disappeared. Sidney offered the simple homage of a shepherd and forester contending for their Summer Queen, (5) and yielding judgment to the Queen—

> *Judge you, to whom all Beauty's force is lent.*
> *Judge you of love, to whom all love is bent.*

Then Spenser published his pastoral vision of the Queen of Shepherds, celebrating the mysterious union of the monarch with the whole countryside, the whole flowery realm of natural beauty.

> *See where she sits upon the grassy green,*
> * (O seemly sight)*
> *Yclad in scarlet like a maiden queen,*
> * And ermines white:*
> *Upon her head a crimson coronet,*
> *With damask roses and daffadillies set:*
> * Bay leaves between,*
> * And primrose green*
> *Embellish the sweet violet.*

Elizabeth reigned over an English spring; the magic sympathy between monarch and people and Nature had gained imaginative form in words. She had become not only a brilliant Presence but a poetic Image, mutable and varied. 'Some call her Pandora, some Gloriana, some Cynthia. . . .'

As Cynthia, goddess of the seas and woodlands, a title which Ralegh made his own, she wielded a general power over Nature. The health of the sovereign mysteriously charmed crops and seasons; the planet Cynthia spread divine influence. Pandora was Lee's title: Astraea, John Davies's.

At Shrovetide, in February of Armada year, the young

lawyers of Gray's Inn presented a play on *The Misfortunes of Arthur*. In their Induction, they abandoned their own study of Astraea for the Muses, but proclaimed their readiness, if need be, to take up arms in the Queen's cause. They explain why they act a tragedy.

> *How suits a tragedy for such a time?*
> *Thus, for that since your sacred Majesty*
> *In gracious hands the regal sceptre held,*
> *All tragedies are fled from state to stage.*
>
> p. 223, ed. J. W. Christopher (Oxford 1912)

A second Presenter describes the story of crime and revenge, but against these old unhappy far-off things he sets the present happiness of England:

> *That, that is yours; leave this to Gorlois' ghost.*

Yet the play reflects darker facets in England's recent history. Guinevora, the wicked adulterous Queen, with her guilty desire for revenge, would serve to recall that the play was given almost on the anniversary of the execution of Mary Queen of Scots; Mordred the archtraitor, who brings in foreign aid against his rightful sovereign, causes Arthur, in Act III, to debate in great anguish whether it can ever be just to kill treacherous revolted kin. He pleads Nature; his councillors tell him 'A King ought always to prefer his realm . . . no worse a vice than lenity in kings.' Finally, as if they had all been taking the Bond of Association, (6) they exclaim:

> *Seems it so sour to win by civil wars?*
> *Were it to gore with pike my father's breast,*
> *Were it to rive and cleave my brother's head,*
> *Were it to tear piecemeal my dearest child,*
> *I would enforce my grudging hand to help.*
> *I cannot term that place my native soil*
> *Whereto your trumpets send their warlike sounds.*
>
> (3, 3, 76-82)

Yet the whole kingdom is felt to be mysteriously implicated and wounded by civil strife; the future changed by reason of children never to be born.

> *What hopes, what haps, lie wasted in these wars?*
> *Who knows the foils he suffered in these fields?*
>
> (4, 3, 48-9)

For epilogue, Gorlois comes forward, leading the spectators out of the play as he had led them into it, with his prophecy of Elizabeth's reign.

> *Let Virgo come from heaven, the glorious star . . .*
> *Which time to come, and many ages hence*
> *Shall of all wars compound eternal peace.*
> *Let her reduce the Golden Age again . . .*
>
> (5, 2, 14-23)

Bold words with the invincible Armada already assembling in the ports of Spain; but this show gains its significance by the time of its presentation, as did Robert Wilson's City triumph ten months later. In offering their service and their historical mirror, the young lawyers anticipated the more splendid use of old story on the common stages. Nor was an element of the dark and sinister at all out of place in Christmas revels. Yet one of the consequences of a feminine ruler was that this darker aspect of the revels, together with deliberate breaking of decorum and order, disappeared. Elizabeth imposed her own style, which was not that of her predecessors, and this style was imitated elsewhere.

Some of Henry VIII's festivities had been as boisterous as any country merriment; once, his rich masquing habits were torn off his back by the crowd. When, however, in 1545, he appointed Sir Thomas Cawarden as first Master of the Revels, the casual improvised reign of the annual Lord of Misrule was doomed. (7) The last courtly Lord of Misrule, George Ferrars, served Edward VI; but his letters, written in full regal style, were coldly received at the Revels Office.

In his masques, the sinister tone that can be found in Carnival was clearly heard. Masks of meyoxes—half men and half death's heads—were ill-calculated to distract the young king from the fate of his uncle, the attainted Protector Somerset, who lay in the Tower under sentence of death. Nevertheless, this tight-lipped young ruler was invited one year to watch a 'drunken mask' and again to fight a combat himself with Will Somers, the jester, perhaps with longspoon and custard.

If Mary tried to provide entertainment elegant enough for Spaniards, at her first Christmas festivities less than a week before the Coronation Entry, Elizabeth was entertained on Twelfth Night with an anti-papal show, in which cardinals, bishops and abbots appeared grotesquely changed to the likeness of crows, asses and wolves. But such performances did not recur; and even in the first month of her reign, when the players overstepped the bounds they were 'commanded to leave off'.

Six years later, after a visit to Cambridge, the Queen was followed to Hinchingbrooke by scholars with a similar dumb show, depicting the imprisoned Catholic bishops in a parody of the Mass. Bonner was shown eating a lamb, and a dog appeared with the Host in his mouth. Elizabeth administered the crowning snub of walking out of the show, and taking the torchbearers, leaving the players in darkness as well as disgrace.

Such rude and popular forms of detraction, traditionally sanctioned, found no place in her Christmas revels and sank to country pastime. (7a) Equally, a projected Masque of Amity, designed to be played at a meeting between Elizabeth and her prisoner Mary Queen of Scots, in which their reconciliation was to have been celebrated by consigning Discord and False Repute to the dungeon of Perpetual Oblivion, would have carried smoothness beyond the bounds of decency.

Unlike her father, her brother, or her successor, Mary's

son, Elizabeth did not personally take part in the Revels; she preferred her masques 'simple' without elaborate properties, and kept her state during performance, rising only to dance a final measure. Five or six plays would be presented each Christmas, as chosen by the Master of the Revels. No longer improvised Offerings of the Household, but the work of trained Comedians, they were interposed with other masks and shows. Invitation was an honour, and precedence a matter of such importance that the Lord Chamberlain was driven to elaborate shifts to content both French and Spanish ambassadors.

Others followed the Court fashion. The City appointed no Lords of Misrule after 1554; the Lord Mayor pulled down a Maypole in Fenchurch in 1552, and in 1557 a Christmas Lord (who may of course have been drunk and disorderly) when he rode from Westminster to the City was put, with his followers, into prison at the Counter.

The older forms of revel, with Lords of Misrule, Boy Bishops and Abbots of Unreason, had depended on mockery or parody of unquestioningly accepted powers. It was at the words 'He hath put down the mighty from their seat' that the subdeacons took over in the Feast of Fools. The new forms of power which had come at the Reformation were still too novel to allow of parody. An early reformer had proposed to replace the traditional Christmas feast with a four-course feast of reading in divinity, spread out on a fair white cloth, in a banqueting hall decorated with the tables of the law and

a table also which containeth in it the office of all degrees and estates. It teacheth us what we owe to our most noble prince, to our parents, and to our superiors. In this table, every man from the highest to the lowest may learn his office and duty.

T. Basill (i.e. Thomas Becon), *A Christmas Bankett* (1542)

No longer were the offices of all degrees and estates to be inverted by old customs. Heavy attempts at morality were introduced—such as William Baldwin's project for a moral play called *Love and Life*, which was to have a cast of sixty-four, every one of whose names should begin with L. This gigantic pedantry, to be given by the Inns of Court for Christmas 1566, was fortunately not produced. The Inns had become a centre of dramatic experiment during the sixties; the new Christmas revel they evolved was an imitation of the new form of government. (8) In particular at Gray's Inn, the largest and wealthiest of the four, detraction and mockery were replaced by stateliness and pomp. The Christmas Lord was selected not to present misrule but to curb it. Young lawyers looked forward to public office; it was suggested that such Christmas sports might teach them their 'office and duty' in affairs of state. From being an occasion of licensed foolery, Christmas sports grew to be an imitation of royal state; the Christmas Prince was less a Lord of Misrule than a Mirror of Monarchy. He was forbidden to make the traditional 'gatherings' from friends and neighbours, though he might send out his 'privy seals' to exact 'benevolences' from senior members of the Inn. The Prince might himself defray much of the expense for the honour of his house. His sports included witty parody, lively paradox, and ready improvising.

The most famous of all such revels were the *Gesta Grayorum*, in 1594. 'I trust they will not mum, nor masque, nor sinfully revel at Gray's Inn' wrote the Puritanical Lady Bacon to Anthony Bacon this year; nevertheless Francis Bacon wrote the Counsellors' Speeches, which ended by advising the Prince to 'dismiss your five counsellors and take counsel only of your five senses'. The new Christmas Prince stood for all those worldly values which the older moralities had condemned; Worldly Man, Mundus, and the Prodigal now received a rhetorical justification. 'Henry Prince of Purpoole' was solemnly proclaimed, defended by a champion, and received the homage of Staples and Barnard's Inns on St Thomas's Eve, 20 December. A series of revels followed, with now a Parliament being 'dashed' by absence of the chief speakers, and again the ambassador from Templaria being crowded off the stage by tumult and the thronging in of 'worshipful persons that might not be displaced, and gentlewomen whose sex did privilege them from violence'. He was appeased by a quickly devised Masque of Amity, and admission to the Order of the Helmet which bound him not only to the service of ladies, to prodigality and reading the *Arcadia*, but also to frequent 'the Theatre and such like places of experience'. A magnificent procession by the Prince to dine with the Lord Mayor gave the City such a splendid spectacle that the streets were as thronged as though some great Prince indeed were passing through.

On a voyage past Greenwich, the Prince paused to send a letter of homage to the Queen and received a spirited and gracious reply:

That if his letter had not excused his passing by, he should have done homage before he had gone away, although he had been a greater Prince than he was; yet she liked well his shews . . . that if he should come at Shrovetide he and his followers should have entertainment according to his dignity. (*M.S.R.*, p. 55)

And as he passed by the Tower, the gunners shot off a royal salute.

The Shrovetide masque of 1595 at Court marked the dissolution of the Prince's reign, at the same time that it acknowledged the irresistible power of the Queen. The elegant simplicity of this, the first true masque of the new kind, (9) made it a model for Ben Jonson and all later writers. 'The plot of those sports was but small; the rather that tediousness might be avoided and confused disorder, a thing which might easily happen in a multitude of actions.' Young lawyers had learned much since Baldwin's day, and even since the five-act play of *The Misfortunes of Arthur*. They knew how to avoid the proliferation that still was a common idea of splendour.

DRAMA AS OFFERING

The merriment of a Christmas Lord depended on his true state and his mock state being recognized together; the rôle was transparent, though maintained in utmost ceremony. By witty self-mockery, the Prince of Purpoole kept his part from declining to a mere fantasy of greatness. Traditional sports were in the blood but no longer in the brain; something had perhaps been learnt from the 'sort of base and common fellows' from the Theatre, whom the Grayans called in when their own sports were held up by tumult.

Once more then in 1595, as at the time of the Armada peril, young lawyers came to offer their service; in the fantasy of *Proteus and the Adamantine Rocks* they proclaimed the Queen's true source of greatness to be her subjects' love

> *Excellent queen, true adamant of hearts . . .*
> *What can your iron do without arms of men?*
> *And arms of men from hearts of men do move . . .*
>
> (*M.S.R.*, p. 64)

Elizabeth now ruled a wider realm than England, the kingdom of the seas; 'Russia, China and Magellan's strait' had witnessed to her power. The Prince, issuing from the rock with his masquers, bore on his shield 'in a bark of cedar tree, the character "E" engraven', and after his measures had been danced, the withdrawal marked the end of his reign.

> *Shadows before the shining sun do vanish:*
> *Th'iron-forcing adamant doth resign*
> *His virtues, where the diamond doth shine.*
> *Pure holiness doth all enchantments blemish:*
> *And counsellors of false principality*
> *Do fade in presence of true Majesty.*
>
> (*M.S.R.*, p. 66)

This youthful Offering touched the old Queen, who asked the young men to Court next day, gave them her hand to kiss; she invited the Prince to join in the day's fight at the barriers, in company of such lords as Essex and Cumberland, where he acquitted himself so valiantly that he was given the prize. Elizabeth had already seen two plays by Shakespeare's company and one by Alleyn's, as well as a masque by a courtier who was seeking to regain lost favour; yet 'she wished their sports had continued longer for the pleasure she took in them'.

The bravura and forensic speech of some of the Grayans did not escape that 'tediousness' which the Masque so nimbly avoided; yet they had discovered the true form for revels in a society where acting was by now in the hands of the players. Shakespeare could take their airy trifles and toss off his reply in *Love's Labour's Lost*. (10)

Meanwhile, in the years following the Armada, Summer Welcomes had revived; and in the lyric there appeared a new note of poignancy, as the poets began to insist that the Queen was not growing old, that she must not grow old. The Fairy Queen's mortality exposed her land to peril; more than the life of one old woman was involved. Civil strife and civil disorder arising from a disputed succession were the worst imaginable catastrophe to an Elizabethan audience, as the history plays of the common stages reiterated again and again. Recalling perhaps the coronation pageant of Truth the Daughter of Time, the aged poet Churchyard wrote *A few plain verses of Truth against the Flattery of Time* to

> *call you poets to account*
> *For breaking of your bounds*
> *In giving of your fame to those*
> *Fair flowers that soon doth fade,*
> *And clean forget the white red rose*
> *That God a Phoenix made.*

He had little need for reproach. When in 1590 Sir Henry Lee resigned the office of Queen's Champion, it was his own old age that was lamented and not hers: 'His golden locks

Time hath to silver turn'd'. When in September 1592
Elizabeth visited him at Ditchley, the story of Woodstock
was taken up once more, showing how time had visited the
host, but spared his goddess, to revive him to new life:

The sole virtue of your sacred presence, which hath made the weather
fair, and the ground fruitful at this progress, wrought so strange an
effect and so speedy an alteration.

(Ed. J. W. Cunliffe, *P.M.L.A.* XXVI, p. 136)

At Bisham she was greeted by sylvan gods and country
maids, Ceres and Pan:

Green be the grass whereon you tread; calm the waters where you
row; sweet the air where you breathe; long the life that you live;
happy the people that you love; this is all I can wish.

(Nichols, II, 4)

At the next house an old shepherd gave her a lock of Cots-
wold wool and a shepherd's coat, like the Offering in a
Mystery play.

By now it was Gascoigne's stepson Nicholas Breton who
was penning the lines; when another century dawned still
the praises of Cynthia were being sung, in brave words which
by now must have sounded hollowly:

> *Lands and seas she rules below,*
> *Where things change and ebb and flow,*
> *Spring, wax old and perish:*
> *Only Time, which all doth mow,*
> *Her alone doth cherish.*

> *Time's young hours attend her still,*
> *And her eyes and cheeks do fill*
> *With fresh youth and beauty:*
> *All her lovers old do grow,*
> *But their hearts they do not so,*
> *In their love and duty.*

In the last years of her life, reviving the ancient custom of her father's day, Elizabeth went maying to Highgate and Lewisham; when her courtiers protested, she bade the old to stay behind and the young to follow her. The last of her Summer Welcomes, at Harefield in July 1602, showed Time standing still in her presence, as at Kenilworth so many years before.

CHAPTER XII

THE PRIVATE AUDIENCE

Collegiate Revels at the University

The private audience in the choristers' theatres—in the Inns of
Court—in the Universities—the traditional mockery in Christmas shows—the Parnassus Plays at Cambridge—*The Christmas
Prince* at Oxford—decline of this form—behaviour
of the audience—general conclusion.

T H E 'private' audience, almost as incalculable as the
public one, must have varied its behaviour according
to the authority of the players and the presence of a
Chief Spectator. That give-and-take between actors and
audience characteristic of the interlude, with characters
popping out of the audience to play a part, or having one
thrust upon them, may have developed into something like a
wit combat between the stage and the spectators. To break
the play or put the character 'beside his part' was a form of
jest that spectators might find more attractive than an
indifferent performance; Elizabeth was pleased when Harry
Goldingham tore off his headpiece and proclaimed himself
for who he was, the Cornish countryfolk enjoyed the discomfiture of the Ordinary at their 'guary' and Shakespeare
showed how the youthful wits of Court would find it smart
to interrupt a country show or 'dash it, like a Christmas
comedy'. This kind of recognition of the players' Offering
may not have seemed bad-mannered—flouting is at least one
form of recognition; if the jester might speak to the king as
'Harry' or 'Ned', or pour a flagon of Rhenish on the
courtier's head, he was inviting the same sort of reply. (1)
Such plays lacked the authority of art; they were a form of
'commoning'.

Yet attentive audiences must have sometimes been needed
in the boys' theatres; the concert of music would have been
ruined by interruption, and their little voices have quavered
into silence if matched against brawling gallants. To the men,
the children's audience of the seventies must have seemed a
model of propriety. Its interest in the boys may not have been
without risks of another sort, of course; Middleton speaks of
'a nest of boys able to ravish a man' and perhaps the Puritan
objection to boys wearing women's dress had a crude and
simple explanation. In *Poetaster* Tucca refuses to hire his boy
players to Histrio because 'you'll sell them for enghles'.

The choristers' theatre depended on exclusiveness; there
was no risk of a fine gentleman finding himself 'pasted to the
balmy jacket of a beer brewer' at Paul's or Blackfriars, and
there was plenty of chance for self-display by late arrival,
smoking and banter. Scandal, smut, or huff-snuff rhetoric
were demanded, and the would-be critic prided himself on
being difficult to please. Such characters as Detraction, Envy,
Damplay appear in Inductions (2); Dekker's Gull exploited
the art of self-advertisement by rising with a 'screwed' face
and leaving a play in the middle, or sought 'to heap glory
upon glory' by 'talking and laughing like a ploughman in a
Morris'.

In so far as genuine private playing still went on in great
households, it was intermittent, depending on the fancy of
the lord or the ability of his servants. What evidence remains
would suggest that, as traditional forms waned, the relation
of actors and 'private' audience became more and more un-
settled; while the themes of the shows simply magnified
those rôles played by the spectators in ordinary life, provided
a celebration of times and seasons, or, in closed groups such
as colleges, indulged in mockery of outsiders. The fear of
detraction caused ill-will and sometimes led to brawling; the
charm of these shows depended on readiness to improvise and
turn misfortunes to good account. Tumults at Gray's Inn in
1594 gave rise to the Masque of Amity to reconcile the

Templarians; the failure of the first English play at St John's, Oxford, in 1607 provided an Induction for its successor.

Reversion to the old seasonal basis of plays was shown at St John's, not only by the election of a Christmas Prince, the first for thirty years, but by the favourite themes of the shows. The Twelve Days of Christmas, the Seven Days of the week, and the Chimes of the great clock were all presented.

Christmas revelry, other than Court revels, is represented by four substantial plays. Nashe's *Summer's Last Will and Testament* has been mentioned in Chapter VI; it was given before the Archbishop of Canterbury in the plague year 1592 by the boys of Paul's, at his palace in Croydon. They were helped by an adult actor called Toy. Nashe inserted an invective against poets and gave his leading actor some jests against the play, while the children mock at Toy. Dramatic illusion is constantly being broken; the spirit of a country 'game' persists, and many of the episodes are merely shows or 'entries', made to songs.

The other three texts are the *Gesta Grayorum* of 1594, considered in the last chapter; the group of Parnassus Plays, given at St John's College, Cambridge, in 1599 and 1600; and lastly, the collection of five plays in Latin and two in English, with minor shows, all linked by a commentary which are known as *The Christmas Prince*. These constituted the Christmas revels at St John's College, Oxford, in the winter of 1607/8.

By this date, the new and splendid form of the Jacobean Masque had evolved at Court, but regular 'private' performances of the choristers in London were now at an end. *The Christmas Prince* marks the end of a tradition, for it is still in the sub-dramatic form of an exercise. The disturbances which these plays provoked show how such a 'vaunt' could be taken for a challenge by other colleges, and may perhaps be considered to prove that the City Fathers' original fear of plays was rooted in the nature of the earlier form of pastime. A show becomes a challenge; 'dashing' a comedy then becomes the duty as well as the privilege of the audience: like the mock-fight of country mummers, the witty exchanges of a select audience could equally soon develop into sheer disorder, as the students at St John's discovered too plainly.

The Parnassus plays coincided with the reopening of the choristers' theatres in London, and echo the tone of the critical prologues and epilogues that became fashionable there, when actors came on to discuss their parts, and sometimes the tireman put in a word. They established a green-room atmosphere of sophistication and familiarity, invited the audience to act like connoisseurs, and undercut sneering by putting it in the mouth of fools. The best-humoured example of jesting at outsiders from the private theatre is the treatment of the citizen and his family in *The Knight of the Burning Pestle*: they are characters who have strayed from a public playhouse and expect a popular play. Later, Ben Jonson made use of strayed simplicity in the antimasques of his Court revels—the simplicity of Robin Goodfellow, 'old Christmas of London', or Notch and Slug.

The comic burleques of *The Christmas Prince* in the old-fashioned tradition of Laneham were by 1607 thoroughly provincial and out of date. Although the writers of this collection of Christmas plays show an engaging sense of humour, they were quite unpractised in drama; the charm of their 'game' depends on its being truly improvised and intimate; it still is a form of academic exercise or of social intercourse, rather than a form of art.

Oxford and Cambridge did not pretend to the splendour of the Revels at the Inns of Court, sometimes called the Third University of the Kingdom. University men were younger and poorer than the students of the Inns; they met only rarely with the chance to enjoy noble festivities or the art of the common players. Those who kept Christmas in college were likely to be poorest of all; however, Colleges had their Christmas sports and Christmas Lords (though forbidden at Cambridge by the Visitors of Edward VI) and plays were occasionally provided. Cambridge's tradition lay mainly in comedy and Oxford's in tragedy.

The visits of the Queen in 1564 to Cambridge and 1566 to Oxford were of course occasions of great splendour, when the whole university united to present stately shows; scaffolds were built, streets were decorated, famous authors were called in to help. The Christmas sports of a college were on a smaller scale. The similarity in style between the Gray's Inn sports of 1594 and the St John's College sports of 1607 should not disguise their difference; one provided a Court entertainment and the other, by careful budgeting, managed till Twelfth Night on what they considered the costly outlay of £64, 5s. od. Although the Grayans did not publish their budget, they mentioned that they had received, unasked, a single gift of £10, in a purse of rich needlework, from Cecil, the Lord Treasurer of England.

The college would in its turn appear very grand when it received the Christmas Lord of the local parish; as for instance, Christ's College at Cambridge entertained the Lord of St Andrew's parish, and St John's, Oxford, their neighbours of St Giles. But the clownish and rough entertainment with which the Cambridge students pursued the Queen to Hinchingbrooke in 1564, as described in the last chapter, must have been nearer to the antics of the village green than to the stately performance at King's.

Plays were a means of establishing the credit of a college—in other words, they were competitive; for these actors, playing still largely meant *impersonating*—assuming the rôles of others. The difficulty of a moral play is that there is no necessary particular action for such an abstraction as Love, Conscience, or Lucre, except the reflection of some highly topical and local event. Their life and being is a timeless one; to get them reflected in a flesh and blood situation meant too often the borrowing of topical examples; this, coupled with the spirit of emulation, led players and audience to cry up themselves, their founders and benefactors, and to scorn their rivals. They used the same method as Lyly, but they lacked Lyly's polish and skill. Detraction was mercilessly applied to the unpopular Gabriel Harvey in the Trinity College play of *Pedantius* (1581), in which he was shewn cheated of his money and his mistress by a lively student. According to Nashe, his very clothes were purloined to strengthen the jest, as his phrases most certainly were. Nashe in turn was accused by Harvey of having been disciplined for a saucy play. In 1598, when *Club Law* was staged at Clare Hall, attacking the townsmen and their allies the common lawyers, the occasion was said to have been improved by inviting the victims, and holding them captive by judicious seating so that they could not walk out.

Students were used to acting in Latin; the Vice-Chancellor of Cambridge, when asked in 1592 to provide a play for the Court revels, replied 'English comedies, for that we never used any, we presently have none'. The action would be formal, corresponding to the prescriptions of Oratory. In *The Christmas Prince*, the majority of plays are in Latin, and the first English show given at St John's on this occasion was very hesitatingly performed, the actors being apparently unnerved by the novelty of it, for their Latin was delivered fluently enough. They improved rapidly; but their academic tragedy is written with wretched stiffness, and only the burlesque English shows have any life; this derives from the familiar popular tradition of the folk play. There is more sophistication in the three Parnassus Plays, given at St John's College, Cambridge, which are written in the style of the College's most popular writer, Thomas Nashe, and could be modelled on his lost merriment, *Terminus and Non Terminus*. The general theme is one he had used in *Piers Penniless*—the problem of graduate employment. Witty, topical, and calculated to come home to the audience very nearly, the story of Ingenioso, Studioso and Philomusus

strings together a series of lively but separable scenes, showing the baffled schoolmaster, the quack doctor, the printer's
reader, the humble suitor for a benefice flouted by a former
fellow-student who is now a foppish member of the Inns of
Court. The scholars wish they 'could cross the Styx and go
live with Tarlton', and at the very end of their painful
journeying are driven to seek help of Burbage and Kempe.
Burbage receives them kindly if loftily, observing that
scholars have often 'a good conceit' in a part and may
improve with 'a little teaching'—he tries them with the safe
old stock parts of Hieronimo and Richard III. Kempe, however, mocks their formal and unpractised way of moving
downstage, and doubts their ability to write:

Few of the university pen plays well, they smell too much of that
writer Ovid and that writer Metamorphoses, and talk too much of
Proserpina and Jupiter. Why, here's our fellow Shakespeare puts them
all down, ay and Ben Jonson too.

    (2 *Return from Parnassus*, 4, 3, ed. Leishman, 1949, p. 337)

He informs the scholars that 'I rode this last circuit pur-
posely, because I would be judge of your actions'. To the
scholars, Kempe praises the player's life in grand terms.

Be merry, my lads, you have happened upon the most excellent
Vocation in the world; for money they come North and South to
bring it to our playhouse, and for honour, who of more report than
Dick Burbage and Will Kempe?

    (2 *Return from Parnassus*, 4, 4, ed. *cit.*, p. 339)

    The scholars however turn up in the next scene leading a
consort of fiddlers—preferring the lower ranks of the
entertainment industry to the shame of taking wages and
being told by Kempe to follow their betters.

    Better it is 'mong fiddlers to be chief
    Than at a player's trencher beg relief.
    But is't not strange these mimic apes should prize

Unhappy scholars at a hireling rate? . . . .
England affords those glorious vagabonds
That carried erst their fardels on their backs,
Coursers to ride on through the gazing streets,
Sooping it in their glaring satin suits,
And pages to attend their masterships:
With mouthing words that better wits have framed,
They purchase lands and now Esquires are named.

(5, 1, ed. *cit.*, p. 350)

At the end, they retire to a shepherd's life on the Kentish hills, save for Ingenioso, who seems desperately bound for the London playhouses, as a satirist.

Faith we are fully bent to be Lords of Misrule in the world's wide hall—our voyage is to the Isle of Dogs. (3) (5, 4, ed. *cit.*, p. 360)

The pitiful fate of Nashe and of Spenser, both lately dead in poverty, is lamented; the mixture of admiration, envy and scorn for the common stages cannot be reduced to final coherence. The writer is candid enough to show Burbage as courteous, even though he also indulges in the sort of invective that might have been learnt from Gosson or Greene:

And must the basest trade yield us relief?
Must we be practis'd to these leaden spouts
That naught do vent but what they do receive?

(4, 4, ed. *cit.*, pp. 343-4)

Rambling and shapeless, though improving in satiric precision as they go on, the Parnassus plays derive their interest from the London stages; they are a contribution to the War of the Theatres on the side of Ben Jonson and the Poets against the Common Players, but they represent primarily the local scene and the audience's own dilemma. They are the last of the true academic interludes, the latest work of the old Theatre of the Hall.

In the same Christmas of 1601, some whiffs of 'that writer Ovid' might have been detected at St John's College, Oxford, where the play of *Narcissus* was staged. (4) This gay Twelfth Night parody of a townsman's show is supposed to be acted by the 'lads of the parish' who called with a Christmas wassail-bowl but were persuaded to act a tragedy. Even these 'townsplayers', however, are made to boast of their superiority to the common stages:

> *We are no vagabones, we are no arrent*
> *Rogues that do run with plays about the country,*
> *Our play is good, and I dare further warrent*
> *It will make you more sport than cat in plumtree.*
> *We are no saucy common playing skipjacks,*
> *But town born lads, the king's own lovely subjects.*
>
> (ll. 125-9, ed. Lee, 1893, p. 5)

This kind of haughtiness was not practised by genuine mummers, who were more likely to come on with an apology:

> *We are not the London Actors*
> *That act upon the stage,*
> *But we are country plough lads*
> *That plough for little wage.*

The mockery of a country show is borne out in the play by the mockery of Narcissus, a cockered mother's boy who would be scorned by any right-minded freshman; the show ends with his metamorphosis:

> *And so I died and sank into my grandam,*
> *Surnamed old earth; let not your judgements random,*
> *For if you take me for Narcissus y'are very silly;*
> *I desire you to take me for a daffadowndilly.*
>
> *For so I rose, and so I am in troth,*
> *As may appear by the flower in my mouth.*
>
> (ll. 737-9, ed. *cit.*, p. 26)

273

and it is wound up by the college porter, who remarks as he comes to take away the bucket which had stood for Narcissus' well

> *I swear by the water,*
> *I have seen a far better play at the Theatre.*
>
> (ll. 750-1, p. 27)

It might be thought that the author was not unacquainted with the common players' *Midsummer Night's Dream*, printed in this same year.

Six years later, in 1607, largely to prevent fighting among the first and second year students, St John's, Oxford, elected one of their Bachelors, Thomas Tucker, as Christmas Prince. The custom had been unused for thirty years, and as the scribe remarks, those who proposed it had little idea how expensive it was to prove. Chosen at All Saints, the Prince was installed on St Andrew's night, when other college officers came into power, and his sports began modestly enough with a play given upon the college tables after supper; but 'every man bringing his friend, had filled the hall before we thought of it'. The play was a debate on the forms of government, culminating in the Prince's visit to the altar of the Goddess Fortune, and his installation; it was so well liked that four plaudites were given

at ye second whereof ye canopy which hung over ye altar of Fortune (as it had been frighted with ye noise or meant to signify that two plaudites were as much as it deserved) suddenly fell down; but it was cleanly supported by some of ye standers by till ye company was voided, that none but ourselves took notice of it.

(*M.S.R.*, pp. 27-8)

Throughout the sports there was a conflict between the desire to impress the rest of the university and a sense that college revels were much pleasanter when they were not 'troubled with strangers'. The comfort and exclusiveness of privacy and the glory of publicity struggled uneasily together.

For this reason, among others, merriments might succeed, but tragedy came to life only on the common stages. Declamation, exhortation and spectacle were possible; in *Philomela* (a Latin tragedy from *The Christmas Prince*) the Prince, who played the tyrant's part 'stood like a prince and fell like a prince', but his English *Periander* can hardly compete with *Richard III*.

> *Mischief herself fears openly to come.*
> *Scurrility will not spend her pains upon me,*
> *Justice yet cannot find due punishment*
> *I have anatomiz'd myself and find*
> *Myself a brief of mischief general kind.*
>
> (*M.S.R.*, p. 274)

Constant uneasy fear of detraction would not allow of the large freedom of the tragic mood; satire alone was possible. This is as true of the boys' theatres in London as of the University. *Caesar's Revenge*, which was an earlier Oxford tragedy, is a mere reminiscence of Kyd and Marlowe, derivative and flat. The children in London could declaim the long tragic tirades of Chapman, but in general they wisely did not attempt tragedy. Jonson makes fun of their efforts in *Poetaster*, where the boys spout tragedy and mount pick-a-back to play 'the Moor'. Nor except as a tribute to classical models, or by way of paradox, could tragedy be thought suitable for the Christmas Revels. The scholars of St John's in *The Christmas Prince* had prepared *Philomela* for Innocents' Night, because they thought the story of Itys a suitable one; but the majority of their shows were comic.

Their 'scholarlike devise' of the opening play, *Ara Fortuna* was in Latin; so was a private show in 'manner of an interlude' given after supper on Christmas Day. On St John's night the genuine 'lads of the parish' came with a Morris dance; an attempt to give a show in mixed Latin and English failed so miserably that the Prince rose and left the Hall. Upon New Year's Night the public show of *Time's Complaint*

was an even more disastrous failure, where the Prologue
dried up and

after him Good Wife Spigot coming forth before her time, was most
miserably at a nonplus as made other so also whilst herself stalked in
the midst like a great Harry-Lion (as it pleased the audience to term it)
either saying nothing at all or nothing to the purpose.

(M.S.R., p. 130)

The drunk man overacted, the stage was so crammed with
spectators that there was no room to move, and the comic
parts were suspected to be aimed at particular persons.
Several Latin plays succeeded well enough, even though the
Prince, who descended from his chair of State as Chief
Spectator to play Tereus, was heavily afflicted with a cold.
A little Mock-play privately given in the Lodging 'by
them which could do nothing in earnest' succeeded and was
replayed. Here the students once again personated the town
players, led by the Clerk of St Giles's. Hesitating between a
morris and something grander

> *we had adventured on an Interlude,*
> *But then of actors we did lack a many,*
> *Therefore we clipt our play into a show.*

(M.S.R., p. 137)

The procession of the seven Days of the Week, who 'beat
in' the Nights in turn, and then are themselves 'beaten in',
is in the same tripping style as the play of *Narcissus*; each
character announces himself:

> *I Monday am, not he surnam'd the black,*
> *But any ordinary one besides . . .*

(M.S.R., p. 138)

and the whole little show could almost have been written by
Lydgate for Henry VI. The public sports continued till
Shrove Tuesday (when the Prince resigned his state) and
even beyond, ending with the English tragedy, *Periander.*

Although some exception was taken to this—'a language unfit for the University, especially to end so much late sport withall'—the play succeeded so well that 'in the end they clapped their hands so long that they went forth of the College clapping'.

The 'Christmas Prince' of St John's, though he kept his full state with a complete Household, issued his privy seals and made a proclamation, anticipated 'exceptions' and 'objections', 'mistakings', pilfering and unauthorized climbing into college. The Fellows of the college gave him modest support, friends and college tenants also sent in supplies, but many shows were laid aside for want of money. In two things only the humbler college students matched those of the City; they were fertile in turning misfortune to good advantage, and once they were well started, it was very difficult to get them to stop. In 1594/5, the ancients of Gray's Inn had torn down the scaffolds after Twelfth Night, but their Prince returned for Candlemas none the less. The scholars of St John's succeeded in getting their vacation extended for a week, with the stage and scaffolds standing in the Hall; in vain did the president and seniors urge the cold weather, and the sufferings of the poor, which made revelling unfit; even after the scaffolds were pulled down on 16 January, there was a private show in the President's lodging, and a vigilate, or all-night party at Candlemas. On Shrove Tuesday the scaffolds were set up again for the show of the Prince's resignation, and suffered to stand till the next Saturday when the last of the plays was given.

The enthusiasm and excitement of these learned Revels could not have differed much from the enthusiasm and excitement which sent young prentices so regularly to the playhouse in London or set the handkerchiefs of morris dancers swinging madly. In its variety of entertainment, the revelry of the Christmas Prince faithfully recalls the style of thirty years before; the aim is also the same (in little) as the Princely Pleasures of Kenilworth. There is the 'ridiculous device' played in the private lodging—and played with the same burlesque double and triple rhymes as Laneham's merriment of the Minstrel of Islington. In contrast stand the especially stately shows of welcome and farewell. Plays that succeeded and others that remained unacted, half finished or abandoned, grand triumphs, little side-shows and impromptu jests make up the full Offering, the ceremony of Hospitality.

The rich profusion of shows at the Revels matches the rich profusion of parts and events within the medleys and gallimaufreys of older common stages. As tables should groan and sag with good cheer, as clothes should drip with jewels, so in plays, proliferation was an admired feature; confusion, loss and muddle were not even noticed.

The Christmas Prince gives the most extended picture of Christmas sports, and of the constant misconstruction and suspicion that dogged the actors. The conditions of playing were of the kind which London magistrates had perhaps sometimes imagined, but had surely never faced.

Those that were without and could not get in made such a hideous noise and raised such a tumult with breaking of windows all about the college, throwing of stones into the hall and such like riot that the officers of the college (being first dared to appear) were fain to rush forth in the beginning of the play, with about a dozen whifflers, well armed and swords drawn. Whereat the whole company (which were gathered together before the chapel door to try whether they could break it open) seeing them come behind them out of the lodging, presently gave back and ran away, though it was thought they were not so few as 4 or 500. . . .

After this all was quiet only some were so thrust in the hall that they were carried forth for dead but soon recovered, when they came into the air. (*M.S.R.*, pp. 285-6)

To say that this performance began 'very peaceably' seems a large toleration; but at least, when the Induction was presented by the figure of Detraction, appearing from the body of the hall to condemn the actors, he was 'like to have been beaten for his sauciness' (for no one took him for part of the play). The difficulties and pleasures are those of all amateur performers; the modesty of the students in casting themselves for the part of parish players, when they played in English, was an act of discretion. (5)

Yet this did not prevent their flinging a little learned scorn upon the common stages. In the show of the Prince's deposition, Momus, traditional enemy of poets, comes to taunt him and to suggest that he might go reopen the boys' theatres in London or set up another playhouse under the sign of his goddess Fortune:

> *Fortasse pueros alere pulchellos cupis*
> *Qui faeminarum splendide partes agant,*
> *Aut histrionum propria haec fiet domus*
> *Fortuna quae appellabitur.*
>
> (*M.S.R.*, p. 221)

Only a few months before, in September, the King's Men had visited Oxford; and even the most countrified of the students had had his chance to see Burbage and Shakespeare. But social prejudice still worked as it had thirty years before, in Oxford as in London.

Having surmounted the harrassing double disability of their own inexperience in English and the ill behaviour of their audience, the students ended their sports in some disillusion.

We intended in these exercises the practice and audacity of our youth, the credit and good name of our college, the love and favour of the university, but instead of all these . . . we met with peevishness at home, perverseness abroad, contradictions everywhere.

> (*M.S.R.*, p. 288)

Taxed for every mistake and envied for all that was well done, mocked, as they suspected, by the Christ Church show of *Yuletide* where Christmas Lords were much jested at, they end with a warning of how they 'paid dear for trouble and in a manner hired and sent for men to do us wrong. Let others take heed how they attempt the like, unless they find better means at home and better minds abroad.'

The warning was not needed, for such plays grew very rare. Bound up with the English Tragedy of *Periander* is a *Christmas Messe* of 1619. (6) This combat between Beefe and Brawn, Souse, Mustard, Mincepie and other Christmas characters does not rise above the level of simple invective.

> BRAWN: *Descend from words to blows, upbraiding Varlet,*
> *Thou art my object, with thy Queen, that Harlot.*
> MINCEPIE: *What? doth he call me Harlot? stand aside.*
> *By Cock and Pie, I'll make the rogue one-eyed.*

Later still *The Christmas Ordinarie*, 'first-born of a young Academic head', presents a masque of the Four Seasons which 'would have passed for an indifferent masque in Guildhall, had it been hammered out by a company of joiners'.

The poor little masque, which is depicted so scornfully, is all that remains of the medieval festive tradition. This play was given privately at a gentleman's house among other revels; and as a charade, might have been copied down with the Christmas recipes and the stillroom secrets.

In the seventeenth century, the private audience survived chiefly in virtue of *not* being a common audience. It represented either a small exclusive London set, or a closed society like the University, or a casual assembly of friends: but it utilized old popular forms, which, except for such lingering traces, had vanished long before. The witty Theatre of the Hall had ceased to exist. Of the four main branches of playing which existed at the beginning of Elizabeth's reign, the common stages alone survived the first decade of the seventeenth century. Town sports, household sports, and academic sports had disappeared—

including the children's theatre, a disguised form of public entertainment.

The older kind of merrymaking, with performers only casually and momentarily distinguished from the rest of the assembly, was fecund but it lacked form, and therefore lacked the power to survive which comes with art; it lacked 'a soul diffused quite through to make it of a piece'. On the common stages, the poets supplied this form by the objectivity and detachment of their presentation. Their triumph of observation and insight resulted in a new kind of self-consciousness, shown at its most powerful in the tragedy of *Hamlet*. The celebrations at Kenilworth, the greatest festivity in the older mode, were attended by Common Players who in less than twelve months' time were to build the Theatre. From the planks of the demolished Theatre the Globe, where *Hamlet* was staged, was to be erected. From the very heart of the old kind of play came materials for the new kind which was to supplant it.

EPILOGUE

THE rise of the common player from the insecurity and uncertainty in which troupes fluctuated at the beginning of
Elizabeth's reign, to general acceptance by reputable society
in the later years of James is inseparable from or involved in
the emergence of the great metropolitan companies. It was a
member of the first of these companies, James Burbage, who
built the Theatre in 1576; a fixed home for drama permitted
strollers to become citizens, and pastime to become art.

Elizabethan drama rose to the greatest heights English
poetry has ever attained about thirty years later. It began to
do so in the mid-eighties, when the Theatre had existed for
a decade, evoking the new phenomenon of the common
audience—a homogeneous body as distinct from a crowd of
merrymakers. Control of the new social activity, a matter of
trial and error, was achieved by dividing authority between
the Office of the Revels, the magistrates, and the players'
lords. The development of drama, or the 'traffic of the stage',
in which poets, actors and audience shared, although it
required the social opportunity provided by the London playhouses, was primarily the creation of one or two great
dramatists, especially Marlowe and Shakespeare. Their new
poetic drama made new demands upon the actor; it enriched
his art, calling for new professional skill.

The economic self-sufficiency and prosperity of the better
actors reduced the rôle of their aristocratic patrons; it led
also to the decline of other forms of entertainment, which
could not compete with the common stages. The choristers' theatres kept alive for a while older courtly forms of
entertainment, the plays of Lyly providing an exercise in
'commoning' or the use of poetry in the arts of personal
compliment and detraction. Later, the choristers' theatres
confined themselves more decidedly to satire and social criti-
cism.

EPILOGUE

Courtiers, lawyers and university students continued to write and act plays as part of any great festivity, whether a royal welcome during the Queen's summer Progress, or a Christmas revel. The legend of Elizabeth lent itself to a certain elegant improvising; but other forms of festivity declined, and by the end of the sixteenth century had almost disappeared.

Poetic drama had passed the peak of its greatness before the death of Shakespeare in 1616; but the form of theatrical enterprise was by then stabilized, the men's companies had taken over the closed theatre of the choristers, and the main traditions of the English stage had evolved.

Social acceptance of the common player was fairly general by the end of the sixteenth century; it came slowly because there had been no place for players in the Tudor social structure. The player had gained this by keeping to the traditional rôle of serving man, while gradually consolidating a new position, in which the organization of leading companies resembled in some ways that of a trade guild.* Practical recognition was conceded, but social theory, especially as displayed in the sermon, or other works of the clergy, was never adjusted to include the actor. Successful individuals—Shakespeare, Burbage or Alleyn—or successful companies, such as the King's Men, received ready acknowledgment; but Heywood's *Apology for Actors* called forth the old general arguments against the stage, which reappeared without modification as late as 1615. In time of social instability, the actor remained vulnerable to attack; similar arguments from later Puritans were eventually to lead, in 1642, to the closing of the theatres by the Parliamentary forces.

---

* In the British Academy Annual Shakespeare Lecture for 1961, *Shakespeare and the Actors*, R. David stressed this, recalling the case put for it by C. S. Baldwin. Baldwin pushed likeness to the point of identification, ignoring, for instance, the differences in mutual financial obligation between sharers in an actors' company and separate masters in a trade guild.

TABLE OF DATES 1558–1616

Date	Main and Metropolitan Events	Choristers	Academics	Festivities
1558	Accession of Elizabeth (17 Nov.)	—	—	—
1559	Queen's proclamation on plays Dudley's (Leicester's) Men formed	—	—	—
1562	—	—	*Gorboduc*, Inner Temple	—
1564	Marlowe born Shakespeare born	—	—	Queen at Cambridge
1566	Alleyn born	—	*Supposes*, *Jocasta*, Gray's Inn	Queen at Oxford
1567	Richard Burbage born Nashe born	—	—	—
1572	Leicester's Men seek licence Act Restraining Vagabonds	—	—	—
1574	City protests against players. Patent for Leicester's Men issued Admiral's Men appear	Protest includes Paul's Boys	—	—
1575	*Laneham's Letter*	—	Cambridge bans players	Princely Pleasures of Kenilworth (July)
1576	Theatre opened by James Burbage Lord Strange's Men appear	Chapel Boys at Blackfriars	—	—
1577	Curtain opened. Northbrooke attacks plays	—	—	—
1578	Stockwood attacks plays	—	—	—

Date	Main and Metropolitan Events	Choristers	Academics	Festivities
1579	Gosson's *School of Abuse*. Tilney at Revels Office	—	—	—
1580	—	Farrant of Chapel dies	—	—
1581	Tilney reforms Revels Office / Wilson's *Three Ladies of London*	—	—	Tourney of Four Foster Children of Desire
1582	Gosson, *Plays Confuted* / City attack renewed	Westcote of Paul's dies. Oxford and Lyly at Blackfriars	—	—
1583	Stubbes, *Anatomy of Abuses*. Queen's Men formed	Blackfriars closed. Lyly in prison for debt	Tumults at Oxford	—
1584	Whit Monday riot at Theatre	—	—	—
1585	—		—	—
1586	Leicester's Men in Netherlands / Rose opened by Henslowe	Lyly restarts Paul's Boys	—	—
1587	Rankins, *Mirror of Monsters*	—	—	—
1588	Death of Tarlton / Wilson's *Pleasant and Stately Moral*		*Misfortunes of Arthur* Gray's Inn	—
1589	Marprelate plays. Theatres closed	Paul's Boys close	—	
1590	Greene's *Never Too Late* / Wilson's *Cobbler's Prophecy*		—	Lee resigns as Queen's Champion

285

Date	Main and Metropolitan Events	Choristers	Academics	Festivities
1591	—	*Summer's Last Will and Testament*	—	—
1592	Death of Greene (Sept.) Alleyn marries Joan Woodward (Oct.) Theatres closed for plague Greene's *Groat's Worth of Wit*		Cambridge ban renewed	Ditchley, Sudley Entertainment
1593	*Venus and Adonis* published Death of Marlowe.	—	—	—
1594	Theatres re-open. Lord Chamberlain's Men formed. Henslowe at Paris Garden	—	*Gesta Grayorum*	—
1595	Swan Theatre built	—	—	—
1596	Players forbidden in City Inns. Burbage buys Blackfriars theatre. Grant of arms to Shakespeare	—	—	—
1597	Theatres closed after *Isle of Dogs* (Nashe) Alleyn sells stock in Admiral's Men	—	—	—
1598	Demolition of Theatre (December)	—	—	—
1599	Opening of Globe (by May)	—	Parnassus Plays at Cambridge 1599-1601	Kempe's Dance from London to Norwich
1600	War of the Theatres 1600-02 Fortune Theatre built by Alleyn	Paul's re-open Chapel re-opens at Blackfriars	—	—
1603	Death of Elizabeth; accession of James (24 March) King's Men formed Theatres closed for plague	—	—	—
1604	Alleyn and Henslowe Masters of the Royal Game	Queen's Revels at Blackfriars	—	—

Date	Main and Metropolitan Events	Choristers	Academics	Festivities
1605	—	Eastward Ho! Chapman, Jonson and Marston in prison Paul's close New prohibition on Chapel playing	—	—
1606	Red Bull Theatre built	—	—	—
1607	—	—	Christmas Prince at Oxford	—
1608	King's Men take over Blackfriars from Children of the Revels	—	—	—
1609	—	—	—	—
1610	—	—	—	—
1611	—	—	—	—
1612	Heywood's *Apology for Actors*	—	—	—
1613	Globe burnt down (June)	—	—	—
1614	—	—	—	—
1615	I.G., *Refutation* of Heywood Death of Shakespeare (April)	—	—	—
1616	Jonson's *Works* published Alleyn's chapel at Dulwich consecrated	—	—	—

NOTES

1. The promised new edition of J.T. Murray, *English Dramatic Companies*, by Giles Dawson, is expected to reveal much more. See Glynne Wickham, *Early English Stages* (Routledge, Kegan Paul, 1959), for the scenic aspect of medieval art. The work of G. R. Kernodle and Alice Venezsky stresses also the decorative and scenic qualities of Elizabethan drama. Performances of the Mystery Plays in recent years have shown how much their vitality depends on production. The purely literary approach is not likely to mislead many readers of the present time.

2. The devil 'pomps' in *The Castle of Perseverence*; the banners dip in the York Play of the Trial of Christ; Alice Perrers appeared as Lady of the Sun in 1374; in 1597 she was represented on the Elizabethan stage (maybe in a replaying of this tournament) by Alleyn's boy prentice, John Pyk. The play of St Apollonia was illustrated by Jean Fouquet.

3. See C. J. Sisson, *Le Goût publique et le Théâtre Elizabethain* (1922), 15, for the Coventry play; for the Bishop of Exeter, E. K. Chambers, *M.S.* II, 190. The theatre at Tintagel I observed during a visit there.

4. *The Paston Letters*, ed. J. Gairdner (1904), V, 185. Cf. John Stevens, *Music and Poetry in the Early Tudor Court* (1961), chapter 13, for the similar developments in music.

5. But compare the attempts to evade military service by players who plead their livery, p. 34, p. 43 below.

5a. See E. K. Chambers, *M.S.*, II, Appendix G. Thomas died in 1313 as Archbishop of Canterbury.

6. See E. K. Chambers, *E.S.*, II, 98, for the full 'flyting'. Thomas Newton, *The Touchstone of Complexions* (1576), fol. 100 r, and cf. J. Stevens, 302-3.

7. The 'youths of the parish' who put on a play against John a Kent, in Antony Mundy's play; the 'politician players' of *Histriomastix*; the ballad seller and conjurer who appear in Chettle's *Kind Hart's Dream* are all examples. Shakespeare's Christopher Sly had been a bear-ward before he became a tinker.

8. This is obvious from the work of E. K. Chambers; though much

288

more remains to be done on the times of Henry VIII, Glynne Wickham being here inadequate. For Royal Entries, see Jean Jacquot, *Les Fêtes de la Renaissance* (1956).

9. The Midsummer Watch developed from the events of Ill May Day; it was discontinued, or rather replaced by the Lord Mayor's Show on Simon and Jude's Day in the mid-sixteenth century.

10. See C. R. Baskervill, 'Dramatic aspects of Elizabethan Folk Festivals', *Studies in Philology*, xvii, I, June 1920. Compare the mockery in the Summer Lord's play at South Kyme as described by N. J. O'Conor, *God's Peace and the Queen's* (Cambridge 1934), C. J. Sisson's account of another mocking summer play at Wells in *Lost Plays of Shakespeare's Age* (Cambridge 1935) and the rustic's play in *John a Kent and John a Cumber*. Baskervill quotes MS. Harley 2253:

> *Hii mayden kyng of somere, so hii nere ne sholde,*
> *Hii sitten on ys heved a crowne of red golde.*

11. See below, Chapter VII. Lydgate supplied a mumming for a summer feast at Brentwood, 'every man bringing his own dish'; and a series of Christmas shows for Henry VI (Chapter V, p. 121).

12. These players give an idealized picture of what acting sixty years since appeared to an Elizabethan playwright. Helped by More, invited to play before the Mayor and Aldermen, the troupe of four players must have appeared to their harassed descendants to be enjoying a golden age. This strong sense of the *history* of their art is marked in Elizabethan players; compare Tarlton's portrait of Lydgate.

13. *M.S.C.* II, 3, 287-8. But cf. below, pp. 35-6, for plays at St Botolph's and St Olave's. Cf. for plays in churches by common players, Chapter III, note 4, and Chapter X, note 5.

14. See the abrupt breaking off of the plays in *Sir Thomas More* and *Histriomastix*; also in Shakespeare's *Love's Labour's Lost*, and the masque in *The Tempest*; in Massinger's *Roman Actor*, the Empress cuts the play because she knows the story.

15. For further discussion see Chapter V, p. 124, and Chapter XII, p. 269. The plays of Heywood are studied in A. W. Reed, *Early Tudor Drama* (1926), and in the works on More by R. W. Chambers. University Drama is best studied in F. S. Boas, *University Drama in the Tudor Age* (Oxford 1914). The dramatic qualities of the Tudor Interlude have been worked out in the detailed study of T. W. Craik, *The Tudor Interlude* (1958).

16. See F. M. Salter, *Medieval Drama at Chester* (Toronto 1955): H. C. Gardner, *Mysteries' End* (Yale 1946).

17. See W. H. Dunham, *Lord Hasting's Indentured Retainers*

1461-1483 (Trans. Connecticut Academy of Arts and Sciences, 39, 1-175), chapter 5. For the case of cobblers and tinkers, see p. 103.

'Instead of coming up at his lord's call to take his part and quarrel defensively arrayed, the retainer of the midsixteenth century was often costumed for a pageant. The fifteenth century retainer's second function, to satisfy his lord's vanity, his love of ostentation, was gaining ascendancy over his martial duties' (p. 115).

An amusing story of a Parliamentary candidate assuming the livery of a serving man for special purposes of his own is given by Sir John Neale, *Elizabethan House of Commons* (1949), 24, 175.

18. See I. M., *A Health to the Gentlemanly Profession of Serving Men*, 1598, and cf. below, Chapter II. For the change of their livery, see *Ratsei's Ghost*, 1605 (*E.S.* I, 340). The Preface to Shakespeare's First Folio speaks of 'purchast letters of commendation'.

19. C. R. Baskervill, 'Early Romantic Plays in England' (*Modern Philology*, 6, 1916, 97). This may have been an attempt to imitate the fashionable late performances in noblemens' houses, which came after supper. See also Chapter II, note 6.

20. For a general discussion of the problems of government control, see Virginia C. Gildersleeve, *Government Regulation of Elizabethan Drama* (Columbia 1908); the facts are also set out by E. K. Chambers in *The Elizabethan Stage*. Neither of these writers has considered the social implications for the actors as a profession. For some parodies of town players see Chapter XII, pp. 273, 276.

CHAPTER II

1. Prologue to Robert Wilson's *Three Ladies of London*. See Chapter VIII.

2. The stigmatizing of opponents, as being the diabolic version of what they claimed to be, was familiar in religious controversy. Plays of Antichrist showed the juggler parodying the whole life of Christ; reformers' tracts, such as the fifteenth-century *Lanthern of Light*, depicted the Papacy as controlling the 'devil's church' – its hierarchies Satanic, its ceremonies black art. This familiar method was applied by preachers to the theatre. See Chapter III, p. 69.

3. The Lord Chamberlain was of course the head of that department of the Queen's household which was responsible for her Revels; the children of the Chapel, equally with the Men of his own troupe, were under his control. The Lord Admiral had at one time held the office of Lord Chamberlain (in 1583); so that both these officials

NOTES

would be men to entertain leading troupes of players during the nineties.

4. Robert Crowley, *The Last Trump* (E.E.T.S.), pp. 1173–6. *Vox Populi Vox Dei* (Ballad Soc. Publications, I, 133). Sir Thomas Smith was exceptional in recognizing the possibility of rising from one vocation to another. In 1578 George Gascoigne could write his *Steel Glass*, and model it on the social categories of Piers Plowman's day, with popular applause; he showed the king who governed all, the knight who fought for all, the husbandman who worked for all, and the priest who prayed for all. When Sir Philip Sidney wrote a defence of his uncle Leicester against the scurrilous attack of *Leicester's Commonwealth*, he spent much time trying to disprove the undeniable fact that the Dudley's were a new family. It was more intolerable to Sidney that his uncle should be an upstart than that he should be a murderer—or so it would appear.

For a general discussion, see Ruth Mohl, *Three Estates in Medieval and Renaissance Literature* (Columbia 1933), chapter V.

5. The irate Queen later declared it had been played forty times in open streets and houses. In the play of *Sir Thomas More*, the Lord Cardinal's Men expect £3, £5 or £10 and are sure the eight angels they receive cannot be what was intended; a servant had withheld two (this coin, at the old value 13s. 4d., was worth £1 at the new value). The rascals of *Histriomastix* demand eight angels, saying their large number and brilliant costumes entitle them to £10. In this play, Lord Maverton dismisses his old servants who served his father in the fields, to pay for his pleasures:

> *I keep a Taylor, Coachman and a Cook*
> *The rest for their board wages may go look.*
> *A thousand pounds a year will then be saved*
> *For revelling and banquetting and plays.*

6. As late as 1580, plays were given in houses in Cheapside, beginning at 7 or 8, ending at 11 or 12 (*M.S.C.* II, 3, 310). Plays were staged by merchants either in the street or in their houses (*ibid.* II, 3, 305) or in 'Yards, courts or gardens'. A similar prohibition in 1553 refers to 'Houses, yards, gardens or orchards' (*ibid.* II, 3, 300). In 1575 Inn-holders *and other persons* are cited (*ibid.* II, 3, 309). The city also reserved the right to decide what would constitute such a performance, which implies that disputes had arisen about it. Some of these plays may have been by craftsmen or prentices, but others by common players.

7. See E. K. Chambers, *E.S.* IV, 237. The comment is by S. Cox.

NOTES

See also Chapter III, pp. 71-6, for other examples of the immorality of living by Play instead of by Work. The latest example is that of Father Colleton in 1618 (Chapter III, p. 95), answering Father Leak.

8. As even E. K. Chambers seems to think it is (*E.S.* II, 75).

9. See e.g. the articles of Peter Laslett (*The Listener*, 7, 14, 21 April 1960). See also below, Chapter III. English society consisted of householders and heads of family who *represented* their little community in all social obligations, 'not such as carried their houses on their backs, and were in this place today and another tomorrow' as Stockwood puts it.

10. *M.S.C.* II, 3, 286. Several of the later players and dramatists were free of the City; John Webster, for instance, of the Merchant Taylors.

11. Cf. W. H. Dunham on royal policy towards retainers 'in principle it was one of repression; in practice it amounted to connivance and control'. W. S. Holdsworth, in *A History of English Law* (1924), IV, 165, observes 'The coercive power of the Council (i.e. the Privy Council) was comparatively weak.' For the events of 1597-1600 see below, pp. 60-1, and cf. Virginia Gildersleeve, *op. cit.*, 183-94.

12. See below, Chapter IV for a fuller discussion of the fear of assemblies.

13. See Virginia Gildersleeve, *op. cit.* 176. Tarlton knew how to defend himself at need. And of course Richard Burbage took by the nose the man who in 1590 invaded the Theatre and 'playing scornfully with this deponent's nose' uttered threats of bodily violence. Ben Jonson killed a fellow actor in a duel. Such evidence must be set against the unwilling testimony of embittered opponents that some of the players were quiet respectable men. See below, Chapter III and Chapter IV.

14. Quoted by F. S. Boas, *University Drama in the Tudor Age* (Oxford 1914), 192. For the risk of turbulence at University performances, see Chapter XII below.

15. Exemplification was not finally abolished till 1616, when the Lord Chamberlain forbade it (E. K. Chambers, *E.S.* IV, 343). For the protective power of these letters see Gosson's remark (Chapter III, p. 71).

16. *M.S.C.* II, 3, 305, 310. Compare the activities of Langley and Henslowe, the arguments of Chettle in *Kind Hart's Dream* (below, Chapter III, p. 87).

17. See Gildersleeve, *op. cit.* pp. 33-4, for the full text, and *M.S.C.* I, 3, 262-3. Notice that the company is licensed for music as well as acting. This was dropped in King James's Letters Patent of 1603.

This patent is the first mention of the licensing function of the Master of the Revels, which was much extended in the eighties.

18. *M.S.C.* I, 2, 175-9. In 1587 the Admiral's Men were said to have killed a woman and a child and injured a man by discharge of a culliver (E. K. Chambers, *E.S.* II, 135). From the players' point of view the apparently reasonable forbidding of 'unchaste, seditious and unmeet matters' while permitting 'lawful honest and comely use of plays' meant that everything turned on the definition of these terms.

19. Father Leak was paying this way still on the Bankside in 1618 (cf. Chapter III, note 21). Note that admission to bear-baiting in 1550 was only a halfpenny, and two or three hundred attended every Sunday (R. Crowley, *Epigrams*, E. E. T. S., p. 17). Yet in a country town, a bear-ward might get a better reward than a troupe of players.

20. See the description of the procession to the Chapel of Adultery in William Rankins's *Mirror of Monsters*. Fencers and other performers entered through the streets in procession to play their prizes. Playbills were known from the mid-sixteenth century, and from *Histriomastix* it appears that they bore the poet's name by the turn of the century, as well as that of the play and players.

21. See E. K. Chambers, *E.S.* IV, 316, and *M.S.C.* I, 1, 75; for Stockwood's querying of the general term, E. K. Chambers, *E.S.* IV, 200.

22. This reaffirmed their minute of 13 February 1598, limiting the London theatres to these two. The pattern of allowing two licensed houses persisted after the theatres in question had passed away. There is little real evidence for the belief of Martin Holmes that the Bankside was an altogether more unsavoury district than the north side of the river. The suburbs on both sides, being out of the City's control, were dangerous. The Bankside was also inconvenient.

23. It has already been mentioned that Alleyn in 1597 sold his stock to the Admiral's Men for £50. Richard Jones of Worcester's Men sold his wardrobe, books and instruments for £37, 10s. 0d. to the Alleyns on 3 January 1589, and in 1602 he and Shaa were paid £50 for their joint share in the Admiral's Men (Greg., *Henslowe's Diary*, 288). In estimating a player's share at £200, Greene was therefore multiplying by four (Chapter III, p. 85).

24. *M.S.C.*, I, 3, 264-5, and *E.S.* II, 208-9. This licence was so favourable that it must have been drafted by the players' friends. The Master of the Revels is not safeguarded in it; but when the patent was copied for the Prince Palatine's players at the Fortune, this was righted. Universities have also slipped in among the places allowed; but

evidently they took protective action, for a year later, in July 1604, James forbade in Cambridge

> . . . common plays public shews interludes comedies and tragedies in the English tongue and games at laggets and nine holes whereby the younger sort are or may be drawn or provoked to vain expense loss of time or corruption of manners.
>
> (J. T. Murray, *English Dramatic Companies*, 2, 221)

25. Chapters 38, 47 (Stow, *Annales* (1631), 1082 and 1086). Buc still thinks of Revels as close to Heraldry—as continuing in fact the alliance of the ancient minstrels. The arms of the Master of the Revels are differenced from the arms of the College of Heralds – 'gules, a cross argent and in the first corner of the scutcheon, a Mercurius Petasus argent and a Lion gules in chief or'. This decorative and heraldic quality of the players' art remained among common players; Shakespeare and Burbage designed and produced *imprese*.

An account of Sir George Buc may be found, written by Mark Eccles, in *Thomas Lodge and Other Elizabethans*, ed. C. J. Sisson (Harvard 1933). The Master of the Revels is not to be confused with George Buc of the Chapel Royal.

CHAPTER III

1. See M. Maclure, *The Paul's Cross Sermons* (1958), 14, 139. Stockwood's immensely long Bartholomew tide sermon appears to have some detailed facts supplied for his use. He is full of the sense of reverence due to his 'masters', who would attend the sermon sitting in their wooden gallery. In the play of *Sir Thomas More*, I, 1, 116-35, I, 3, 79-83, the players represent a preacher being approached by City rioters seditiously to publish their 'wrongs' in a City sermon.

2. See below, Chapter X. It is piquant to think that the boys were acting within a few yards of the scene of John Stockwood's eloquent denunciation. But their theatre was *socially* acceptable. The 'lost' pamphlet *The Children of the Chapel Stript and Whipt*, rumoured to have been written in 1569, has turned out to have been a figment of the imagination and never to have existed. See D. Nichol Smith, *Proceedings of the British Academy*, XV (1929), 96.

3. M. C. Cross, *Historical Journal* (Cambridge 1960), 3, I, 'Patronage in the Elizabethan Church'. In 1572 Stockwood dedicated a translation to the Earl, and another in 1592. Huntingdon, leader of a powerful Parliamentary group, who represented his views in the

NOTES

Commons was an influential shaper of Puritan policy, according to Sir John Neale.

4. See above, Chapter II, p. 49. In the Bartholomew Sermon of 1578 he records that Thomas de Cabham's infamous naked dancers (see Chapter I, p. 22) were still about. Among 'Lords of Misrule, Morris dancers and May Games in so much that in some places they shame not in the time of divine service to come and dance about the church, and without to have men naked dancing in nets, which is most filthy . . .' (T7 r and v). He adds that on the stage the clowns come on and lose their trousers ('slops').

5. This bears out a letter sent to the Privy Council by players in 1581 where they petition to act in London during the winter 'having no other means to sustain themselves, their wives and children but their exercise of playing, and were only brought up from their youth in the exercise and profession of music and playing'. Alleyn's apprentice John Pigge or Pyk sent his charming letter to Mrs Alleyn when on tour with his master some time in the early nineties. He was still playing women's parts in 1597, the year when Henslowe 'bought' a boy from a stroller (Chapter II, p. 59; cf. Chapter IX, p. 196).

5a. Cf. Greene's *Groats Worth of Wit*, D4 r. 'But Roberto now famazed for an Archplaymaking poet, his purse like the sea sometime swelled, anon like the same sea fell to a low ebb: yet seldom he wanted, his labours were so well esteemed.'

6. For Mundy's authorship see J. D. Wilson, *Modern Language Review*, 4, 484-7; *Cambridge History of English Literature* (1910), VI, 391; and Celeste Turner Wright, *Anthony Mundy* (Berkeley 1928), chapter V.

7. In *The True Triall of a Man's Self*, also published in 1586, Newton inconsistently classes Stageplayers as Thieves, pp. 227-8. The point needed elucidation even in Charles II's time; Flecknoe on Burbage said:

Those who call him a Player do him wrong, no man being less idle than he, whose whole life is nothing else but action: with only this difference from other men's, that as what is but Play to them, is his Business; so their business is but a play to him.

(*A Short Discourse of the Stage*, 1664)

See E. K. Chambers, *E.S.* IV, 370. For a genuine though exceptional case of begging see chapter IV, note 16.

8. *The Mirror of Monsters*, 1587, fol. 2 v. Rankins's allegory may yet contain some facts about the theatre embedded in its picturesque scenes; it is a highly dramatic work, and a few years later this writer became a writer of plays.

NOTES

9. For an account of Gosson see *Stephen Gosson: a Biographical and Critical Study*, by William Ringler (Princeton 1942). Lodge's *Defence* was largely a translation of Badius Ascanius, according to Ringler (*Review of English Studies*, xv, 1939, 364-71). In *An Alarum Against Usurers* (1584) dedicated to Philip Sidney, Lodge contents himself with rebutting Gosson's personal slanders, and adding some 'damnable iteration' about *Philippics*, which suggests he knew of Sidney's own defence. In a verse of praise, Barnaby Rich exhorts Lodge to ignore 'Goose son or Gander's hiss'.

10. The mummers' tradition is described in N. J. O'Conor, *God's Peace and the Queen's* (Cambridge 1934), C. J. Sisson, *Lost Plays of Shakespeare's Age* (Cambridge 1935), C. L. Barber, *Shakespeare's Festive Comedy* (Princeton 1959). See also below, Chapter XI.

11. *M.S.C.* II, 3, 315. For the general situations discussed here see E. K. Chambers, *E.S.* I, 290-8.

12. S. D'Ewes, *Journals of Parliament* (1682), 360. I am indebted for this reference to Lloyd E. Berry. Fletcher was the uncle of John Fletcher the dramatist, and brother to the Bishop of London. The City Remembrancer was an official much seen in the controversy against players.

13. From Barnaby Rich, *Faults, faults and nothing but faults* (1606). This witticism is repeated by the rascal players of *Histriomastix*.

14. For the penalties for libel, see the work of N. J. O'Conor (note 10 above) for the case of the Dymokes at South Kyme; another Star Chamber case against a barrister involved a fine of a thousand marks, the loss of both ears, the riding from Westminster to the Temple 'with papers' (i.e. stuck over with papers as a public humiliation) and perpetual imprisonment. This case was heard 5 May 1602 (*The Inner Temple and its History*, ed. F. A. Inderwick, 1896, appendix V).

15. Sir John Harrington, *Preface to Orlando Furioso*, 1590. The play is called 'A London Comedy' and may have been Robert Wilson's. The boys had put on a Play of the Cards eight years earlier, in 1582, but it is unlikely that Harrington was referring to this performance.

16. *M.S.C.* 3, 166. This arose from an appeal to the Archbishop of Canterbury from the Lord Mayor, asking that Tilney should not licence playing houses (*M.S.C.* I, 68-70). Cf. Chapter II, p. 55 (quoting *E.S.* IV, 271).

17. Nashe's preface to Greene's *Menaphon* (see E. K. Chambers, *E.S.* IV, 236). I have written on Greene and Shakespeare at more length in *Shakespeare Survey*, 15 (1962).

18. 'This is somewhat like (thought I) if he had said anything

NOTES

aginst cozening tooth drawers, that from place to place wander with banners full of horse teeth to the impairing of Kind Hart's reputation. ... But I perceive master doctor was never a tooth drawer; if he had, I know he would have touched their proceedings.' D3 v. For further discussion see below, Chapter VII.

19. This description tallies with that of Hotson's waggon stage— but note that the theatre is a *half* moon only. For an even more remarkable example of anachronism see Gosson's assertion that St Gregory Nazianzen wrote his dramas 'detesting the corruption of the papist Corpus Christi plays that were set out by the papists', and therefore designed his work for closet reading 'that all such as delight in numerosities of speech might read it, not behold it on the stage' (*Plays Confuted*, E5 v-E6 r).

20. The comparison is of course especially with Jacques' speech and with Prospero.

21. MS. 4787, Folger Shakespeare Library, Washington. It appears that the prohibition really issued not from the archpriest, William Harison, but his assistant, John Colleton, who had been given the power to waive the prohibition, but who writes the lengthy defence of it. Colleton, who had stood trial with Campion, was an old man of seventy and may have been trying to control the conflict over plays between Catholics and Puritan's (James's 'Book of Sports' having inflamed it); was Leak perhaps of the same family as the play-loving Sir Francis Leek of the north? (Cf. Chapter I). The notice of withdrawal of the prohibition occurs on fol. 87.

CHAPTER IV

1. In *Liberality and Prodigality*, probably 'Sebastian's play' of 1567, the instruction *Flie goldknaps*, I interpret as flinging 'buttercups'— perhaps sweetmeats in this form. The play is an offering to the Queen and at the end dissolves in compliment to her. Wilson's play was also perhaps designed for private performance (see Chapter VIII). For von Wedel see E. K. Chambers, *E.S.* II, 455. For a similar device at York in 1485, see Glynne Wickham, *Early English Stages*, I, 95. In the Masque at the end of Middleton's *Women Beware Women* Juno flings a shower of gold which is poisoned and kills the nymph who gets it in her lap.

2. Cf. Chapters V, VIII for praise of variety; the request to Robert Wilson Chapter VIII.

3. For the popular sport of 'horse and jack an apes' see Chapter IX, p. 198, and C. R. Baskervill, *The Elizabethan Jig*, 121. For clowns'

K* 297

vaudeville, see Louis B. Wright, *Anglia*, heft I, xl (1933). Cf. also *Modern Language Notes*, xxxii, 215-21; xxv, 248-9. A picture of the roughness of traditional sports is given in the two Scots poems of the early sixteenth century, *Peblis to the Play* and *Christ's Kirk on the Green*. For nobler sport, see W. Dunbar, *To Aberdeen*.

4. See the epilogue to *Liberality and Prodigality*; there is an analysis of the play in T. W. Craik, *The Tudor Interlude* (1958) 110-118. See the arrangement at King's College in 1564, where the Queen was placed on the stage opposite the actors, described by Glynne Wickham, and by Leslie Hotson in *Shakespeare's Wooden O* (1959).

5. See Chapter XI and compare the behaviour of a Christmas Prince, Chapter XII.

6. This may account for the suggestion (see Chapter III) that it was wrong for an actor to impersonate men above him in station. The sudden descent from stage grandeur to real humility is of course a theme for the great writer to use, as in the epilogue to *The Tempest*; but the effect on simple people may have been felt to be dangerous. Coriolanus begging voices of the plebs perhaps reflects a natural distaste not unknown to his creator. Shakespeare's crowds scenes contain many traces of his experience of the theatre crowds.

7. See *M.S.C.* I, i, 74-80. Alfred Harbage mentions this in *Shakespeare's Audience* (1942), 67. Crosse's use of Greene makes an interesting illustration of the way in which such set descriptions were slightly twisted.

8. Plays were many times forbidden for plague. For the constant comparison of plays and players with 'filth' see E. K. Chambers, *E.S.* Appendix D, *passim*.

9. Middleton, *The Roaring Girl*, I, i.

10. A fragment only; reprinted in Student Facsimile Edition. 'A new play for to be played in May Games. Very pleasant and full of pastime' it is also subtitled 'Very proper to be played in May Games'.

11. Froissart, translated by John Bourchier, Lord Berners (1525), ch. ccxlii, fol. cccxii v. Compare the boast of Sir John Fortescue in *The Governaunce of England*, ch. xiii. 'There be more men hanged in England in a year for highway robbery and manslaughter than be hanged in France for such manner of crime in seven years'—a proof of English courage.

12. See Alfred Harbage, *Shakespeare's Audience*; the passages quoted are from p. 14 and p. 139.

13. Henry Crosse, *Virtue's Commonwealth* (Q1 r), says the rebellion broke out 'at a stage play (according to a drunken custom

there used)'. It occurred at Wymondham, on the feast of the translation of St. Thomas à Becket, whose chapel was there (S. T. Bindoff, *Kett's Rebellion* (1949)).

14. See Virginia Gildersleeve, *Government Regulation of Elizabethan Drama*, 180. The most hopeful clause runs:

> Especially you shall take order that this watch of householders may be of that strength with their weapons as they may be able if there be any uproar, tumult or unlawful assembly, to suppress the same.

The Midsummer Watch of the mid-century was a decorative procession of the liverymen with torches and weapons (see Chapter I).

15. Robert Willis, *Mount Tabor* (1639), p. 113; cf. Chapter V.

16. J. T. Murray, *English Dramatic Companies*, II, 326. The evidence is given by 'Richard Errington of the City of London pewterer, aged 50 years or thereabouts'; he was one of the players, who was taking money at the door. For Barnstaple, see Murray, II, 200. Players were sometimes given rewards to go away but insisted on playing none the less; Worcester's Men did so both at Leicester and Norwich. Lady Elizabeth's Men on one occasion admitted that they came not to play but to ask the gratuity of the town (Murray, II, 340).

17. Cf. Chapter I, p. 33.

18. *Letters of Philip Gawdy*, ed. Jeagues, 120-1. (I owe this reference to Harbage.) A letter, however, is not written upon oath, and anything 'credibly reported' may be taken as 'generally rumoured' at most. This 'great Press' is parodied in *Eastward Ho!* 4. 1.

19. See Chapter III, p. 89, Chapter X, p. 219.

CHAPTER V

1. This is the notion implied in *The Cobbler of Canterbury* (see Chapter VII, note 10), a collection of jests; and in the reproof of it, *Greene's Vision*, where Chaucer is contrasted with the 'moral Gower', and described almost as if he were another Tarlton:

> *His stature was not very tall:*
> *Lean he was; his legs were small,*
> *Hosed within a stock of red:*
> *A button'd bonnet on his head,*
> *From under which did hang, I ween,*
> *Silver hairs both bright and sheen.*
> *His beard was white and trimmed round,*
> *His countenance blithe and merry found.*

(Greene's *Works*, ed. Grosart, XII, p. 209)

He tells a merry, bawdy tale about Tomkins and a Trinity scholar.

2. Lydgate, *Troy Book* (E.E.T.S. 1906) II, p. 169. Lydgate's mummings, published by the same society in volume II of his *Minor Poems*, have been discussed by Glynne Wickham, Chapter VI, *Early English Stages*, and Walter Schirmer, *John Lydgate* (1961).

3. See Richard Southern, *The Medieval Theatre in the Round*, 1957, p. 174. Compare the deafness of the dreamer in Chaucer's *Book of the Duchess*; at the beginning he overhears the Black Knight say his lady is dead, but does not take it in till he is directly informed at the end.

4. See John Lough, *Paris Theatre Audiences in the Seventeenth and Eighteenth Centuries* (Oxford 1957), Chapter I, especially pp. 39-43.

5. In the very early Oxford play *Thersites* (1537) a giant snail challenges the hero to fight and an old woman charms away the worms from a child in a parody of cure by holy relics. Martin Marprelate, in ape's form, was similarly treated on the stage (cf. Chapter VI, p. 159). Compare Elizabeth's rejection of a dumb show in 1564 (Chapter XI, p. 257); in popular procession, such mockery lasted till the end of the seventeenth century (Chapter XI, note 7a).

6. See Chapter I, p. 30, and Chapter XII, p. 270.

7. Henry Crosse, *Virtue's Commonwealth* (1603) Q2 v. The use of separate 'houses' on the stage, the vestigial remains of multiple staging such as Southern describes and Leslie Hotson would postulate for the Elizabethan public stage (see his *Shakespeare's Wooden O*, 1959), must have supplied a visual basis for the confused lack of perspective in the poets.

8. Robert Willis, *Mount Tabor* (1639), published in the author's seventieth year. See also Chapter IV, p. 114. This play is mentioned in the repertory of 'my Lord Cardinal's players' in the Shakespearean *Sir Thomas More*.

9. Thomas Heywood, prologue to Perkins's revival of *The Jew of Malta* in 1633. Note that 'shape' and 'tongue' are still kept apart. Perkins was measuring himself against Alleyn, as Alleyn was invited to measure himself against Knell and Bentley (see Chapter IX, p. 195).

10. See Bernard Spivack, *The Anatomy of Evil* (New York 1959), for a penetrating discussion of the Vice and his relation to the later parts of Richard III and Iago.

11. See Stubbes, *Anatomy of Abuses* (1583) N2 r, on the wickedness of 'enterlacing' the word of God in wanton shows; Crosse gives an example of 'a certain poet, who mixing the word of God in a heathenish play, was suddenly smitten blind for his prophaneness' (*Virtue's*

NOTES

Commonwealth, P3 r) and condemns 'this blasphemy, that a man may edify as much at a play as at a sermon.' In *Greene's Vision*, Chaucer is rebuked—'The meaning is good, but the method is bad' and some of Greene's own sentences are quoted with the comment 'If they had been placed in another humour, how much more had they been excellent?'

Spivack does not take this sufficiently into account, or allow that the social context of the plays would convert a good many of their 'sermons' to mock-sermons, reducing the Vice also to a mockery of evil.

12. Cf. Chapter VII, p. 165, and Chapter XII, p. 271. Burbage is made maliciously to say to one student, 'I think your voice would suit for Hieronimo', and more maliciously still to the other, 'I like your face and the proportion of your body for Richard III'—a part for the ugly and misshapen. They run through a few lines, and then Kempe tries them with a comic Justice's part.

CHAPTER VI

1. See Paul Hentzner, *Travels in England* (Rye, *England as seen by foreigners*, p. 107). T. Heywood at the end of his *Apology for Actors*, says wrestling replaced the summer plays at Clerkenwell.

2. C. L. Barber, *Shakespeare's Festive Comedy* (Princeton 1959), gives an account of these summer games and their connexion with plays. C. J. Sisson, *Lost Plays of Shakespeare's Age* (Cambridge 1935), tells of another mocking summer game at Wells in 1607. Mockery of gentlemen was suspected at the Curtain in 1601 (Gildersleeve, *Government Regulation of Elizabethan Drama*, p. 100).

3. For these and other entertainments, John Nichols, *The Progresses and Public Processions of Queen Elizabeth*, 2 vols., 1788, provides the best collection. See below, Chapter XI, for other aspects of the Kenilworth festivities.

4. The text I have used is that of the Folger Library copy, checked with a photostat of the Harvard copy. The pagination runs 1-54, 56-87; the signatures A-E8, F1-4. The Bodleian and Harvard copies represent the first edition; the second edition, of which eleven copies are known, exists in two states, of which the Folger Library copy represents the first. I have rechecked with the B.M. copy.

5. For the facts about Langham, Martin and Bompstead, I am indebted to the Clerk to the Mercers' Company.

6. See C. J. Sisson, *Lost Plays of Shakespeare's Age*, 192, 195, for use of these phrases in May Games. The most famous use of a slightly

distorted name is Greene's 'Shake-scene'; the trick is essentially that of the Vice—see Chapter V, pp. 129-30.

7. The house Sir Roger built at Long Melford is riddled with priest-holes. Leicester knighted Sir Roger, then Lord Mayor of London, at Westminster on 14 March 1567/8 (William Shaw, *Knights of England* (1905), vol. II).

8. See E. K. Chambers, *E.S.* II, 385, for Bompstead. For the Visitation of Suffolk see Harl. Soc. Pub. 4, xli. The name Laneham occurs in a will from Bury dated 1540 (Camden Soc. Pub. xlix, 137).

9. See F. Peck, *Desiderata Curiosa*, pp. 58-9; S. Pegge, *Curialia*, (1791) ii. 7; and E. K. Chambers, *E.S.* I, 45. 'Clerk of the Council Chamber-Door' is the sort of mock-title that might be devised for the 'household' of a Summer Lord or Christmas Prince.

10. See above, Chapter II. The office of grooms of the chamber continued to be the one assigned to players under James I. In his case it involved ceremonial attendance on ambassadors. Laneham describes how he scrutinizes those who go in when the Council sits and how he lounges outside while it is in session, chatting to friends.

11. See *The Queen's Majesty's Entertainment at Woodstock*, ed. J. W. Cunliffe, P.M.L.A. XXVI (1911), discussed below, Chapter XI. The opening of this work is missing, but the epistolary form is clear.

12. See Chapter VII for the description of Tarlton. The 'low' vivid style of description in terms of a character's appearance is a hallmark of this kind of writing. For other mock marriages see C. R. Baskervill, *Studies in Philology*, xvii, I (1920), p. 74.

13. 'The destruction of the Danes at Hoptide' was cited by Sir Richard Morrison in 1542 as suitable matter for a show (E. K. Chambers, *M.S.* II, 221). For later history of the Coventry play see C. J. Sisson *Le Goût publique et le Théâtre Elisabethain*, p. 15 n.

14. The real device of Islington (Nichols, II, 200) is a milk churn —the town seal. Famous for its curds and cream, Islington was much visited by Londoners on holiday and the horn joke may rise from the danger of these excursions. Mock arms were given to the famous player family of Duttons in verses from the Inns of Court, beginning 'The field, a fart durty', which confounded them with minstrels (see E. K. Chambers, *E.S.* II, 99); such arms were born by Summer or Christmas Lords. For various social levels among musicians, see John Stevens, *Music and Poetry in the Early Tudor Court*, chapter 13, and the *Autobiography* of Thomas Whythorn, *passim*.

14a. Greene's *Orlando Furioso* has a fight with spits and pans: and also compare the double and triple rhymes in the burlesque townsman's play of *Narcissus* and *Seven Days of the Week* (see Chapter XII).

15. See Richard Robinson, *The Ancient Order Societie and Unitie Laudable, of Prince Arthur and his knightly Armoury of the Round Table* (1583), dedicated to Mr Customer Smith, with verses in praise of the Bow by Thomas Churchyard. A grand assembly of three thousand archers in the year of publication marched from Merchant Taylors' Hall to Smithfield, where they shot at the target for glory; their leaders had such titles as Marquess of Clerkenwell (Nichols, II, 304). See also Nichols' account of another shoot organized by Sir Hugh Offley. Justice Shallow who 'played Dagonet in Arthur's show' was evidently one of these knights.

16. It is a challenge to King Arthur's knights by a giant who vows to take all their beards in tribute. See Malory, *Le Morte D'Arthur*, Book I, chapter 27. The burlesque remained current in a debased form; Percie Enderbie copied it from a manuscript of Lord Herbert of Cherbury in *Cambria Triumphans*, 1661 (ii, pp. 197-8); it appeared also, recognized as burlesque, in J. Mennies, *Musarum Deliciae* 1651, where it is attributed to J. A. and also in Percy's *Reliques*, III, p. 25. In addition to Laneham and Enderbie, Percy used a Bodleian manuscript, but it seems that the manuscript texts derive from Laneham.

17. The Black Prince was the sign of a mercer's shop in Cloth Fair, near West Smithfield, as late as 1760 (Ambrose Heal, *The Signboards of Old London Shops* (1947), p. 134). This was 'the cloth quarter', a natural home for the mercer; and a natural sign for the City Archer, for whom the Black Prince, according to Richard Robinson, was a patron. (He skilfully avoids the question of how either the Knights of the Round Table or the Black Prince could have adopted so plebeian an infantry weapon as the bow.)

18. Cf. the Latin letter asking for plays from Robert Wilson mentioned, Chapter VIII, p. 180. T. W. Baldwin, Shakespeare's *Small Latin and Less Greek* (ii, p. 126), accepts Laneham's statement; it gives correctly the curriculum for St Paul's up to the fifth form, the lowest form of the upper school, which is the one he claims to have reached. There were eight forms in all.

19. Vergil's phrase is 'invidia rumpantur et ilia Codro'. Codrus' name as an enemy of poets was used also by Robert Wilson; see p. 191. A contemporary translation in manuscript in one copy of Laneham runs:

> *While that oour neighbourz Reamz (alas) uprore doth rend asunder*
> *In mirth among the subjects that her Majesty ar under*
> *She (thanks too God) leads pleazant daies; let spite and malice wunder.*

20. *A Whip for an Ape*, April 1589. It begins

> *A dizard late leapt out upon the stage,*
> *But in a sack that no man might him see:*
> *And though we know not yet the paltry page,*
> *Himself hath Martin made his name to be.*

The boy players and their dramatist were anti-Martin but might also have been anti-Laneham. Cf. C. L. Barber, 'The May Game of Martinism' in his *Shakespeare's Festive Comedy*. Laneham was still alive in 1591, but Heywood, in his *Apology for Actors*, while praising him, lists him among the older comedians with whom he was personally unacquainted. This would mean that he was no longer about in the mid-nineties.

John Nichols, in his reprint of Laneham's Letter in the second edition of his *Progresses*, says, 'In Herbert's Ames, p. 1689, this tract is intitled "A Whip for an Ape, or Martin displaid" '—a curious but suggestive confusion.

CHAPTER VII

1. Robert Wilson so describes Tarlton in *Three Lords and Three Ladies of London* (see Chapter VIII). Tarlton is described as an innkeeper by William Percy, and in *Tarlton's Jests*, which though largely apocryphal, appeared before the end of the sixteenth century and therefore has some value as evidence for the facts of Tarlton's life.

2. *Calendars of State Papers, Domestic, 1581-90*, pp. 541-2. These papers were printed privately by J. O. Halliwell in 1866 in full; his edition of *Tarlton's Jests* (New Shakespeare Society, 1844) has a valuable preface. The Tarlton scrapbook from the Halliwell-Phillips collection is now in the Folger Shakespeare Library, Washington.

Tarlton appealed to Walsingham since Sidney his son-in-law was dead, and Walsingham investigated the situation. The lawyer Robert Adams had several of Tarlton's relatives arrested for slander, after Katherine Tarlton had filed a bill of Complaint alleging that Adams refused to pay legacies, which Tarlton had made after the will was drawn. (He had also tried to revoke the will, perhaps under pressure from his relatives.) Katherine Tarlton also alleged that Adams would not pay her son's debts.

3. The ballads included *Tarlton's Farewell*; *Tarlton's Recantation*, *A sorrowful new sonnet upon this theme given him by a gent at the Belsavage without Ludgate* (*Now or else never*) *being the last theme he sung*; *Tarlton's Repentance of his Farewell*; and *A pleasant Ditty*

dialogue wise between Tarlton's Ghost and Robin Goodfellow. Tarlton, like Greene, was given a number of edifying 'repentences'. Kempe objects to the ballad singers foisting ballads upon him at the end of his *Nine Day's Wonder*, and says his principal reason for writing it was to give a true account of what happened.

4. *Cal. State Papers, Domestic,* 1581-90, p. 541. Reprinted by Halliwell with some further rhymes which perhaps were added by Collier.

5. Jonson, Induction to *Bartholomew Fair*; H. Peacham, *Truth of our Times* (1638), p. 103.

6. Humphrey King, *An Halfpenny worth of Wit* (1613). Cf. the similar 'rustic' view of Chaucer, chapter V, note 1.

7. Greene's 'country author' in *A Groats-Worth of Wit* extemporizes, so do the country players in *Histriomastix*. Of John Shanks, who began in the nineties, it was said perhaps only by Collier:

> *There's the fat fool of the Curtain*
> *And the lean fool of the Bull*
> *Since Shanks did leave to sing his rimes*
> *He is counted but a gull.*
> (See E. K. Chambers, *E.S.* II, 339)

8. *A Brief Discourse of War* (1590), address to the reader.

9. See his dedication to the *Tragical Treatises* for a display of his Latinisms; he evidently liked to lard his talk with tags and malapropisms.

10. *Tarlton's News, The Cobbler of Canterbury* and *Greene's News* are all mixtures of nonsense, scurrility and 'invective' in the ancient tradition of Thomas de Cabham's minstrels. The collection of *The Cobbler of Canterbury* was attributed to Greene, but when the posthumous *Greene's Vision* appeared (in which Chaucer and Gower appear to Greene) his authorship is denied. This last pamphlet, however, is very unlike Greene in style, and was again probably making use of his name as a selling device. These scurrilous little pamphlets probably represent something fairly near the lost stage merriments of Tarlton and his generation.

11. See Chapter III, p. 87, and Chapter IV, p. 104.

12. 'There is a grass widow in the world complains against one or two of them for denying a legacy of forty shillings; some pity it is, poor soul, being turned to their shifts, they should hinder her of her portion, for had she that, she intends to set up an apple shop in one of the inns. If they pay her, so it is; if not, she hath sworn never to be good, because they have beguiled her.'

A grass widow in Elizabethan terms was an 'unmarried wife'. Em Ball may also have associated with Robert Greene; in *A Groats-Worth of Wit*, Roberto had a companion, 'brother to a brothel he kept' who 'was trussed under a tree, round as a Ball', i.e. hanged.

13. See *Shirburn Ballads*, ed. Andrew Clerk (Oxford 1907), p. 351.

14. *Tarlton's Tragical Treatises, contayning sundrie discourses and pretty conceits, both in prose and verse.* Imprinted at London by Henry Bynneman An. 1578. It contains a dedication to Lady Frances Mildmay and three commendatory sonnets, by T. A., Ferdinando Freckleton, and Lewis Ph. A small black letter octavo, it was originally among the Lamport Hall books. *Tarlton's Toys*, of which no copy is known to survive, was published in 1576.

15. The source of this story is late (1693). I cannot believe that so skilled a performer would ignore the signs of displeasure on the Chief Spectator's brow. Compare the description in the Shirburn Ballad, which seems more likely.

CHAPTER VIII

1. Another Robert Wilson, who matriculated at St John's, Cambridge, in Michaelmas was ordained by 1575; and a third who took his B.A. at Oxford in 1572 was likewise ordained by 1578. Both these men held benefices. The notion that there were two player-poets named Robert Wilson, originally Fleay's, has nothing to recommend it, and has been rejected by Greg and Chambers. For a recent statement see H. S. D. Mithel, *Notes and Queries*, vol. 6, No. 3, March 1959.

2. See R. C. Bald, *Notes and Queries*, March 1955.

3. G. L. Hosking, *Life and Times of Edward Alleyn*, 61.

4. This was the actors' church: the Fortune theatre was in the parish. See Mary McManaway in *The Shakespeare Quarterly*, IX, 4 (1958), pp. 561-2, on the registers.

5. See E. Nungezer, *Dictionary of Actors* (Yale 1929), under Bayleye, for the full text of this letter.

6. A reference to the noisy bells of St Michael's might apply to either University; but a joke against Cambridge 'I came from Oxford, but in Cambridge I . . .' (B4 v) appears in the first edition but is cut in the second.

7. For an account of these, see Roy C. Strong, 'The Accession Day of Queen Elizabeth I', *Journal of the Warburg and Courtauld Institutes*, XXI, 1958, 92-3.

8. Here all the sins attendant on plays were disguised as virtues, such as Honest Recreation or Modest Audacity. Lust the bride 'painted her fair face with spots of shadowed modesty' (fol. 14) as did the spotted Conscience of Wilson. Pride carries the idol of the little God Cupid in procession to the Chapel—Wilson uses the 'little God' Contempt as the villain of *The Cobbler's Prophecy*.

9. Englishmen who steal brides from foreigners were a favourite topic; compare *Englishmen for my Money*. Pleasure, the youngest of the lords, is distinguished by his sprightliness as the younger brothers generally are in these plays. The Lords of Lincoln may be aimed at the Earl of Lincoln's players, a rival troupe. Someone, as Gosson mentioned, had put on a rival play, *London against the Three Ladies*, written in envy of Wilson's success; this is referred to briefly at the opening:

> *They were slandered late with liberty*
> *And marriage to three far born foreigners.* (B1 v)

10. These are said to be spies planning insurrection, thieves marking booty, or engrossers testing the state of the market in wood. It must have been in some episode of the previous play, now lost, that Tarlton captured Simony 'in Don John of London's cellar' (*E.S.* IV, 229), i.e. on the premises of the Bishop of London.

11. Among his lost plays in Henslowe's lists are *The Chance Medley* and *The Madman's Morris*.

12. Compare the burning of the temple in the Digby play of Mary Magdalene. Contempt is the child of the old churl Ingratitude by Security; he seduces the false goddess Venus, alias Lust, who bears him the bastard Ruin. All this might be made a reflection of the players' overweening, in which case the play would be a recantation, in a humble form, like *Summer's Last Will and Testament*.

13. Peter of Pomfret appears in Shakespeare's *King John*, 4, 2. In the romance, Thomas of Erceldoune receives political prophecies from his fairy bride, as Ralph does from Mercury.

14. See Alice Venezsky, *Pageantry on the Shakespearean Stage* (New York 1951).

CHAPTER IX

1. The facts of Alleyn's life are set out by W. W. Greg in the volume *Shakespeare and the Theatre*, by members of the Shakespeare Association (Oxford 1927), pp. 1-34, and more recently in a book by G. L. Hosking, *Life and Times of Alleyn* (1952). Greg's editions of the

NOTES

Henslowe Papers and *Henslowe Diary* (1904, 1907) are invaluable; much material is found in W. Young, *History of Dulwich College* (1889), which takes the story down to the dissolution of Alleyn's original foundation by Act of Parliament in 1857.

2. The letter refers to Peele, which places it probably in the early fifteen nineties. For examples of similar challenges see Chapter II, p. 62.

3.
> *The gull gets on a surplice*
> *With a cross upon his breast,*
> *Like Alleyn playing Faustus,*
> *In that manner he was dressed.*
> (S. Rowland, *The Knave of Clubs*, 1609)

The Vestments Controversy was one of the sharpest ecclesiastical disputes of the time; Alleyn must have seemed either superstitious or sacriligious. In *Dr Faustus* Mephistophilis assumes the Franciscan habit. Compare the appearance of the devil in full pontificals, seated in the papal chair, at the end of Barnabe Barnes's *The Devil's Charter*.

4. See above, Chapter II, p. 60, for the proceedings. It was the building of the Fortune which led to the Privy Council assuming responsibility for controlling the playhouses of London, at least for a time.

5. See above, Chapter III, p. 93: 'Most worthy, famous Edward Allen' is ranked by Heywood among actors of the past, though 'yet living'. Within the playhouse, Alleyn's reputation for bounty was remembered till the end of the century (*E.S.* IV, 371-2); without, he was probably treated with some inconsistency; e.g. Peacham specifically exempts from gentry those 'who by mechanick and base means, have raked up a mass of wealth, or because they follow some great man, wear the cloth of a noble personage, or have purchased an ill Coat [of arms] at a great rate; no more than a player upon the stage for wearing a Lord's cast suit' (*The Compleat Gentleman*, ed. Gordon, p. 3).

6. See e.g. Thomas Newton, *A Treatise Touching Dice Play* (1586), G2 r and v. He approves only of games sanctioned by magistrates, as shooting competitions (cf. Chapter VI, note 15), or those where the winnings are spent in treating the losers.

7. John Stevens, *Music and Poetry in the Early Tudor Court* mentions that a chorister from the Chapel Royal may have become a tailor (p. 306). See Young, chapter 3, for the Statutes and Alleyn's will. Alleyn seemed to be envisaging something like the Chapel Royal at Windsor; his scholars correspond to the choristers, his minor fellows

NOTES

to the minor canons, his fellows to the canons, and his poor brethren to the poor knights. For general comparisons, cf. W. K. Jordan, *The Charities of London, 1480-1660* (1960).

On one occasion, in 1595, Alleyn was described officially as a musician.

CHAPTER X

1. For the quotation see *Liber Familicus of Sir James Whitelocke* (Camden Society 1858), p. 12. It refers to Mulcaster, who was master first of Merchant Taylors and then of St Paul's Grammar School. Udall moved from Eton to the Court, then to Westminster, where he was allowed to call on the Master of the Revels for supplies.

As mentioned below (p. 215), after the founding of the theatres the grammar schools ceased to appear at Court; Merchant Taylors made one last appearance in 1576. St Paul's presented two dialogues before the Mercers in 1584 and 1586, each interpreting a dream that the Company would provide more University scholarships for the boys!

2. See Chapter I, p. 30, and Chapter XI, p. 245. The tradition about early plays at Paul's is derived from Dodsley, preface to *Old English Plays* (1780), I, p. xxxix, and it seems very unlikely that Old Testament plays alone were given. Dodsley's authority is unknown.

3. One doorkeeper was probably sufficient for the small theatre at Paul's. Westcote's plays probably included *Liberality and Prodigality* (see T. W. Craik, *The Tudor Interlude*, 1958).

4. Metrical Life of Thomas Tusser, prefixed to *Five Hundred Points of Good Husbandry*, 1573. Redford shows a full appreciation of his charges' point of view in his *Lamentation of Boys Learning Prick Song* (see C. C. Stopes, *William Hunnis*, 1910, 151). Tusser was sent on to Eton—where Udall beat him unmercifully—then to Trinity College, Cambridge.

5. See William Langham, *A History of the Three Cathedral Churches of St Paul* (1873), 55-6. Plays were forbidden inside churches; yet in 1602 players were given 1s. not to perform in the church at Syston, Leics.

6. Nashe mentions the convenience to those 'loathe to go too far to seek sport' (*Have With You to Saffron Walden*, Works, ed. McKerrow, 1904-10, III, 46).

7. The attack on Martin had been in form of a Maygame; he was shown as 'a coxcomb with an ape's face, a wolf's belly, cat's claws'. Lyly despises the common players and wishes 'those comedies might

be allowed to be played that are penned', while suggesting that Martin himself in his 'gleeks and girds' should 'pen some play for the Theatre, with some ballads for blind Davie and his boy, devise some jests and become another Scogan'; *Pappe with an Hatchet*, D2 v.

8. See C. L. Barber, *Shakespeare's Festive Comedy* (Princeton 1959), for a full discussion of this play. It is about as far from a simple 'bringing in of Autumn' as is *The Shepherd's Calendar* from a rustic almanack. Note in particular the sophisticated treatment of the Presenter, Will Somers. But mock spontaneity was probably what the boys' theatres did aim at. Hillebrand, 148-9, states the case for assigning this play to Paul's.

9. A transcript of Farrant's indenture, which appointed him as clerk, organist and master of choristers at an annual fee of £81, 6s. 8d. plus 'spur money' for recruiting journeys and other fees, is printed by E. H. Fellowes, *Organists and Masters of the Choristers of the Chapel of St George at Windsor* (1939), pp. 25-6. Farrant came upon 'special request and desire'. His fellow organist was John Marbeck (the Chapel Royal also had two) and on Marbeck's death in 1585 Nathaniel Giles was brought from Worcester on the same special terms as Farrant, the chapel 'being destitute of an expert and cunning man to teach, inform and instruct' the boys. Cf. John Stevens, *Music and Poetry at the Early Tudor Court*, 305, on special appointments.

10. See E. F. Rimbault, *The Old Cheque Book of the Chapel Royal* (Camden Society, 1872), p. 97, for these as given in 1604, on the reformation of the Chapel. The quarter from St Peter's Day to Michaelmas, eight other weeks, Shrove Monday and Tuesday, all 'removing weeks' and whenever the King is from a standing house are claimed; the last and three other items are struck out again.

For the Statutes of Eltham, see *Household Ordinances* (Society of Antiquaries, 1790), pp. 160-1. Cf. however, the Patent issued to Crane as Master that year (Hillebrand, 59) which raises the number of choristers, and gives his fee as £40. As late as the time of Laud there were singing men who belonged both to Paul's and the Chapel Royal (Hillebrand, 94). For evidence of lax attendance under Elizabeth, see Rimbault, 66-7, and cf. 71-3, 79.

11. For the petition see Chambers, *E.S.* 2, 37-8, Hillebrand, 102-104. The Statutes of Eltham gave the Master 'wages and board wages' of £30, and for the boys, £50, 13s. 4d. yearly (*Household Ordinances*, 169-70). Queen Elizabeth's Annual Expenses *c.* 1578 (*Household Ordinances*, 252-3) gives a fee of £40, and £16 for breakfast allowance. Hunnis says in 1583 he gets 6d. a day apiece for diet—which is 42s. a week—for the boys, and £40 a year clothing allowance,

NOTES

but no fees or wages besides; and that some former supplementations have vanished. At Windsor, chantries survived as sinecures for supplementing the lay clerk's fees.

Two years after presenting his petition, Hunnis received a substantial grant of crown lands. He had charge of the gardens at Greenwich; enjoyed toll rights on London Bridge, and sold his patent; left his shop to his wife, and followed the Court where his handsome presence and poetry secured him favour. The terms on which Farrant acted as deputy for him are unknown. From the Household Book of James, of July 1604 (*Household Ordinances*, 301), it appears that choristers were allowed 'one mess of meat a day as lawfully accustomed' and therefore it is probable that Hunnis had regained their dining rights, without lodging and breakfast; he also, it would appear, kept the full dietary allowance, for this was raised by James from sixpence to tenpence in the Chapel augmentation of December 1604. By the class of persons listed with the boys in the Household Book, it appears that the boys ate whenever their duties brought them to Court, and not merely at great feasts, for example, they are classed with glaziers, painters, etc. For the chapel augmentation of December 1604, see Rimbault, 60-1; this had long been pressed, and in 1596 a deputation had been made by 'six of the ancients of our company (most commonly waiting)', of whom no doubt the aged Hunnis was one.

12. For Nathaniel Giles, see Fellowes, 31, and Sabol, *Renaissance News*, xiii. 3. One of Giles's expedients was to try to get the father of one of his choristers, a Somerset carpenter, to breed horses for riding journeys, (Hillebrand, 330-1). One of Hunnis's later sources of income was fines levelled on the widows of recusants—which casts a curious retrospective light on the title of his New Year's gift of 1578 to the Queen, entitled *The Widow's Mite*.

13. See the newly found entertainments at Mitcham and Chiswick, edited by Leslie Hotson (Oxford and Yale 1953). A new biography of Lyly by G. K. Hunter is due to appear shortly.

14. 'Near St Paul's Church, being then in the hands of one Mr Pierce' (Hillebrand, 215, from the Keysar-Burbage suit of 1610). It was circular (Prologue to *Antonio's Revenge*) with a very small stage (Induction to *What you Will*). I do not know why Martin Holmes identifies it with Whitefriars (*Shakespeare's Public*, 1960, p. 114) which was down Ludgate and across the Fleet.

15. In 1596, dwellers in Blackfriars affirmed 'there hath not any time heretofore been used any common playhouses within the same precinct': even in 1619, the old name persisted 'The owner of the said house doth under the name of a private house (respecting private

NOTES

commodity only) convert the said house to a public playhouse' (Hillebrand, 155-7 from *Cal. S.P.D. James I*, 260, 116); it could be recalled as late as 1699 (*E.S.* IV, 372). Cf. William A. Armstrong, *The Elizabethan Private Theatres, Facts and Problems* (1958), 2-3.

16. For *The Old Joiner of Aldgate*, the play in question, see C. J. Sisson, *Lost Plays of Shakespeare's Age*.

17. I share the scepticism of Chambers (*E.S.* II, 19) about a possible appearance in Gloucestershire.

18. For the Clifton case, see Chambers, *E.S.* II, 43-5. For the German's report, *ibid.* 46-7: he gives an account of a mixed concert preceding the play, so that some of the boys at least were singers.

19. Both commissions to Giles are printed by Chambers, *M.S.C.* I, 4; pp. 359-63. Hillebrand remarks that this is the solitary instance he recalls of the revocation and reissue of a writ, to the same person.

20. See the Induction to John Day, *The Isle of Gulls*; Thomas Dekker, *The Gull's Horn Book*; and cf. Chapter XII, pp. 278-9.

CHAPTER XI

1. Speech of 6 November 1566, on the succession. Printed by J. E. Neale, *English Historical Review*, XXXVI, October 1921, from B.M. MSS. Sloane 354 18a-19a. See Elkin C. Wilson, *England's Eliza* (Harvard 1939), for an account of the literary aspects of the legend of Elizabeth.

2. This and other Progresses quoted in this chapter are to be found in John Nichols, *Progresses and Public Processions of Queen Elizabeth* (2 vols., 1788). For the growth of Accession Day celebrations, see Roy C. Strong, *Journal of the Warburg and Courtauld Institutes*, XXI, 1958, 86-103, and cf. also below, note 7a.

3. See above, Chapter IX. Gascoigne's career has been studied by C. T. Prouty, *George Gascoigne, Elizabethan Courtier, Soldier and Poet* (New York 1942). His plays were produced by the Inns of Court, and his lyric and satiric poetry was among the first work of this kind from the court circle to receive publication—in theory anonymously, and against his knowledge (*A Hundreth Sundrie Flowres*, 1573).

4. Hunnis, Master of the Chapel Children, may have used his boys as nymphs in one of the many shows. For Ferrars see below, p. 256: he was also represented in *The Mirror for Magistrates*; he appeared as

NOTES

a typical early reveller in the scurrilous *Beware the Cat* (see above, Chapter V, p. 124).

5. In *The Lady of May* (1578). The most spectacular offering in which Sidney took part was the Whitsuntide tourney of 1581 when he appeared as one of the Four Foster Children of Desire who besieged the Fortress of Perfect Beauty, with dummy cannon, and melting lyrics, only to yield themselves as captive slaves to the invincible Elizabeth.

6. The oath subscribed by many members of the gentry to avenge Elizabeth's death, if she were assassinated, by pursuing not only the assassins but any who might benefit by her death. This was largely subscribed by the gentlemen of the Inns of Court. It was of course directed against Mary Queen of Scots.

7. The Lord of Misrule was elected annually and came out of some strange region—Ferrars one year arrived 'from the moon' another 'from Vastus Vacuum'. Churches, parishes and colleges elected their Lords of Misrule; the Sheriffs of London had theirs. Christmas lords were forbidden at Cambridge by Edward VI's Visitors, and in the mid-century they tended to decline.

7a. The same rough anti-papal sport, with the use of grotesque animal forms was used as late as 1681 to celebrate the accession day of Queen Elizabeth in London. Processions culminated with the burning of an effigy of the Pope before her statue at Temple Bar. See Sheila Williams in *Journal of the Warburg and Courtauld Institutes*, XXI (1958), 104-18.

8. Among the famous productions of the Inns were *Gorboduc* (1562, Inner Temple); Gascoigne's *Jocasta* and *Supposes* (1566); and *Gismond of Salerne* (1566). The Inns were given to 'arguments of state' in their plays. The household of the Christmas Prince was furnished with a full complement of officers, and practised the full ceremony of a real court. This had been carried out in great splendour at the Inner Temple in 1561, when Lord Robert Dudley was elected the Christmas Lord.

9. For the historical significance of *Proteus and the Adamantine Rocks* see Enid Welsford, *The Court Masque* (Cambridge 1927). The 'discovery of the masquers', their presenting a slight story in speech and song, and then descending to dance with the spectators form the pattern of the Stuart masque.

10. For the use of the players at *Gesta Grayorum*, see above, Chapter II, p. 51. For the relation of these Revels to Shakespeare's play see Frances A. Yates, *A Study of Love's Labour's Lost* (Cambridge 1936).

313

NOTES

1. The fool in *Friar Bacon and Friar Bungay* calls the Prince 'Ned'. For Goldingham, see Chapter XI, p. 251, and for Cornish 'guary' see Chapter V, p. 121.

2. See the Induction to Day's *Law Tricks*; to the Oxford play of *Periander*; to *Mucedorus*; and many of Jonson's Inductions, from *Cynthia's Revels* to *The Magnetic Lady*.

3. *The Isle of Dogs* was the scandalous play by Nashe which brought about a general inhibition of plays in 1597; the real Isle of Dogs was a beggars' refuge opposite Greenwich. For the connexion between the Parnassus plays and the Poets' War see the edition by J. B. Leishman (1949) and my *Growth and Structure of Elizabethan Comedy* (1955) chapter 5.

4. St John's College, Oxford, had been founded by Sir Thomas White, who also founded Merchant Taylors' School; it may be that the strong acting tradition at the school supplied this college with good actors. The probable author of *Narcissus* and *The Christmas Prince* is John Sainsbury, a Merchant Taylors' boy who later became the incumbent of St Giles, Oxford, parish church for St John's.

5. For similar disturbances at King's College, Cambridge, on 20 February 1607, see Cooper, *Annals of Cambridge*, III, 24; others at King's (1595) and Trinity (1601) are noted earlier, II, 539, 601. For a well-behaved audience, see the Vice-Chancellor's directions for regulating the conduct of the scholars in March 1613, when Charles Prince of Wales visited the University (Cambridge University Library, Baker MS. xxvii, 145). No one was to applaud till the Vice-Chancellor led off. (I owe this reference to Professor Helen Cam.)

6. Folger Shakespeare Library MS. J.a.I.

INDEX

Biographical dates are given for players only ('*fl.*'—flourished—indicates the birthdate is unknown). Literary works are entered under authors; references in the notes expanding those in the text are not separately given.

315

INDEX